How to Bring a Product to Market for Less Than $5,000

Don Debelak

John Wiley & Sons, Inc.

New York   *Chichester*   *Brisbane*   *Toronto*   *Singapore*

Copyright © 1992 by Don Debelak.
Published by John Wiley & Sons, Inc.

Library of Congress Cataloging-in-Publication Data

Debelak, Don.
    How to bring a product to market for less than $5,000 / by Don
Debelak.
      p.   cm.
    Includes bibliographical references and index.
    ISBN 0-471-53278-9 (cloth).—ISBN 0-471-53279-7 (paper)
    1. New products—Management. 2. New products—Marketing.
    I. Title.
    HF5415.153.D43   1991
    658.5′75—dc20   91-13572

Printed in the United States of America

10 9 8 7 6 5 4 3 2 1

Preface

I've yet to meet a person who hasn't thought of a better way of doing something. Some people are inventors who design complicated products, like inspection equipment, electronic diaries, or complex machinery. Other people think of a simple innovation—a Chip Clip, a slap bracelet, or a bicycle clamp that holds a soda. Almost everyone has thought of tiny product variations, such as putting black pumpkin faces on orange garbage bags, or adding neon-colored bows to sunglasses. Every year, products from all of these categories are put on the market.

I believe anyone with the right product idea can create a profitable company. Yet, according to business start-up statistics and income tax returns, over 250,000 individuals lose money on product concepts every year. Many of those people spend over $50,000 without ever getting their product in front of customers.

I wrote this book because I don't think people should spend their life's savings on what they *hope* is a "million-dollar idea." Instead, I want every person to have a chance to pursue and evaluate an idea for less than $5,000.

Another purpose of the book is to give product creators a better chance of launching their product idea. Currently, only 1 in 500 to

1,000 people successfully introduces a new product concept. I believe entrepreneurs can raise their chances to between 10 and 20 percent if they are willing to work hard, are properly prepared, and know when a product can be successfully marketed by an individual. I can't make anyone work hard, but I can describe the steps that must be followed to pursue a "million-dollar" idea.

Readers will find that my advice changes: sometimes I'll stress how difficult it is to introduce a new product idea, and at other times I'll stress how anyone can take the right product to the market.

The reason for this apparent conflict is what is sometimes called the PGL syndrome. PGL stands for paranoia, greed, and laziness. Even one of these three traits will doom anyone trying to introduce a product. Paranoia prevents people from receiving the outside input they need; greed pushes them to overlook investors who could be instrumental in their product's success; laziness stops them from creating the extra drive that every product idea needs before it will sell. When I emphasize that product creators have a difficult challenge, I'm encouraging readers to put forth every ounce of effort they have.

One of the book's goals is to help entrepreneurs understand the new-product introduction process. I use examples of the right and the wrong moves that other people have made. The product creators named don't mind being identified or their stories have been told earlier in newspapers or magazines. Others who preferred anonymity have been given fictitious names or first-name-only identification.

The vast majority of the examples given involve products created by individuals. I've modified some of the products discussed, because the creator of the idea isn't quite ready to put the product on the market and does not want the idea disclosed or has asked me for a confidentiality agreement. I have not, however, changed the market situations that these product creators confronted.

Sources for the statistics given in several places throughout the book can be found in the References listing.

DON DEBELAK

Mounds View, Minnesota
September 1991

Contents

Introduction: The Five Key Criteria for Success   1

Part I   Before You Start   5

1 Facing Realities: Hard Work Lies Ahead   7
2 Financing: Forget the Myths—Here's the Truth   16
3 Drop Your Paranoia: Secrecy Can Hurt You   31
4 Professionalism: Know What You're Doing   44

Part II   The Go/No-Go Decisions   63

5 Distribution: Nothing Is More Important   67
6 Product Appeal: Will Customers Buy?   94
7 Manufacturing: Not Every Product Can Make Money   113
8 Inside Help: Everyone Needs Key Contacts   142

Part III   Selling Product   161

9 The First Sales Period: Proving a Product Will Sell   163
10 Evaluation Time: Before You Spend Big Money   185

v

11 The Transitional Period: Establishing the Business   207
12 The Business Plan: Turning into an Operating Company   235

Part IV Now You're Ready   **255**

13 New Product Failures: Nine Reasons Why Entrepreneurs
    Don't Succeed   257
14 Exhilarating Times: You Too Can Be Successful   269

    Appendix: Sample Patent Documents   273
    Glossary   281
    References   287
    Helpful Sources   289
    Index   291

Introduction: The Five Criteria for Success

There are five criteria for determining whether a product idea can be successfully marketed:

1. The product is easy to distribute.
2. The technology is simple.
3. The product is perceived to be unique.
4. The benefit is obvious.
5. The product can be sold at four to five times its manufacturing cost.

Consider the effects when those criteria were met by two new products: a real estate lock box and a foam lock-box cover. Neither product was on the market in 1982, when my wife and I were shopping for a house in Pennsylvania. The real estate agent drove us from house to house; for almost every showing, she had to go to another realtor's office to get a house key. Sometimes, the key wasn't there, primarily because another agent had not yet returned it. I estimate that nearly half our time with her was spent tracking down house keys.

In 1989, when we were again house shopping, not one minute was lost looking for keys. In those seven years, someone had created the real estate lock box. The box has a U-shaped hook that slides over the back of the door knob and then locks into the back of an empty box. The front of the box has a combination lock that opens the box's door. The keys to the house are put inside this locked compartment. All a real estate agent has to do is call the seller's real estate office to get the lock's combination. I'm not sure who created this nifty product idea, but it saves real estate agents hours of time.

The real estate lock boxes had one problem. When the front door was opened, the boxes would swing out a few inches and then bang into the door. This is where Darnell Krell entered the picture. When she and her husband had their house up for sale, she noticed the damage caused by the lock boxes. When she saw the same damage on virtually every house with a lock box, Darnell created knitted mittens for lock boxes, as an experiment. Real estate agents loved the idea, and Darnell decided to market a molded foam lock-box cover. Her product protected the front door *and* provided an advertising spot for mortgage bankers and real estate agents.

Darnell worked hard to market her product, but her efforts were aided by the fact that both the lock box cover and the lock box met the five criteria for successful marketing:

1. The distribution system was obvious and available. Not only were real estate offices and mortgage bankers easy to locate, but they represented a virtually untapped market, because few products were sold exclusively to them.

2. Combination lock and foam molding technology were well-known and relatively simple.

3. The products were unique; nothing like them had ever been sold.

4. The products' benefits were obvious to the real estate agents.

5. Lock type products and foam molded products typically sold at four to five times their cost.

All the go/no-go decisions discussed in this book are based on the five criteria for successful marketing of a product idea. Can an individual, operating alone, market a product that doesn't meet the criteria? Yes. But the product creator will need more money for advertising, distribution, and/or manufacturing than most people can afford to spend. Meeting the criteria will offer the best chance for a successful introduction and the only chance for marketing a product with a small investment.

What should you do when a product that you feel has profit potential doesn't meet the criteria? You have two choices: try to sell or license the idea to a corporation, or drop the idea. Corporations have advantages that individuals don't—already developed distribution systems, established research and development (R&D) and marketing departments, and extensive financial resources. Corporations can produce many products that small entrepreneurs can't. Because manufacturers often buy and license products from individuals, licensing should certainly be considered.

The other choice is to drop the idea. I believe firmly that you have to be willing to move on to new ideas when you discover that a product doesn't meet the five marketing criteria. Otherwise, you'll invest your time and energy in the wrong products.

In my experience, out of 100 ideas that may have market potential, only five to ten can be introduced by an individual. At least nine out of ten times, you won't have a "million-dollar idea."

Part I

Before You Start

Yoshiro Nakamatsu ("Dr. NakaMats"), who invented the floppy disk, digital watches, and approximately 2,000 other products, is probably the world's leading inventor. Dr. NakaMats believes that the first element of inventing is *suji*, which translates into English as knowledge. I agree with Dr. NakaMats. Before you start to take a product concept to the market, you need to know and understand the importance of the product introduction process.

Part I covers some important questions that you should consider before deciding whether you want to try to introduce a product concept.

- How much time should be devoted to the product?
- How much money will an introduction take?
- How can the needed money be raised?
- How can a product idea be protected, for the lowest possible cost?

5

- How much market information is needed, to have a chance of being successful?

To put an idea on the market, you need to make a commitment of time, money, and effort. Part I will help you realize the extent of that commitment and will prepare you to face the rigors of the product introduction process.

1

Facing Realities: Hard Work Lies Ahead

Jon Kittleson was a hockey player in high school. He was required by state rules to wear a mouthguard whenever he was on the ice. The strapless mouthguards that Jon and his teammates preferred were easily lost. The alternative strap model was unpopular because it was made out of a heavy plastic that stiffened and curled up, making the mouthguard uncomfortable.

Jon came up with the idea of putting a strap on the much more comfortable strapless mouthguard. He began by cutting a hole in the strapless model and looping a piece of flexible nylon cord around the face mask and through the mouthguard. When Jon furnished the mouthguard to a number of his teammates, all of them loved his idea.

Jon spent the next seven years trying to promote his product. He spoke to most of the major mouthguard dealers around the country, presented his product more than 200 times to potential investors, and invested over $15,000 of his own money.

During Jon's eighth year of promotion, he was able to find a manufacturer that would help distribute his product. At last word,

Jon hoped to start introducing the mouthguard during the winter of 1991–1992.

The Odds for Success

Which of the following statements do you think applies to Jon?

1. Jon took a long time to put his product on the market, because he made too many mistakes.
2. Jon didn't have enough money to introduce the new mouthguard.
3. Jon's new mouthguard wasn't innovative enough.
4. Jon did a great job with his product. His performance was better than that of 90 percent of all the people who try to market new product ideas.

Most people who hear about Jon's venture pick one of the first three statements. I don't agree. Jon made some mistakes, but he also correctly covered most of the steps recommended in this book. His major mistake was that he didn't know how to enter the transitional sales period (Chapter 11), but that mistake is made by most people who are trying to introduce an idea. The $15,000 to $20,000 that Jon spent was more than enough money to introduce the product; Jon probably could have gotten by for under $5,000. The product seems to have been unique. Jon had his teammates test it, and he showed it to numerous mouthguard dealers.

From my experience with over 200 people who've spent more than $15,000 promoting a product idea, I'd say that Jon did a better job than 90 percent of the people who create and try to introduce a new product idea.

Am I saying that Jon did a great job? Not quite. He should have been able to introduce his product in no more than two years. Jon's main roadblock was that he kept looking at how he could introduce the product to the *whole market,* which made the introduction a big and expensive affair. Jon should have started by selling the product to Minneapolis high school hockey players. He could have continued to expand to other markets from this initial sales base. I also think Jon should have obtained an endorsement from a well-known Minnesota hockey player. He might have been able to persuade the player to become an investor and partner, which would have greatly increased the mouthguard's chances for success.

After hearing about Jon, one product creator responded: "Wait a minute! After eight years, Jon hasn't introduced his product and you say he's done a better job than 90 percent of the people trying to introduce products? That doesn't make any sense at all. After all, a good product has a 25 to 50 percent chance of making it on the market." I'd agree with this statement if product creators had a 25 percent chance of introducing their ideas. But they don't. According to income tax reports, business start-up statistics, and patent recipient information, 250,000 people try to introduce new products every year. From my research and my experience working in the new product business, I'd say that no more than 250 to 500 individuals successfully market a product each year. That means that out of every 500 to 1,000 people who try, only one finally succeeds. Considering those odds, Jon Kittleson did fairly well.

Why do so few product creators succeed? Most readers would probably answer: Not enough people have good ideas. I don't agree. Well over 75 percent of the people I talk to have ideas that are just as marketable as the products that manufacturers are introducing. However, most people don't know how to market a product. Another important reason is that only 10,000 consumer products have a significant introduction each year, and they include products by 3M, Sony, Procter & Gamble, Mattel, and other major manufacturers.

The market for products is limited. Retailers have only a certain amount of shelf space; only so many TV commercials and space advertisements can be run; only so many sales calls and mailings can be made, at only certain times of the year. Product creators have to be prepared to compete not only with other product creators, but also with established companies that are trying to introduce new products.

Most people who create a product idea aren't overly interested in what happens to other entrepreneurs; they are only interested in the reasons they might fail. The two most common reasons for failure are that the creators didn't pick the right type of product and/or they made too many mistakes.

It takes hard work to introduce a product, but individuals still bring their products to market every year. In 1985, Lynn Gordon was a divorced mother with three children. Her only asset was a recipe for an old-fashioned bread that contained no oil, honey, or dairy products. Lynn started selling the bread through a small number of health food stores in her home town. As a result of dedicated effort, Lynn was soon selling 40 loaves per week. Then a buyer for a chain of bakeries saw her product at a store. This buyer, by coincidence, couldn't eat bread with oil or honey, and was overjoyed to find Lynn's old-fashioned bread. Using that chain's contract as a springboard, Lynn was able to start French Meadow Bakeries, which now sells its products around the world.

Raising Your Chances

The 5 to 10 percent chance of success I've promised is certainly better than the 1-in-1,000 chance that faces most product creators. You can raise your odds to over 50 percent with one simple tactic: be willing to drop an idea. Why does dropping ideas raise odds? Because it allows you to pursue other product ideas that might have a better chance for success.

Any discussion of the odds for a product creator's succeeding contains a number of negative statistics. Books about how to market product ideas should be positive, but I decided to include this information because I don't believe that an individual can introduce a product idea unless it meets all the criteria for successful marketing. When you start a project, it won't always be apparent whether a product can be introduced. As you move through the introduction cycle, you will get a better idea of your product's profit potential. If you learn, even after a year or two of work, that your product falls short of meeting the criteria, drop it and move on to another product. Dropping a product can be very painful, but it needs to be done if you want to raise your odds of success to over 50 percent.

I had a painful experience with a tire cutter that I once worked on. The tire cutter was designed to cut the tire along the line where the sidewalls meet the tread. This product was originally created by a Ron R., a tire dealer. He never had enough room for his waste tires, which became a breeding ground for mosquitoes. Ron wanted to cut his waste tires up quickly, at a minimal cost. He saw that cutting the tires at the junction of the sidewall and the tread would greatly reduce space requirements. The sidewalls would lie flat, like a stack of plates, and the tread, without the sidewall support, would form a flat strip on the ground. He would eliminate the mosquito problem by eliminating the open space inside the tire.

Ron made cutting the tires easy, and inexpensive, by designing an attachment for the hydraulic machine he used to mount tires onto wheel rims. When Ron was over 70 years old and had given up on his idea, he gave it to me and my partner.

We tested the product with several tire dealers, all of whom liked the product. We had several positive meetings with a tire equipment dealer who sold tire mounting equipment throughout the Upper Midwest. These contacts helped us as we modified the product, to give it an acceptable price/value relationship. The contacts also helped us realize that the tire cutter would only cut tires when they were still on the rim. Most waste tires were already off the rim, and therefore couldn't be cut on tire mounters. We developed a second product, a tire expander, which could be placed in a tire in about 15 seconds and would then act as a wheel rim.

Everything sounded pretty positive, but we had a problem: Waste tires from large tire dealers don't go from the dealers to a landfill or tire shredder. Instead, a junk tire dealer picks up the tires. The junk dealer picks out the best of the discards and then sells the rest to a tire retreader. Any tire that still has a respectable amount of rubber gets a new tread, and only the remaining tires go to a tire shredder or landfill. The junk tire dealers did not like our product, which had the potential to put them out of business. The large tire dealers would use our product only if free tire pickup was part of the package. The retreaders didn't seem to care one way or the other about our product, because they could get used tires from companies that owned fleets of cars. Only the small tire dealers, who stored tires for a long time, were eager to use the cutter.

Normally, these complications would be more than enough to persuade me to drop a product. However, one feature of tires still gave us a strong chance for success. Tires have a high steel percentage, which makes them difficult to recycle except as a highway roadbed or in other filler-type applications. The sidewalls have a very high percentage of steel, and the treads have a low percentage. Because the steel percentage is not the same throughout the tire, there was a strong possibility that treads, recycled alone, could be turned into new rubber products like garbage cans.

I knew that I didn't have the time, money, or energy to change the waste tire industry. But I had support from Andy Ronchak, who was in charge of waste tire disposal for the State of Minnesota. Andy's position was important, because Minnesota is a leading state in addressing the problem of waste tire disposal. Andy's department circulated a nationwide newsletter, and Andy was a well-known figure in the recycling industry. Andy told us that our product could open up new markets for waste tires, and that he was prepared to help us get local shredders to test the potential of recycled tire treads.

But then Andy left his job. His replacement didn't have Andy's knowledge or contacts, and we dropped the product—a big disappointment for me. I had spent a lot of time and almost $1,000 on the idea. The tire cutter had the potential to result in a steady business that could be run with minimal effort. Because I'm concerned about the environment, I would have liked to introduce an environmental product. But I had to drop the tire cutter, because, without Andy's help, the product would no longer be easy to put on the market.

The Step-by-Step Approach

One purpose of telling the tale of the tire cutter is to show how you must be willing to drop ideas whenever new information becomes available. The story demonstrates another point: Product creators have to take a slow, step-by-step approach. If they don't, they might spend all their money before they discover complications that will prevent them from introducing a product.

Many product creators have told me: "I can see why developing the tire cutter was complicated. After all, it is a somewhat complex mechanical part. But my product is real simple. It will be a snap to introduce." The tire cutter did have more mechanical features than most products, but most of the complications came from the junk tire dealers, retreaders, and tire shredding companies, none of whom was directly related to our product. Five to ten problems have surfaced unexpectedly during the introduction of every product I've worked on. Some inevitable problems can be overcome, if entrepreneurs have spent their money sparingly.

Time Management

My experience with a variety of projects indicates that product creators have to devote at least 10 hours each week to launching a project. This is a significant commitment, especially for someone who needs to keep a full-time job in order to meet current bills. The task gets even tougher when a product creator has to make the most of his or her important contacts during regular work hours.

To keep a product moving, I recommend establishing goals, with a specific timetable, for each month. My April 1990 timetable for introducing the tire cutter (Figure 1.1) can serve as an example of a timetable, and my comments on each goal will explain the sequence and time frames that were assigned.

You're headed for trouble if you don't prepare and follow a timetable. Roy L., for example, created a soda can holder that attached to the handle of a bike—a well-designed product that was easy to manufacture and had a manufacturing cost of less than 15 cents per unit. Roy developed a prototype and then tried to obtain large orders from soft drink distributors and from a chain of convenience stores. Roy had a very strong response from one chain of

Goal 1. Finalize contract manufacturing arrangements.

Actions:
- Visit the final three contract manufacturing choices on April 9 and 12.
- Choose the final contract manufacturer by April 18.

Time Required:
- Half-day on April 9.
- All of April 12.

Comments: We had three considerations guiding our choice of a contract manufacturer. (1) We needed design help. The original product was put together with a variety of parts purchased from a farm implement store. Although the product worked well, it didn't look finished. We needed a manufacturer that would redesign the product, at its expense, using commonly available, inexpensive materials. (2) We had to have product liability insurance. The tirecutter, which cut through a tire in about 15 seconds, was capable of injuring someone. If we could find a manufacturer that had other products with similar safety problems, we could obtain a rider on the manufacturer's already existing insurance policy. The alternative was a $2,500–$5,000 insurance deposit from our own funds. (3) We wanted the product's manufacturing costs to stay low, to allow us to make money on the project. All in all, we had quite a few points to negotiate, especially since we were willing to pay only $250–$300 for our initial prototypes.

Goal 2. Obtain an insurance company's preliminary approval for a new product design.

Action:
- Present the design from the contract manufacturer to the insurance company on April 23.

Time Required:
- Four hours on April 23.

Comments: The original product design didn't have some safety features required by the insurance company. Before moving ahead, we wanted to be sure the tire cutter's new design was acceptable.

Goal 3. Prepare a preliminary product flier to be shown during market tests.

Actions:
- Develop preliminary ideas for the flier, April 1–10.
- Work out the final flier layout, April 11–20.
- Have artwork completed by a high school art student by April 30.

Time Required:
- Two to three hours every Tuesday night and Friday night in April.

Comments: When you are showing a new product, prepare a sample product sales brochure to help people quickly understand what you feel are the benefits of your product. Response to your flier will help you determine which product features are important to potential customers. You don't need to spend a lot of money on a flier. Photographs, headings prepared with stencils or press type, and simple artwork are usually enough to capture the benefits of a product.

Figure 1.1   Timetable for Introduction of Tire Cutter, April 1990

convenience stores. The buyer told Roy in January to come back with an actual production model and appropriate proof that Roy could deliver a large order. The buyer was prepared to issue an order if the product was as good as the prototype and if Roy could hold his price to 22 cents per unit or less.

Because Roy had to start working overtime at his regular job, he couldn't give the buyer a response until June, when the spring buying period was over. The buyer he had contacted had left the convenience store chain, and a new buyer had not yet been hired. Roy's other contacts all asked how his product was doing. When they heard Roy had failed to sell any units during the spring, they lost whatever enthusiasm they had had for the product.

Your continual progress on a project is crucial to its success. Distributors, retailers, buyers, and virtually every other contact will at least partially judge a product's merits by how well it is doing at other locations, or by how much progress you've been able to make between visits. You must commit enough time to your project, and you must stay on your original schedule, to maintain the momentum you need to succeed.

2

Financing: Forget the Myths—Here's the Truth

I get 15 to 20 phone calls a month from people who state, in effect: "I've got a sensational idea. Where do I go to get financing?" My answer to almost every underfinanced entrepreneur is: "Look in the mirror, because you're going to have to come up with the money yourself—from savings, from borrowing against personal assets, or from recruiting investors among family and friends."

The truth of financing is that virtually no one will loan money to an unproven entrepreneur for an untested idea. According to Jerry Christenson, an Assistant District Director of the Small Business Administration, 90 percent of start-up money comes from private sources. Most of the other 10 percent goes to people who have proven business backgrounds.

What about that "fantastic source" of start-up money, venture capitalists? In 1987, less than 2.5 percent of the money invested by venture capitalists went to people who had only an idea, according to Venture Economics, a Wellesley, Massachusetts research firm. Venture capitalists prefer to invest in companies that are already up and running.

Most product creators don't like to believe that *they* will find it hard to obtain financing. To reinforce my warning, look at the test for obtaining financing for *established* businesses, shown in Figure 2.1 on page 18. Notice how all but three of the questions listed involve, in some way, how long the business has been in existence.

Am I saying that underfinanced entrepreneurs shouldn't try to start a business? Not at all. People with very little money start businesses every year. Keith Kendall designed a line of expensive fashion clothing. He wanted to market his product, but he had only $1,000. Keith didn't even have a sewing machine, but he borrowed one and started sewing his product in his basement. After receiving positive responses from a few stores, Keith went on to sew $10,000 worth of clothes in his "factory." Keith has 13 employees now, and sells $400,000 of product a year.

My point is, you won't be able to count on borrowing money from outside sources. You need two strategies to overcome this problem:

1. Conserve your money, spending as little as possible on each introductory step.
2. Court potential investors during your initial development steps.

The best people to court are "insiders," people who work in the market where you want to sell your product. Distributors, retailers, and marketing people for other manufacturers in the industry are all insiders. They won't look at a product as a profit-and-loss statement, but they'll be able to evaluate the product as a potential sales winner.

Some Hard Financial Facts

When you start a project, all you'll have is an idea—and trouble borrowing money from anyone, at this point. As you start to work on the project, you'll have models, prototypes, market research, and, eventually, a small number of actual sales. My goal is to

CAN YOU GET THE MONEY?

This test can help you determine whether your business is strong enough in the key areas that attract lenders and investors. The questions are based on a test developed by the accounting firm Price Waterhouse. A score of 200 or more means your chances of getting the funds you need at a reasonable cost are above average. A score of 100 or less should send you back to the drawing board.

	Points		*Points*
How will you use the funds?		**How does your business's current ratio**	
Expand the business	20	**(assets divided by liabilities) compare**	
Operate the business	10	**with others in your industry?**	
Start a new business	0	Above average	20
		Average	10
How long have you been in business?		Below average	0
Three or more years	20		
One to three years	10	**Do you have a business plan?**	
Start-up	0	Formal	20
		Informal	10
Do you have established bank or		None	0
funding relationships?			
Several connections with banks		**How many of these key functions do**	
and other sources	20	**you manage by yourself: production,**	
Account at local bank	10	**marketing, finance, administration,**	
None	0	**policy, personnel?**	
		Two	20
What is your personal and		Three or four	10
business general credit rating?		Most or all	0
Good	20		
Fair	10	**Do you have adequate business**	
Poor or not rated	0	**insurance?**	
		On all important areas, including	
Are you known in your community?		"key man" coverage	20
High profile	20	Average for my industry	10
Known to some extent	10	Little or none	0
Unknown	0		
		Do you have formal financial and	
How does your business's return		**internal accounting controls?**	
on investment, or profitability,		In most areas	20
compare with the average for		In some areas	10
your industry?		Little or none	0
Above average	20		
Average	10	**How would your key employees be**	
Below average	0	**evaluated for loyalty, competence,**	
		and experience by an objective	
Does your business have a history		**outside observer?**	
of and prospects for continued		Above average	20
profitability?		Adequate	10
Strong trend	20	Below average	0
Steady	10		
Inconsistent or losses	0	TOTAL SCORE	_____

Reprinted with permission from *Changing Times* magazine, © Kiplinger Washington Editors, Inc., May 1990.

Figure 2.1   Test for Availability of Financing

get you to that point for $1,000 to $5,000. When you're finally in a position to borrow money, you'll still face some financial facts that you'll need to overcome.

You Always Need Your Own Money

No one cares how much money you've spent on a product; all that matters is how much money you have left to invest. For example, Tony G. and three partners created a product called Pizza Stick. The product resembled a corn dog but had cheese and sausage, or cheese and pepperoni, on the inside, and a pizza crust outside. Tony and his partners sold the product for three or four years at the Minnesota State Fair, the Minneapolis Aquatennial parade, and a host of other outdoor events. Pizza Stick was always popular.

Tony and his partners thought Pizza Stick would be a great supermarket product. A frozen Pizza Stick could be heated up and eaten for a snack, or a dinner for one. Tony and his partners invested $175,000 in developing the product and its packaging, and then spent two years trying to put it on the market. They weren't successful, primarily because Pizza Stick couldn't be heated in a microwave oven. Supermarkets and convenience stores felt the product had to be microwaveable.

Pizza Stick's creators went back to their kitchens, developed a product that could be heated in a microwave, and prepared to reattack the market. By now, they were broke, and they needed some investors. They couldn't find any, and their product died. Their problem was that investors looking at Pizza Stick saw a company without any assets. The investors wanted Tony's group to put up half the money before they would participate.

Equity Ratios Are All-Important

Paul Santille started Pasta Mama's, a company that sells 32 flavors of pasta, in 1987. Sales grew by 175 percent in 1988 and were projected to hit $2 million in 1989. Paul needed to borrow $400,000 for a new building, in order to expand. Banks wouldn't loan him the money, because Paul couldn't come up with $50,000 as his share of the equity.

Banks always require an entrepreneur to have some equity in a venture before they will loan out money for it. The amount of equity depends on the stage a business is in. Most banks require a new venture to have a one-to-one equity basis, which means that, in order to borrow $15,000, an entrepreneur must invest $15,000 of his or her own money.

For an ongoing, successful business, banks and investors usually want a four-to-one loan ratio; they will loan $4 for every $1 the business has in cash. A profitable product and a strong business plan are still needed, but the necessary ratios must be met if you are to have even a chance of raising money.

You Must Have Business Experience on Your Management Team

Every potential investor or lender is going to evaluate your ability to run a business. If you don't have substantial business experience, you'll find it difficult to borrow money. Some banks and investors believe that the skill of a company's management team is more important than the merit of a company's product.

This might sound like an insurmountable obstacle if you have little business experience and are marketing a product for the first time. The obstacle will shrink if you can get industry insiders to invest in your idea and help you market it. Chapter 8 discusses how to line up experienced insiders and create a strong management team.

To confirm the importance of a management team (usually yourself and one or two part-time partners), watch the local papers for stories of new businesses that receive start-up financing. You'll find that almost all of these companies are headed by three or four people who have significant business backgrounds.

Self-Employed People Are Bad Credit Risks

A self-employed person needs at least a year or two of proven earnings before he or she is considered a good credit risk. Because entrepreneurs marketing a new product may not make money for a year or two, they may have to wait three or four years before they can take out a personal loan to support their business.

Employed people, on the other hand, are usually granted both personal loans and a high limit on their credit cards. If you decide to fund part of your venture with personal loans, be sure to set your lines of credit before you quit your job. Because you may have to wait 12 to 18 months, or longer, for income, keep your regular job as long as possible, and pay off all your personal debts. I'd also recommend that you save money by driving an "old reliable" car, having garage sales, and selling your boat or any other nonessential products you may own.

Overhead Costs Hurt Your Chances of Borrowing Money

Another name for overhead costs is fixed expenses: rent, utilities, property taxes, or lease costs. Some product creators feel that by leasing a small plant with manufacturing equipment, they become a better credit risk. Just the opposite is true. Fixed expenses represent bills that you have to pay every month, no matter what your sales volume is. You become a bad credit risk because you can be forced out of business by a few months of poor sales.

Instead, try to eliminate all overhead expenses. One technique is to work out of your basement or garage; another is to find a small manufacturer, and then rent out its space and equipment as you need it. If necessary, you might also be able to rent, by the hour, an experienced employee who can help you set up production runs.

To find a small manufacturer who might rent you space and equipment, check for business start-ups in your area. Owners have to file (usually with the office of the Secretary of State in their home state) their assumed name prior to starting a business. These filings are typically announced in small community newspapers. At your state's capital, you can review all the filings processed over the past year or two. A second method is to watch for businesses filing for Chapter 11 bankruptcy protection. These companies are still operating, and they are usually willing to do almost anything to bring in extra money. Bankruptcies are filed by county and can be researched at your county courthouse.

Development Financing

During the development period, a product goes from its initial conception through its beginning sales period. Most product creators obtain development financing from personal savings, family or friends, credit-card cash advances, and personal loans.

Jan Dutton started Paper White with $10,000 of personal savings. Susan Anderson started her company, which sells antistatic kits for computers, with a $20,000 personal loan. Other entrepreneurs I've talked to started out with $25,000 to $75,000 drawn from their personal savings or invested by friends.

Does it sound as though some pretty hefty financial reserves are needed in order to introduce a product? Yes, it does sound that way; but underfinanced entrepreneurs without any wealthy relatives or friends can also take a product to market. They just have to be sure to choose ideas that can be developed in their basement or garage and introduced for $1,000 to $2,000. Of the products I've seen that an entrepreneur could introduce, I'd say that 40 to 50 percent could go through the development stage for $3,000 or less.

That $3,000 still has to be raised, but almost anyone committed to an idea can raise that much money. Many entrepreneurs get a second, and possibly a third, job; they cut their expenses as much as possible, and they save their money until they have the amount they need.

Some product entrepreneurs elect to rely heavily on credit-card advances for development financing. Credit cards are certainly an option, but you risk running up your debts to the point where you can't repay them. The risk affects you personally, because you might go bankrupt, and bad personal credit will hurt your chances of borrowing money later on, when the product has started to sell.

Some readers will be able to easily put up $20,000 to $40,000 for development financing. Your good financial position does not mean that you can afford to spend money freely in the development phase. Of the products that initially pass the go/no-go decision point, I'd estimate that 70 percent become unmarketable for unanticipated reasons. Many of these reasons aren't discovered until the last phase of development—the first sales period—when the product entrepreneur tries to prove the product will sell. (See Chapter 9.) You won't be able to start over if you've spent most of your money finding out that a product won't sell.

Having extra money set aside is helpful in any circumstances. After you prove a product will sell, you'll enter the transitional sales period, a time when extra money is extremely useful.

Transitional Period Funding

The transitional period is the time when a product entrepreneur develops a base of sales in a limited geographic area or in a small niche market. At the end of the development period, a product creator has established only that a product *can be* sold. The creator may have sold the product in six or seven stores. Those few sales don't mean that the product can support a viable business; the distribution network is too small.

In your transitional period, you have to develop a minibusiness in a small part of the market. You will be setting up a distribution network, running a small manufacturing operation, and actually making sales in a competitive market. Your minibusiness is not likely to generate enough sales to support you financially, but it will allow you to prove that your product has merit and can support an ongoing business. That proof should enable you to obtain outside financing.

This period is very tough to finance. You don't have enough sales proof to borrow money. Yet, you have to set up the manufacturing, marketing, and sales functions of a small operating company. Throughout the book, I'll explain how to minimize these expenses, but you'll still need $10,000 and up to enter the transitional period.

If you and/or your family have financial resources, and you've conserved them in the development period, you should be able to fund this period from your own savings or from family investments.

If you don't have financial resources, you're going to have to rely on investments from insiders in the industry. (See Chapter 8.) For example, Richard Worth, founder of R. W. Frookies, which sells a fruit-juice-sweetened, no-cholesterol cookie, received $500,000 in investments in his fledgling company from 30 food distributors. What makes insiders such good candidates for investors? They know the market, and they can understand why a product should succeed.

When you have trouble getting the money you need to start the transition period, there are a few other tactics for raising at least part of the necessary funds.

These tactics include: using actual orders to borrow money or find investors; selling products for cash; selling receivables; and getting extended terms from suppliers.

1. **Using your orders to borrow money.** Ralph Q. had created an elaborate plant stand that sold for about $30. Ralph had sold about 80 units at various craft fairs, but he couldn't afford to start producing the stand in enough volume to enter the transitional period. Because of his shaky work history, Ralph was unable to borrow money from anyone. Ralph went to another fair and took a $10 deposit on each of 50 orders. He showed the orders to a retailer friend, who then not only loaned Ralph enough money to produce the 50 orders, but started to carry Ralph's product.

Your chances of getting a loan from family, friends, or insiders will be greatly enhanced when you have actual orders in hand. Orders seem to make everyone believe that this might be a chance to get in on the ground floor of a winning company. A story about my parents captures the spirit of the small family investor. Medtronics, now a multimillion-dollar producer of heart pacemakers and other products, started out about 20 years ago in a building about a mile from my parents' house. Some of my parents' friends knew the company founders, and they encouraged my parents to invest in the start-up venture. My parents didn't invest. I'm not sure what their modest investment might have been worth today, but I'd bet it would be a tidy little retirement nest egg. Stories like this are common among potential investors. Show people a batch of actual orders, and they'll think seriously about either investing in your company or loaning you money.

If you plan to use this tactic, try to bunch together as many orders as possible, even if you have to hold shipments for two or three weeks. Every additional order will improve your chances of raising money.

2. **Selling your product for cash.** One of the biggest investments you will make is for operating cash, which covers the time between when you pay for materials to make your product and the time when you get paid for the product. You can greatly reduce your operating cash requirements by getting cash at the time you sell the product, rather than using the more common method of accepting payment in 30 or 60 days. You can get cash through down payments and by selling on a cash-on-delivery (C.O.D.) basis.

In the previous example, Ralph was able to get $10 down payments from consumers. You might also get a down payment from a retailer or, if you have an industrial product, from a company. The easiest way to get a down payment from a retailer is to offer an exclusive one-year sales agreement. For example, Steve K. created a patio swing for two, with an innovative seat construction that made it very comfortable. Steve had sold about 40 units at trade shows and at one store in his small home town. Steve couldn't get money to expand. He offered his swing to a small chain of patio stores as an exclusive item, in return for a 25 percent down payment. Down payments are also available on industrial products. I worked with an inventor who sold a piece of testing equipment to the semiconductor industry. This market had quite a few small suppliers of specialized manufacturing equipment. I'd estimate that 15 to 20 percent of those companies required a 25 to 50 percent down payment.

You can also collect cash for orders from small, and even medium-size, retailers, especially small drugstores and convenience stores. Convenience stores already pay cash for some of their merchandise, such as sodas and other drinks. Many small novelties, and items like lighters, are frequently purchased from small distributors that take only cash. Retailers won't pay cash for a major purchase from an unknown supplier, but they will buy $30 to $50 of products for cash if they think the product will sell. For example, I sold a lottery pen in Minnesota during the last three months of 1990. The pen was a novelty item offered by retailers who also sold tickets to Lotto America. For those of you not familiar with Lotto America, it is a lottery held in 12 states, with jackpots ranging from $2 million to as high as $30 million to $40 million. Players pick 6 numbers out of 54. If the 6 numbers match those picked by the lottery, the player wins. Many people have trouble deciding which numbers to pick, which is where the lottery pen fits in. A person shakes the pen, and the pen makes the pick by lining up blue balls on six numbers. About 35 percent of the pen sales were to retail stores for cash. Those sales greatly reduced the need for operating capital.

Another option is to concentrate on selling product for cash to consumers. For example, Victor Toso and Stuart Spector sell annually about 75,000 of their $35 Nada chairs to consumers, primarily at trade shows. Victor and Stuart developed their product while they were learning to meditate. Meditation relaxed them mentally, but sitting on the floor in the lotus position gave them very sore backs. They created a sling that goes around the legs and backs while a person is seated. The support from the legs prevents slouching and, consequently, reduces the problem of backaches. Victor and Stuart decided to market their product after they learned that the product was effective for secretaries, computer operators, and anyone else who sat in a straight-backed chair.

Their product has a very unusual appearance, and it was difficult to get investors. Victor and Stuart got started by setting up booths at trade shows and demonstrating their product. The demonstration helped sell the product, and the cash sales helped keep the business operating.

3. **Selling your receivables.** When you sell a product for terms, the customer won't have to pay you for the period specified by the terms. For example, if you sell a product with 30-day terms, the customer won't have to pay you for 30 days. When a customer has taken delivery but hasn't yet paid for the product, you have a

receivable—an amount of money you expect to receive in the near future. You can sell a receivable to a commercial finance company for 88 to 95 percent of the receivable's value. If a company owes you $100 for a shipment you've made, you can sell the receivable for $88 to $95. The advantage of selling receivables is that you can get a fast cash turnaround. The disadvantage is that you are giving a significant portion of your profits to a finance company.

You can find commercial finance companies in the Yellow Pages of your phone book or by looking for ads in the local business newspaper or magazine. You can also find them at trade shows geared toward small companies.

4. **Getting credit from suppliers.** Another tactic for cutting operating cash requirements is to receive credit, or terms, from suppliers. Before you choose a supplier, explain how you are starting to increase sales. Then tell the supplier that you need 90-day payment terms to fund your growth. Not every supplier will grant you extended terms, and most will probably offer only 30 days (rather than requiring cash on delivery), but every bit of extended terms will help. Suppliers might also become investors, if you can show them how your sales growth will help their business.

Clyde and Jamie Leach and their company, C. J. Leacho, are an example of how a product survives through the transition period. Clyde and Jamie's product was the Wiggle Wrap, a cloth restraint with a Velcro™ closing, originally designed to keep their baby son safely seated in a high chair.

The development phase of a product like the Wiggle Wrap is inexpensive because early models, prototypes, and even the first production runs can be made at home. The Leaches were able to fund the initial product testing with their personal savings. Then they sold 8 percent of their company to get enough money to buy materials for larger production runs. The Leaches also arranged a deal with a contract manufacturer, which kept down their costs for manufacturing and packaging equipment.

However, the Leaches didn't have enough operating cash to support their business during its beginning transition period, when sales were $1,100 per month. They sold their receivables to a commercial finance company at a 5 percent discount. This allowed them to keep cash coming into the business, and it helped Wiggle Wrap's sales to grow, in only two years, to $25,000 per month.

Note that the Leaches had to give up a part of the company to obtain investors. Many entrepreneurs get greedy and don't want to sell off part of their company. They're making a big mistake. In the transition period, a new product creator can't survive without enough money. Being able to line up investors may determine whether a product can be taken to market. Owning a share of an ongoing business is better than owning all of a business that can't get off the ground.

Financing the Growth Stages

In the growth stage, a business expands from a minibusiness selling to a small part of the market to an ongoing company serving most, if not all, of the market. Only after you've sold a fair number of products for a year or two will you be in a position to attract lenders or outside investors to fund your growth. Your company will have begun to show the stability you need to prove that your product can be sold, that you know how to manage a business, and that you have a good chance for continued profitability.

You will have also reached the point where the books and financial advice on "how to finance start-ups" are applicable. You should then write a business plan and seek funding from banks, venture capitalists, and other investors.

You can finance the growth stage of your business a number of ways. Some methods are listed in the following sections. I strongly urge that you supplement this chapter by reading a comprehensive book on financing, such as *Start-up Money*, by Jennifer Lindsey (Wiley, 1989).

What is the best method of financing? There isn't only one right method. Economic conditions change rapidly, and the best method of financing may change from one year to the next. For example, banks were a good source of loans in the mid-1980s, but they are currently strapped for cash and difficult to deal with. Don't settle on just one of the following options. Consider each one, and find the best one for you at the time you need money.

Bank Loans

You can keep control of your business by taking out a bank loan, but interest payments can hinder your ability to operate. Banks usually don't make borrowing easy. If you can, try to get a line of credit from a bank. That's the best way to handle a business's seasonal variations or short-term cash shortages.

Commercial Finance Companies

Because commercial lenders take on riskier loans than banks' standards allow, they can be important to a new company's cash flow. They provide accounts receivable financing, inventory loans, fixed asset loans, equipment leasing programs, and various business-oriented options. Their drawback is that their interest rates are several points higher than those available at banks.

Government Loans

The Small Business Administration will loan a qualifying business up to $750,000, provided the owners put up 15 to 20 percent of the total investment needed. In small cities, favorable financing may be available from rural development programs, sometimes with an investment of less than 15 to 20 percent.

Specialized Loan Programs

Private foundations, independent associations, and government agencies have programs for loaning money, often at more favorable terms than those offered by other sources. For example, the National Association of Female Executives has loan programs available to help its members start a company. Many foundations provide loans for minority businesses, and some industry and state programs are designed to loan money to specific types of businesses. To find these loan sources, check back issues of appropriate trade magazines or contact your state's small business development office.

Investors

Once your business establishes a sales pattern, you can approach outside investors. The best way to find interested investors is to maintain active membership in the local Chamber of Commerce, small business organizations, and entrepreneur networks.

Venture Capitalists

Your state's small business assistance office should be able to provide you with a list of local venture capitalists, but be aware that they tend to invest in large projects that have extensive managerial talent in place, and they don't usually respond favorably to small product entrepreneurs.

3

Drop Your Paranoia: Secrecy Can Hurt You

Susan B. and Linda R. thought they had a million-dollar idea. As workers in retail stores, they noticed that the stores had a haphazard way of shipping merchandise between branch locations. Linda and Susan (an MBA in market research) set out to see whether their idea had potential. After interviewing every major retail chain in their area, they decided that a service business that delivered merchandise between branch stores had tremendous potential.

After only six weeks and expenditures of $35,000, the women were out of business. Why? When they did their market research, the women were afraid to explain their idea thoroughly; they were sure someone would try to steal it. They never asked potential customers whether they would *buy* their service. Instead, they asked whether they transferred merchandise. Linda and Susan found out too late that stores do transfer merchandise but weren't willing to pay to have it done.

One out of 500 product entrepreneurs successfully markets his or her product. One out of 3,000 product ideas becomes commercialized. These odds underline the two main reasons I caution against being overly concerned about secrecy.

1. Manufacturers, sales representatives, and distributors all know the odds of success are long, and they are rarely motivated to steal an unproven idea.
2. Product creators must thoroughly test their product, which means they have to show it to people who will either sell or buy their idea.

Will Your Idea Be Stolen?

Ideas occasionally do get stolen, but the time to worry about theft is after you've started to sell the product, not when the idea is in the concept or prototype stage. Someone who steals an idea in the concept stage won't be sure the idea will sell and will have to do all the work necessary to introduce the product.

By waiting, a thief will save money on product testing and more than likely be able to steal the idea legally. To steal most product ideas, all that's necessary is to change a few features. For example, Mr. Coffee was the first coffee-maker product on the market, and it was introduced with several patents. Now, five to ten different but similar products are available. Many product entrepreneurs would say that Mr. Coffee's competitors stole the original idea. Most businesspeople would say that Mr. Coffee encountered some competition. The company that introduced Mr. Coffee took all the risks of a product introduction. After the product started to take off, competitors entered the market. There is nothing illegal about competing against a patented product, as long as enough modifications are made to avoid infringing on the product's patents.

There are four reasons why your idea probably won't be stolen.

1. Nobody knows what products will sell. Ninety percent of companies' introductions fail, and those products were chosen by experienced marketing people. A potential thief won't be able to look at your idea and know for sure that it's worth stealing.

2. People who know how to promote products have plenty to choose from. They don't have to steal ideas. A marketer who is looking for products to promote can easily find 50 to 60 every year, and many of those products can be bought cheaply from down-and-out product creators.

3. A large initial investment isn't required to buy a product idea. Ideas are usually not bought outright. Instead, they are purchased under an arrangement that pays the product creator a royalty in a range of 2 to 15 percent of the net sales of a product. A person who has a 5 percent royalty agreement would receive $5,000 for every $100,000 of sales. If the product doesn't sell, then the idea's buyer loses only the advance to the product creator, which is usually only $1,000 to $10,000. If the product is a big seller, then everyone makes money.

4. A product can be patented up to a year after it's first shown to the public. If someone steals an idea within a year of the idea's first public introduction, the product creator could still apply for a patent and eventually initiate a lawsuit.

There isn't much motivation for a person or company to steal an idea.

Why You Should Show Your Idea

There is plenty of motivation for a product creator to show an idea. The first advantage is that essential input can be gathered from the people who will buy, sell, or make the product. These people know whether similar products were previously introduced and the market's reaction to those products. They can provide key information about how your new product could be marketed.

I worked as a marketer for a dental company for seven years, taking potential new products to dentists, dealers, and the company's sales force. I never felt that I knew everything there was to know about a product or its market, and I never failed to uncover a key piece of new information while showing a new product idea.

Another advantage to showing your idea is that it gives you a way to make vital contacts. Many key people will offer helpful input when you tell them you're doing market research. Those same people may not even agree to see you when you say you are trying to sell a product.

As an example, when I was in the dental business, Dr. James Pride created a new concept for placing equipment in a dental office in a way that increased a dentist's efficiency. Dr. Pride was offering seminars around the country and had become quite influential. When we were designing a new piece of dental cabinetry, we asked Dr. Pride to come to our plant and evaluate how well our cabinets would work for his office concept. We told Dr. Pride that we would welcome any product changes he might suggest. Dr. Pride benefited because he had the opportunity to influence products that would actually be sold on the market. We benefited because Dr. Pride was a valuable contact. I seriously doubt that we could have made much progress with Dr. Pride if we had been trying to sell him equipment that we had designed.

You absolutely must show people your idea before you spend too much money on it. If you don't, you'll probably lose your entire investment.

Patents

Most product creators, as well as the media, tend to worship the power of the "almighty patent." The patent system, as it relates to individual inventors, has completely run amok. As a result, people are probably wasting over $100 million every year in needless patent applications and litigation.

The original purpose of the patent system was to discourage secrecy. The intent was for inventors to disclose their invention so that other people could use the new technology in other products. For example, a new development in rifle-sight technology could, through information disclosed in the patent, eventually be incorporated into microscope equipment. In return for helping other inventors, a patent was awarded to the original inventor. He could then sue anyone who, without permission, tried to market or manufacture the original product. The goal of the patent system was to share technology—an admirable goal, and one that still exists to some degree in high-technology fields.

How could such a system hurt product entrepreneurs? The problem arises from the word *novel;* to receive a patent, one is supposed to have a product that is novel or unique. I believe that the authors of the U.S. Constitution (particularly Article I, Section 8) thought novel meant a significant technological breakthrough. I'm not sure what novel means today. Virtually any product seems to be able to receive a patent, if the claims are written cleverly enough.

The disposable kitty litter box provides an example of how far the patent system has sunk. Between February 28, 1989, and October 3, 1989, a period of just over seven months, patents were issued for nine disposable kitty litter boxes. All of these boxes had some differences, but I'd hardly call them novel, especially since there were already several disposable kitty litter boxes on the market.

Most product creators don't understand what a patent does for them. They believe that a patent on a disposable kitty litter box, for example, gives them the right to be the sole manufacturers and sellers of disposable kitty litter boxes. That's not what patent holders receive at all! They receive the right to sue anyone who makes or sells their *specific* product design. There may be hundreds of patentable designs for any given product. You can prove this point by going to any large store and looking at competitive products in each section. All of them may have patent numbers listed, even though consumers identify all the products as one category.

Not all patents are worthless; some provide a real benefit. Manufacturers obtain patents on complex manufacturing devices. They know that other manufacturers will redesign the product and eventually compete with them on the same market. But they also know that a product redesign might take one or two years. A benefit of a patent is that it delays the introduction of competitive products.

When I worked for the dental supply company, dental handpieces, the tools dentists use to drill teeth, were one of our products. A competitor introduced a patented fiberoptic handpiece that had a small light next to the drill bit, a feature that gave dentists more light for their work in a patient's mouth. It took our company nine months to perfect a new design, nine more months to complete the tooling, and three additional months to introduce our version of the fiberoptic handpiece. In effect, the patent gave our competitor an extra time without competition.

Another instance where a patent is useful is when only one design of a product actually works. Wind surfboards are an example. For a board to work, the mast needs to swivel and must be able to flop over at a 90-degree angle. For several years, only one mechanism would let the mast work properly. The mechanism's patents were potentially very valuable.

Even if an inventor is lucky enough to have a useful patent, he or she will still find the patent system troublesome. The U.S. Patent Office does not guarantee the validity of a patent. A patent might not stand up in court for a variety of reasons: someone else may have had the idea first; the invention may have been obvious because its patented features were already used in similar products in another industry; the idea may have been used previously overseas; or the patent claims may have been too broad. Of all the patent claims brought before the courts, 80 percent are overturned or held invalid.

A second problem is that an inventor needs to be rich to defend a patent. A person or company does not commit any criminal offense by infringing on a patent. If a patent is infringed upon, the patent holder has to sue, which costs a minimum of $20,000. Ken Hakuta is an example of what can happen to a product creator who tries to defend his or her patent. Ken invented the Wacky Wall Walker, a little plastic spider that walks down a wall. This simple product was easily copied. Once the Wall Walker started to sell, several competing companies started to sell identical products. Ken sued his competitors to stop them from competing with him and he won, but much of the $10 million he had made on the product was spent on legal fees.

Not only are court cases expensive, they can take forever. Jerome Lemelson sued Mattel, claiming Mattel's Hot Wheels Track that features 360-degree loops infringed on one of his patents. Jerome filed the suit in 1977 and finally won it in 1989.

Later in the chapter, I'll show you how you can inexpensively put patents to use. The main point here is that you should not run out and spend $5,000 to $10,000 on a patent every time you get an idea.

My views are in sharp contrast to the beliefs of the general public and most product creators. The consensus seems to be that applying for a patent is the first step anyone should take with a new idea. Many people won't even show an idea to anyone until they have a patent.

Why is the mainstream opinion regarding patents so strong? Among the reasons are: large companies often apply for patents; patent attorneys emphasize that patents are essential; some inventor groups push patents; and the media frequently praise people who have obtained patents.

Large companies obtain patents for two reasons. First, patents sometimes do offer needed protection (the wind surfboard I discussed earlier is an example), especially when a product represents an entire technology, such as the VCR, Polaroid™ camera, or Xerox copy machine. Products of this type are not easily designed around, and the patents are very valuable. Technological products, however, are not within the means of most underfinanced product creators. They require far too much money for development of working models and prototypes.

Second, a product that has "patent pending" status can delay competition from entering a market. Patent pending is a tactic companies use to discourage their competitors. The tactic works because competitors don't know what patent claims a company has made, and, therefore, what patent claims to design around, when a product's patent is pending. The Patent Office keeps this information secret until a patent is actually issued, at which time the patent claims become public information.

When I was at the dental supply company, one of our competitors came out with a new style of dental cabinetry equipment. It was designed to act as both a wall and a cabinet system. The benefit to dentists was in greatly reduced construction costs on a building, because no partitioning walls would have to be built. The product was introduced with patents pending. Our company knew that we could easily design around any patent claims on this product, but we didn't know what the claims were. We were reluctant to introduce a product without that knowledge, because it would have taken us 18 months to tool up and introduce our version of the product, and all of our effort would have been wasted if we had infringed on our competitor's patents.

A curious aside on this example: When the competitor's patents were finally issued, they were worthless. Eight years earlier, our company had tested the parts of the system our competitor had patented. We even had some remaining prototypes in use by a dentist. But the competitor still had a two-year head start in the market.

The patent pending tactic works well for products that take 18 to 24 months to be readied for their market, but it can backfire on a product creator who is trying to market an easy-to-make item. Greg Murtha, for example, created the slap bracelet, a piece of spring steel covered with fabric which, when slapped across the wrist, goes from a flat, straight edge to a bracelet. Greg introduced his product while it was in patent pending status. Once the product started to sell, competitors immediately marketed their own copycat products. Greg couldn't do a thing to stop them because he didn't have a patent. The patent pending status didn't allow Greg to sue anyone. The money Greg spent on filing for a patent is probably going to be wasted. By the time Greg gets his patent, the slap bracelet fad will more than likely be over.

In addition to the fact that patents don't buy much protection for mechanically simple ideas, individual product creators need to realize that companies' financial position is different from theirs. A company might consider $5,000 to $10,000 for a patent to be a minimal expense, worth the money if the patent provides even a small benefit. An inventor may have only $5,000 to spend. For that inventor, investing in a patent is foolhardy unless it provides significant benefits.

Patents are overvalued by the public because some inventor groups promote them. The Minnesota Inventor's Congress, for example, strongly encourages product creators to see a patent attorney before they do anything with their idea. What this group don't tell people is that they are partially funded by patent attorneys, who serve on their boards of directors, and that sometimes the people giving out the advice are the wives of patent attorneys. Is it any wonder that the groups encourage patents? Supporting inventor groups is a clever marketing tactic of patent attorneys. At $5,000 a patent, and with 25,000 patents awarded in a typical year, the patent attorneys have a $125-million-per-year business.

Some inventor groups are independent of patent attorneys, but they are often led by professional inventors, or, as I prefer to call them, professional tinkerers. These inventors tend to create products that solve mechanical problems. Companies may hire these inventors to create a product that solves a specific problem. Patents can pay off for this type of mechanical product, either because of a unique design, or because the product takes 12 to 24 months to introduce.

I don't want to discourage you from visiting inventor groups, where you might find someone who can help with working models, mockups, or prototypes. At the meetings or exhibits, you might pick up names of contacts at small manufacturers who may be able to help you. Be aware, however, that some groups may overemphasize the importance of a patent.

Many misconceptions regarding the importance of a patent arise from media praise for patents and the people who receive them. The media have come to associate technological progress in the United States with the number of patents issued to U.S. citizens. Have the writers and announcers of this praise ever taken a look at what patents are actually issued to individuals? If they did, they would realize that most patents don't represent technological advancement.

The media also overlook the many products that are introduced without patents. The first Apple computer, Ford's Model-T car, and Eastman's first camera were all introduced without any major patents.

How You Should Protect Your Idea

You've noticed that I'm not in favor of investing $5,000 to patent an idea. Instead, I favor taking several inexpensive steps to lower the chances that someone will steal an idea. The steps I recommend do *not* offer legal protection. They encourage some people to believe that your product may be protected or that you may be protecting the idea in the future.

On any project, the steps you should take to document the development of your idea are: keep a notebook; file your product in the Patent Office's Disclosure Document Program; copyright the product; and apply for your own patent.

Keep a Notebook

For each project that you start, you need to buy a bound notebook, preferably one with numbered pages. If the pages are not numbered, take the time to number them yourself. The engineers' notebooks or accountants' ledgers sold in large office supply stores are ideal.

A bound book can't be tampered with. You can't add pages, and you can't rip a page out without leaving a stub. As evidence of your activities, everything you do should be entered into the notebook in sequence, as a dated entry. Include notes on your product design decisions and on conversations with potential vendors or customers. Include the date and time for each conversation, and note whether it was in person (give the location and who was present) or by telephone.

Be sure to tell each person that you want to keep your idea confidential, and indicate in your notebook that you made that statement. Send out a confirming letter to each person you talk to. Thank him or her for the conversation time, and add a reminder to keep your conversation confidential.

Most attorneys will tell you to have a confidentiality form or nondisclosure form signed by anyone to whom you show your idea. The form offers strong proof that the contact knows the idea is to be kept secret. I think an official form hinders an open discussion. When I make a contact, I'm always aware that this person might be a future customer or investor. I don't want to start out the relationship on the wrong foot, and a confidentiality form shows a certain amount of distrust.

Your notebook's value goes beyond showing that you are making efforts to keep your idea confidential. It documents all your activities. When you talk to investors, you have something to show them. When you talk to a contract manufacturer, you can document who liked your product and on what date they said so. When you are lining up distributors, you'll be seen as someone who has done all the necessary homework.

The Document Disclosure Program

The Patent Office will accept invention documents and keep them on file for two years in the Document Disclosure Program. When you file, you will receive back a file number and a date of acceptance. This is not a patent or a patent search. It only gives you evidence of when you filed an idea, but it allows you to tell people that a product is registered in the Patent Office's Document Disclosure Program.

To place your invention on file, send a check or money order for $6.00, two copies of a written description of your invention or product idea, and two copies of a drawing or two photographs to: Document Disclosure Program, U.S. Patent and Trademark Office, Washington, DC 20231. Use a receipted delivery method and keep the appropriate originals or copies of all materials in the package.

You should register in this program when you start out with your idea. Some people will ask you whether you have a patent. You can respond that your product is registered in the Patent Office's Document Disclosure Program. Most people won't know the difference between having a patent and being registered in this program. If they do know the difference, you can explain that you are waiting to file for a patent until the product is ready to introduce, to ensure that the patent you apply for will be on the product's final design.

The advantage of this tactic is that the people you talk to will know that you're aware that you have to protect your idea. Yet, you need only spend about $5 for a notebook and $6 for filing fees.

Copyright the Idea

Copyrights cost only $10, and they can be useful on some products. You can get a copyright on something you publish—a song, a book, game rules, or instructions—but you can also get a copyright on a graphic design, a game board, a T-shirt design, a piece of art, a doll, or a product's visual look. Request an information booklet from: Registrar of Copyrights, Copyright Office, Library of Congress, Washington, DC 20559.

Apply for Your Own Patent

Usually, I get one of two responses when I tell people they can apply for their own patent. One is: "What about the patent search?" You don't have to do a patent search to *apply for* a patent. Let the Patent Office do it for you, as part of your application filing. The second reply is: "I was told I have to use a patent attorney to get a patent." That's what the patent attorneys would like you to believe.

You can apply for a utility patent for a fee of $315 and a design patent for a fee of $125. A utility patent covers the way a product works; a design patent covers how a product looks. To find out how to file these applications, send $2 to the Patent Office for its pamphlet, "General Information Concerning Patents," or ask for it at your public library. The pamphlet includes the forms you need to file your patent. (The mailing address is the same as is listed above for the Document Disclosure Program.) Two patents are reproduced in the Appendix, to give an idea of how patent claims are written.

You won't be able to prepare a patent application as easily or well as a patent attorney would, and your patent might be rejected. But, by waiting as long as possible to file for your patent, you'll be able to have patent pending status for about a year after your product's introduction.

If you are determined to file for a patent, you have a better chance to get a design patent than a utility patent. Design patents are simpler, and most design applications are granted. I think you're in a better situation when you apply for a utility patent. The Patent Office takes much longer to process utility applications. To have a utility patent issued costs $525; a design patent costs $190.

The benefits of all of my recommended steps are mostly psychological. They help you convince people that you are protecting your idea. I don't think you'll be able to win a suit in court with only the evidence in these steps, but I don't think your chances in court are significantly better with patents obtained through attorneys.

I feel some guilt in recommending that you file your own patent. The resultant applications clog the patent system; significant, worthwhile patents get tied up for years in a status of patent pending. However, I'd rather see the system clogged with individuals submitting their own patents at a cost of $315 apiece than have the system clogged with those same ideas submitted through patent attorneys at a cost of $5,000 per application.

The patent system is desperately in need of an overhaul, but that's not my rationale for telling you to show people your idea. My reason is that your chances of success will be much higher if you receive outside input.

4

Professionalism: Know What You're Doing

An investor visited Peter and Lance B., a father/son inventor team. Peter and Lance had worked for five years and spent over $30,000 on an electric surge protector for industrial applications. When the investor arrived, Peter announced that the investor would have to agree to put up $2 million just to see the idea, and Lance threatened to kill the investor if he even thought of stealing it. Peter and Lance thought their little charade would convince the investor they had a product that couldn't miss. Instead, the investor thought they were a couple of crackpots and didn't stay to find out more.

Dan T. spent $48,000 developing and manufacturing a hardware product that helped do-it-yourselfers hammer a nail straight in. The product's benefit was that it prevented nails from being bent as they were being hammered. Now was the time, Dan decided, for someone else to spend money on his idea. Dan offered to give any marketer a 10 percent commission for handling the marketing, sales, order-taking, and billing activities. Dan thought marketing his product would be easy, even though he had already tried and failed to sell the product himself. Dan didn't realize that the vast majority of marketable ideas and products originating from individuals fail because of bad marketing, not poor design. Dan should have expected to pay for all the collateral materials—brochures, price sheets, and so on—and should have offered a 25 to 30 percent commission. He should have been ready to pick up any costs associated with trade shows or other promotions. Are these outrageous costs? Not at all; a range of 20 to 30 percent is the typical percentage that most companies pay for marketing and sales costs.

Leo S. created a product that removed cracked oil filters from the standard oil filter clamp. Over 95 percent of the time, an oil filter clamp, which fits over the outside of a oil filter, will twist off, leaving the filter intact. Sometimes, however, the filter is stuck on so tight that the clamp cracks the filter's housing, leaving a big mess— and the filter still won't come out. Leo's product fit into the broken housing and removed the filter.

Leo had market-tested the product and felt it could sell at retail for no more than $45. Leo's initial production run yielded a manufacturing cost of $28. A distributor approached Leo about carrying the product. Leo said yes, but only if the distributor would agree to buy the product at $40 and then sell it for no more than $45. Needless to say, the deal fell through. The distributor needed at least a 50 percent markup before the product would be carried. Leo should have sold the distributor the product at $30, a tactic that would have developed a sales base to grow from, and then worked toward cutting his manufacturing cost.

Product entrepreneurs have to realize that, before they can sell an idea, they first have to sell themselves. They must convince people that they are persons with whom they will want to do business. Only then will they get an interested audience for a marketable idea.

When I was trying to introduce the tire cutter (see Chapter 1), I ran into circumstances that almost completely stopped the project. I was able to salvage the situation only because I approached it in a professional manner.

This was the bind I was in:

- The product needed to be redesigned, in order to get liability insurance;
- The first redesign raised costs to a point where I would have to charge more for the product than people thought it was worth;
- The redesign had to use stainless steel parts, to add value back into the product;
- The redesign was needed during a short-term financial pinch, and I couldn't pay for the engineering changes.

I was able to persuade my contract manufacturer to absorb about 95 percent of the costs incurred in the redesign, by dealing with the manufacturer in a professional way.

1. I was loyal. I was willing to sign an exclusive manufacturing agreement, as a sign to the manufacturer that I knew he was going out of his way to help me.
2. I shared information. The manufacturer knew that I had laid a lot of groundwork for the product and that the product had a good chance to succeed. The manufacturer became more like a partner in the venture, not simply a vendor.
3. I was candid. I kept the manufacturer advised of my situation and was truthful about why it existed and what I was doing to change it. My upfront honesty helped show the manufacturer that I would be a reliable business partner.

Many product creators fail in similar circumstances. They aren't willing to treat their contacts as partners. They want their ideas and information kept secret, and they want to keep, for themselves, all the control and as much of the profit as possible. Not surprisingly, nobody trusts these product creators, and they have to put up hard cash for everything they need.

Every month, more product entrepreneurs fail because they didn't take the time to develop proper professionalism. That doesn't mean walking around in a suit; it means having the right attitude and understanding the new-product introduction process.

Attitude

You must project four attitude characteristics to every contact, if you want to receive maximum cooperation and have the best possible chance of turning a contact into an investor. Your attitude must say, in effect:

I am appreciative.

I have perseverance.

I am open to suggestions.

I can cope when things go wrong.

By projecting your attitude in each conversation or letter, you'll be able to establish solid, ongoing relationships with all of your contacts.

Being Appreciative

Throughout the introduction process, you will be dealing with people who have seen many products come and go. They'll know your chances of success are slim, but they'll also know that some products do make money. Most people will help you, provided you make their experience with you enjoyable.

Be sure to thank people for the time they spend working on a project with you. Explain to them how you need their help and expertise. After the meeting, send a thank-you note.

Persevering

You've probably read that entrepreneurs need pluck and luck to succeed. Pluck is another word for perseverance. The line between perseverance and recklessness can be quite thin. A product entrepreneur who spends $50,000 on an idea, against progress that is worth only $2,000, is not showing perseverance.

You can use several methods to convince people that you won't be discouraged by obstacles that you might encounter.

1. Take the time to prepare research on the idea (or hire a professional research service). If you can show that you've taken the time needed to really look into an idea, you'll start to convince people that you're serious about getting it onto the market.

2. Develop three or four models or prototypes. This effort will show you are willing to devote time and energy to the quality of the idea or product.

3. Put together a team of three or four people, each with different skills, to work on the project. This approach will show that you know hard work lies ahead and you have taken steps to be sure the work gets done right.

4. Discuss freely other difficult projects you brought to completion.

Perseverance is an intangible quality that is difficult to prove in advance. Still, people will see that you are dedicated to your project and that you know the difficulties of introducing it.

Welcoming Suggestions

The goal in a project's early stages is to obtain input so that you can understand how people are likely to react to an idea. Most people won't give accurate input unless they believe a product entrepreneur is open to suggestions. To receive valid input, you must learn to listen closely to people's comments, take notes, and ask clarifying questions.

This sounds like simple advice, but eight out of ten product creators I talk to don't listen at all. They spend their time telling people how great their idea is, and they argue with anyone who is bold enough to mention any of the product's shortcomings.

Listening to people's criticisms can be very difficult. I remember the first time I did a product brochure. I spent a month on the preliminary layout before I sent it out for evaluation. I was devastated when the brochure came back with suggested changes. We all feel vulnerable when our work is evaluated by someone else.

When you're interviewing people to get feedback, use clarifying questions to determine exactly what the people are telling you. For example, if someone mentions that a product doesn't look like it's worth $20, follow up that comment with: "What makes the product look like it's not worth $20?" or "Why do you say that?" Asking clarifying questions will give you valuable information and will show that you're open to suggestion.

Not asking enough questions can cost you a lot of money. Cameron E. created a little piece of tape that wrapped around the spokes of a bike. The tape was flashy and appealed to kids, and it had the potential of being an outstanding promotional item for a chain of convenience stores or a soda manufacturer. A buyer told Cameron: "This is the type of product we like. Last year, we bought 20,000 units of a similar item. Be sure to stop back when your product is ready." Cameron interpreted that to mean the buyer would buy 20,000 units once the product was on the market.

In reality, the buyer was only telling him to come back when the product was available. Cameron missed the following key points by not asking enough clarifying questions:

- The product purchased last year had its price discounted 70 percent. Cameron couldn't afford that large a discount.
- The buyer's boss approves all large orders. The buyer couldn't project what his boss would think of the idea.
- The chain ran only one big promotion per year. Typically, as many as 10 products were considered for each promotion.

Being open to suggestion does not mean that you must consider making all the changes people propose. Keep a clear vision of what the final product should be, but gather reactions, to know whether an idea will sell.

Coping

Contacts will be wondering how well you will cope with the inevitable problems encountered by product entrepreneurs. Coping with problems is another intangible trait that's hard to prove in advance. A tactic for showing how you can cope is to offer contacts a short explanation of your activities every time you call them. Some examples of short explanations are:

- I've narrowed down my list of potential contract manufacturers to three.
- I've completed the initial phase of my product research.
- I've completed field testing of the product at six different sites.
- I've finalized the layout for the package.
- I've started my initial contract negotiations with several key distributors.

Your summaries should be extremely brief; omit details of the obstacles you had to overcome. The message is that you expected problems and you solved them in a businesslike manner. Giving a short summary shows that you are in control of your project and that it is moving along.

Maintaining Ongoing Relationships

You should keep in touch with all your contacts. Calling them periodically shows that they're important to you and establishes a pattern of your calling on a routine basis. Contacts will then feel that they're part of your project and that you don't call only when you need help.

Whenever you start a project, start a contact file. Include a person's name, address, phone number, and capacity for possible future help. Record the date, time, and agenda, each time you talk. If a contact tells you to call "my Uncle Fred," by all means make up a contact card and call him. You never know when someone might be a key contact in helping you to put your idea on the market. *Making these initial contacts during the development phase of a project is critical.* Rapport with key people has to be established *before* you need their help in manufacturing or selling a product.

What You Need to Know

I believe the two most important ingredients for a product creator's success are having the right product and having the help of people in the market. Knowing a market offers two big advantages:

- Your contacts are much more likely to talk freely with someone who understands their business;
- Your questions about your idea and its potential will be more concise and detailed; you'll know enough to be able to gather more valuable responses.

You're not going to be able to learn everything about a market, nor can you totally overcome any lack of experience you might have. But you can certainly gain a working knowledge about how a market or industry operates. Knowledge by itself doesn't make an idea succeed, but it provides a roadmap for the introduction cycle and it makes contacts confident about your business capabilities.

Before starting to introduce a product, entrepreneurs should know the market aspects that are described in this section. The next section tells where you can find sources and data.

Industry Margins

Most people think businesses that stay in business are raking in sky-high profits. Actually, the vast majority of businesses make less than 5¢ for every $1 of sales.

An industry margin is an important indicator of how many sales are needed before an entrepreneur makes back an investment. For example, if the expected margin in your industry is 10 percent and you've invested $10,000 in a project, you'll need $100,000 in sales ($10,000 divided by 10 percent) to break even.

You can find the margins in the *Almanac of Business and Financial Ratios* (published by Prentice-Hall) at larger public libraries. Look for the line titled "Net profit before taxes as a percent of sales." In most categories, you'll find the average margin is either very low or negative. Find the highest margin in the column and make that your projected margin.

Note particularly the column titled "Other expenses"; these generally run anywhere from 12 to 20 percent of sales. These are the miscellaneous expenses that hurt most new businesses, primarily because entrepreneurs don't anticipate them. Office supplies, insurance, interest expense, postage, freight on incoming shipments, utilities, and so on, are "other" expenses.

Cash Flow-Through Chart

Figure 4.1 analyzes where the money goes when a $100 sale takes place in the hardware industry. (Every industry has a slightly different pattern.)

A small manufacturer in the hardware industry receives only $51 from a $100 sale: $40 goes to the retailer's discount, and $9 to

Item	Cost	Comments
Retail price	$100	
Less: Retailer discount	40	Can go as high as 50% in some industries.
Distributor discount	9	10–15% discounts to manufacturer's reps or distributors are common.
	51	
Less: Manufacturing cost	25	Includes packaging and shipping.
Sales cost	6	Salespeople, telemarketers, and order entry.
Marketing cost	6	Advertising, literature, promotional materials, and so on.
Product support	3	Regulatory approvals, warranty returns, product modifications.
Administrative cost	6	Interest charges, accounting, executive salaries, and miscellaneous charges.
Profit	$ 5	Most companies are lucky to have this much profit.

Figure 4.1 Typical Cost Flow-Through Chart for Hardware Products

the distributor's discount. A $5 profit, which most readers will think is tiny, is actually a very normal 10 percent profit margin ($5 profit/ a $51 sale). Most manufacturers would gladly settle for $5 profit on a $100 retail sale.

Note how closely you have to watch costs of sales, marketing, and administrative expenses. Overspending in these areas could eat up all of a product's profit.

Manufacturing Techniques

A product entrepreneur once boasted to me that his product had a six-cavity mold. I asked the significance of the mold, and he replied that it indicated how sophisticated his product was. In reality, the number of cavities indicates how many units are made at once; it has nothing to do with a product's sophistication. A six-cavity mold produces six units at the same time.

At first glance, the entrepreneur's not knowing the real value of having six cavities doesn't seem like a serious oversight. But a knowledgeable businessperson, hearing about a six-cavity mold in use for a product that has no proven sales history, would know that the entrepreneur is wasting money. If the first cavity for a part costs $3,000 to $5,000, each additional cavity will cost about 60 percent of that initial amount—in this case, $2,000 to $3,000, for a total cost of about $15,000. The tooling for the initial production run could have been completed, using a one- or two-cavity mold, for less than $5,000; or, the initial parts could have been machined for $1,000 to $2,000.

Ernie S. had designed a $5,000 piece of equipment that could inexpensively make concrete blocks. The product was intended for underdeveloped countries, to allow small villages to make their own homes or buildings. Ernie's product called for some heavy metal parts. These parts could have been made from high-quality steel permanent castings, which are expensive, or they could have been from a sand casting, which is a mold made out of sand and a bonding agent. Sand castings are inexpensive, but they last for only one or two parts, and they require more labor. Ernie stopped his project because he thought he couldn't continue without $25,000 worth of permanent castings. I asked Ernie why he didn't use a sand casting; the costs would have been minimal. Ernie could have even made the model for the casting himself. Unfortunately, Ernie wasn't aware that sand castings could be used.

Manufacturing is the area about which product creators know the least. Their lack of knowledge is a tremendous handicap. They make a poor impression on their contacts, and they often end up paying too much for prototypes and initial product runs.

Another factor causing product creators to make poor manufacturing decisions is the conflicting information they receive from various manufacturers, who almost always recommend their own manufacturing process exclusively. For example, if a plastics manufacturer has equipment for vacuum-forming parts, its reps will sometimes recommend a vacuum process, even if another process might be more effective. The result to the product creator may be an ill-designed part that costs too much.

Joe L. and Chris P. created a plastic tool storage compartment that bolted to the underside of a workbench. The part was 6 inches wide, 9 inches long, and $3\frac{1}{2}$ inches deep—too big for economical injection molding, but a candidate for vacuum forming or rotational molding. An engineer from a rotational molding manufacturer told Joe and Chris that the company's process would produce parts with a better finish and would use less material than a vacuum-forming process. Joe and Chris decided to make their parts with rotational molding equipment.

In my opinion, this was a bad decision. The rotational mold cost $3,500, and the manufacturer suggested four molds to speed production. Joe and Chris could have made the vacuum-formed mold out of wood, in a basement, for under $200. The rotational mold would produce parts with a slightly better appearance, but the part wouldn't be visible under a workbench and a vacuum-formed part would have been fine. As for plastic usage, vacuum-formed parts do use more, but wastage could have been minimized.

The net result was that Joe and Chris, before selling even one product, invested $13,000 in tooling. A small production run of vacuum-formed parts would have cost less than $500.

To succeed, an undercapitalized product entrepreneur needs a close relationship with a contract manufacturer. That relationship can only happen if the entrepreneur knows enough to evaluate a manufacturer's advice.

You're going to need to spend a lot of time researching techniques for manufacturing your particular product. No easy-to-use reference source is available. Manufacturing issues are discussed in Chapter 9, but this book can't address all of the different types of products. Use the sources described in the next section, and dig diligently to get the information you need.

Comparative Products

A comparative product isn't identical to yours, but it has characteristics that are similar. For example, suppose you have created an electronic golf aid that you hope to retail for $19.95. Your creation would have two types of comparative products: golf products, with a retail price range of $15 to $25, and other electronic products with similar circuitry.

By finding comparative products in your target market, you can generate valuable marketing information. When you talk to contacts, you can ask them to evaluate your product against that information. A comparison will help you to project potential sales volume and will answer questions such as:

Which product has a more important benefit?

Which product is more unique?

Which product has a better price–value relationship?

You can also ask contacts about the promotional programs and distribution networks used by the marketers of successful comparative products.

Comparative products with similar technology offer a basis for estimating what a product's eventual manufacturing cost should be. If a similar product retails for $24.95, that product's cost should be about 25 percent of the retail price, or $6.25. With this information, you'll be able to tell a contract manufacturer that you can afford to pay only $6.25 for a part. If the manufacturer complains that it can't make the product for that price, you can point to the comparative product, explain its retail price, and project its manufacturing cost. These data should help you to negotiate the price you need.

Typical Packaging

A product's package often determines how effectively its benefits can be communicated, which, in turn, may affect how well an idea will sell. The package can impact on a product's perceived value. High-priced perfumes, cosmetics, and jewelry are examples of items that concentrate on packaging more than low-priced items do. Toys are another example. When sold in cardboard boxes, with 100 or so units per box, toys are priced at 50¢ to $1. The *same toys* will sell in blister packs for about $2.

Marketing Data

Target markets, market size, and distribution outlets are a few of the marketing components that you need to learn. The marketing lingo is another; vocabulary can be different from one industry to another. For instance, the computer industry calls a company a direct response marketer if it sells products at a discount through magazine ads or catalogs. In the dental industry, the same type of company is a mail-order discounter. You'll be able to learn an industry's language by reading the trade magazines discussed in the chapter's next section.

You can really impress people if you know specific information about a local or niche market: the big three distributors, or the last major product introduction, or which retailers control sales promotions, and so on. Every time you talk to a contact, try to find out at least one or two pieces of specific market information.

Regulatory and Other Approvals

Many product areas have a wide variety of requirements, such as liability insurance, bar codes, and U.L. (Underwriters' Laboratories) or government approvals. You should learn not only what approvals are required, but their cost and how long it takes to get them. U.L. approval, which is needed for virtually any electrical item, might cost over $5,000 and take up to a year to obtain. Even a simple bar code number, which is required on products sold in most retail outlets, costs a minimum of $300. Four to six weeks are needed to obtain a new company bar code. Product liability insurance may require $2,500 up front. I'll explain in later chapters how you can minimize your approval problems by working with a contract manufacturer.

Where to Find Information

The Library

At larger libraries, you can find trade magazines, which are the best source of information about a particular industry. *Plastics Technology, Potentials in Marketing, Tire Wholesalers, The Home Shop Machinist,* and *Modern Castings* are just a few examples of trade or specialty magazines that can provide you with data that usually can't be found anywhere else. Try to read at least a year's worth of back issues. Look for competitive products, specialty mail order catalogs that might sell needed supplies, and information about upcoming trade shows.

If your nearby library doesn't have a wide assortment of trade magazines, look at *Gales's Source of Publications,* a reference book that lists almost every magazine and newspaper published in the United States. Publications are listed both by the state in which they are published and by industry category. Look up the trade magazines for your category, including those directed toward retailers, wholesalers, and manufacturers. Many of the magazines will send you a free back issue if you express an interest in subscribing.

Most libraries keep a file of sales catalogs from mail-order houses. These catalogs are an excellent source of competitive information and of examples of comparative products.

Thomas Register of American Manufacturers is the leader among industrial catalogs. It lists manufacturers for virtually every conceivable type of product and publishes a separate catalog in which companies can purchase space for their sales brochures. Look up specialty material suppliers that you might need to make your product. I've always preferred trade magazines to the industrial directories, primarily because magazines have more current information. If you can't find the right trade magazine, then the directories can be helpful.

Another place to look is in the index for your local newspaper. A number of press releases and small stories about developing businesses will appear in almost every edition. Sales volume and market share statistics may be revealed in these news items. *Reader's Guide to Periodical Literature, The New York Times Index,* and other business and scientific indexes offer similar help.

Try to get annual reports from companies in a target market. Your library might have some of these reports on file for local companies. If you can't find the reports you need, look in the *Million Dollar Directory* for addresses of companies whose reports you want to request.

Your library will have books on manufacturing techniques and model building. The Helpful Sources section on page 289 lists some of my favorite how-to books for making models, prototypes, and initial production runs. Your library may have others that are just as helpful.

Salespeople and Manufacturers' Representatives

These individuals, in your targeted market, are selling products similar to yours. They generally know a great deal about an industry and can provide a considerable amount of background information.

Your best contact will usually be either a friend or a referral from a friend. You can often find a contact just by asking people whether they know anyone who sells products in the market that you're hoping to sell to. If that doesn't work, request product information from the market's suppliers and manufacturers. You can locate these companies through trade magazines or industrial catalogs. The information will usually come from a company's local salesperson or its manufacturers' representative. You can call up this person, explain what you're doing, and then ask whether he or she would mind answering a few questions.

If you have a consumer product, you typically can't find salespeople or manufacturers' representatives by requesting product information. Instead, have some business cards printed to display your name and the name of your company, and apply for a sales tax number from your State's Department of Revenue. Having these proofs that your company exists will allow you to visit wholesale merchandise marts and trade shows directed toward retailers. Visiting these events will give you an idea of how the industry works and a chance to meet helpful salespeople, distributors, and wholesalers.

I prefer to work with manufacturers' representatives rather than salespeople. Because they sell products for, on average, four to ten manufacturers, they have a better knowledge of the industry—and they will usually tell you more of what they know. A salesperson, working for just one company, is more likely to look at you as a competitor, and consequently will be more secretive of what he or she might feel is proprietary information.

Retail Stores

Keep track of how similar products are displayed to the final consumer. Check local stores to see how products are packaged, how much of each product the stores carry, what the typical price range is, and what other similar products are originating from small companies.

Utilize any contact you might have, from family or friends, who owns or works in a retail store. This person can explain what a retail store wants to see in a product and can provide names of manufacturers' representatives or distributors that serve the local market.

Packaging Suppliers

A package is important to a product's success. You need to know what your options are, and the benefits and cost of each option. Packaging suppliers seem to know a great deal about how other new products are doing. For example, I wanted to put a small jewelry item in a point-of-purchase display. The packaging supplier's salesman, who wanted my business, told me about four other novelty items he worked with, described how they were packaged, and gave me a rough idea of each product's unit volume.

You can find packaging suppliers in the Yellow Pages or in the local business-to-business phone directory at the library. Other sources for suppliers are trade magazines and trade shows. An alternative is to call up a buyer at a local manufacturer of similar products, tell him or her that you're looking for a packaging supplier, and ask which ones the manufacturer uses.

Small Business Assistance Groups

Local Chambers of Commerce are usually excellent referral sources. If they can't help you, they can at least direct you to a member who can. "The Chamber of Commerce suggested I call you" is a great way to start a conversation. Because Chamber members run successful businesses, they know the problems entrepreneurs encounter and how they can overcome them.

I've never had much luck when I approached state or federal small business groups: their information tends to be too general. The one area where they can be helpful is in regulatory approvals. For example, the Small Business Administration or a state agency is the best place to call if you need to know how to get a bar code number or where you can find out details about U.L. approvals.

How to Package an Idea

When I worked for the dental manufacturer, I used to receive, free, more than ten new product ideas a month. These ideas were submitted by people who weren't hoping for profit from an idea but wanted to be able to buy the product. All of your contacts are exposed to people who give their ideas away and to others who spend only a week or two on their idea before giving up on it. You must do something to immediately prove to contacts that you're serious about putting an idea on the market.

The best way I can recommend to make a strong impression is to package your idea well. When a consumer looks at a product that is properly packaged, he or she immediately knows what the product is and what its benefits are. Marketers know that a first impression is all-important. The same principle applies when someone is conducting market research.

There are two components to packaging an idea before a product is in its final form: the initial materials and the backup materials (those used after someone expresses interest in an idea). Initial materials have four parts:

1. A drawing of what the product will eventually look like;
2. A drawing of how the product will be used (try to get both drawings on one sheet of paper);
3. An ad layout, which consists of a drawing or sketch, with graphics;
4. A model, prototype, or drawing of the package, if you have a consumer product.

You don't need to have professional drawings on ad layouts. Instead, use appropriate pictures from magazines. If you can, find an art student, or drawings done by high school art students, or friends with artistic talent, or, as a last resort, a freelance professional artist. You should be able to prepare the initial materials for under $100.

The second part of packaging the idea is to have the backup materials, which contain thorough marketing information, ready to discuss with a contact. Some of the information you should have prepared are:

1. Projected retail price;

2. Target market;

3. Market size;

4. Key benefits;

5. Product description;

6. Market trends;

7. Competitive products;

8. Similar successful products;

9. Other pertinent information.

If possible, compile this information in a booklet. You won't have to use the information with everyone, but when contacts are interested in knowing more about your idea, having these data will be essential.

Off and Running

Professionalism will help you to succeed; you'll also find it makes your project a lot more fun. Instead of stumbling along, you'll be in control. As an added plus, people who are successful will offer you helpful advice. Most importantly, you'll enjoy the project because your money won't be running away from you. There is nothing more disheartening to a product entrepreneur than to spend $10,000 without making any meaningful progress. The steps I've listed in this chapter will take time to complete, but they will save you time, money, and aggravation.

Part II

The Go/No-Go Decisions

A product creator's decision-making process should be based, at least in part, on an evaluation of risk/reward ratios. At every moment in a project's introduction cycle, a product entrepreneur has to know how much money he or she is willing to risk on the project. I believe that no more than 20 percent of a product's projected yearly income should be invested. The risks involved in taking a product to market are too great to justify a higher percentage.

For example, if you have a product that you can reasonably project will have annual sales of $1 million per year, and your industry's breakout chart (from Chapter 4) lists a profit percentage of 10 percent, you will have a yearly profit potential of $100,000 before taxes, or roughly $70,000 after taxes. You shouldn't invest any more than $15,000 in the project.

The key phrase in the previous paragraph is reasonably project. This isn't just what you feel can be sold, or what you'd like to sell.

Chapter 5 (pages 73-74) discusses how to reasonably project a product's potential sales.

The risk/reward ratios are guides throughout an entire project. I once looked at an interesting dental product that could possibly produce a yearly income of $250,000. But I couldn't be sure. Was the product feasible? Could it be produced at a low enough price? What would the development costs be? For a $300 fee, an engineering group looked at the product and gave me its opinion on my three questions. I felt that the $300 expenditure was worthwhile, because it represented only a small percentage of the $25,000 to $50,000 the project was worth. The study, I knew, would also help in finding investor/partners. Would I have been willing to pay $5,000 for the study (which some companies wanted to charge me)? No; it wouldn't have left enough money to cover all the other introduction costs.

Part II covers the go/no-go decisions you'll need to make on your project. Some decisions will have an absolute guideline, such as: Don't try to sell a product when its benefit isn't obvious. Other criteria aren't absolute. On some projects, a certain dollar risk is acceptable, because the project has strong sales potential. On others, the risk would be too high.

For example, suppose you have a product that makes painting corners and edges easier. When you survey the market, you find that most painting products are sold through chains of paint stores, hardware stores, or discount stores. Now assume that none of these firms has a headquarters near you and that a minimum of $1,500 for travel would be needed to get essential inside help for promoting the product. Is it worth going ahead? I'd say yes, if the product is totally unique, and no, if the product is only an improvement over an existing project.

The risk and rewards of your product can be a guide to the best way to proceed on your project. As the creator of the painting product described above, you might see that getting an industry person to help on the project is worth only $1,000. Instead of trying to visit home offices, you might team up with another entrepreneur and buy a booth at a local or national trade show. This tactic would hold costs down to an acceptable level.

Remember, as you read Part II, that there is not a clearly defined time when you make go/no-go decisions. You make them all the time, over and over again, checking whether to continue. Make it a point to check your go/no-go decisions at least every month or two, and before incurring any major expense.

5

Distribution: Nothing Is More Important

Jan Dutton loved lacy things, whether they were aprons, doilies, tabletop items, or decorative bedroom ensembles. About ten years ago, Jan noticed that there weren't many handmade lace items on the market. Jan formed her own company, Paper White, and started selling a line of lace products, at retail prices of $90 and up, to a few expensive New York stores.

Mike Murphy, a 23-year-old hospital orderly, noticed how some patients had trouble moving in bed and consequently developed painful bed sores. Mike thought bed sores could be eliminated if he could make various parts of the mattress removable. He designed the DeCube Health Care Mattress, a 7-inch foam mattress that contains removable cubes in the areas where the patient using the mattress is likely to develop bed sores. Mike then started to sell the product to hospitals and nursing homes through medical distributors.

These ventures have a common feature: the products created were made to sell in markets that are small, easy to identify, and simple to reach. In this type of market, inventors have the best chance of setting up a distribution network.

The market for Jan Dutton's line of lace products is upper-middle-class and wealthy women who like handmade lace. This small market is an advantage to Jan: she won't encounter much competition, and she'll be able to charge a higher price. Because handmade lace products are sold through a limited number of stores, the market is easy to identify and simple to reach.

The market for hospital and nursing home mattresses may seem, at first glance, a fragmented market. However, medical products are sold through well-established distributors who are happy to handle a new and unique product. The market is simple to reach.

Distribution is the marketing term for the method or process by which a product moves from the manufacturer to the consumer. For example, for clothing, the chain of selling may begin with a manufacturer and continue on to a wholesaler, a distributor, a clothing store, and finally, a consumer. This whole process is called a distribution network. Some manufacturers have a much shorter network; they may, for example, send out mail-order catalogs and then receive orders on an incoming 800-number.

Why do most inventors overlook distribution, when the go/no-go decisions regarding distribution are critically important? Distribution is an activity that most consumers are never aware of. They see only the product on the market, and they take its being there for granted. Most product creators have no idea of the distribution considerations that are involved in introducing a product. Many potential entrepreneurs have worked at companies that have distribution networks in place. These people don't realize the work their company went through to establish its network.

I'm not saying that you shouldn't go ahead with a product that has distribution problems; there is always room in the market for a truly novel product. But be forewarned about the difficulties you'll face before you develop an introduction strategy.

Why You Must Evaluate Distribution

In one word, the reason is *money.* Each distribution network has four concerns that involve money:

1. How much product support is needed?
2. How big is the market?
3. How long will it take to collect receivables?
4. How should the product be designed?

How Much Product Support Is Needed?

Joan P. created a kit of directions for 50 to 60 projects that parents and young children could do together. What made the kit outstanding was that every activity could be done using common household materials. Joan had created her kit because she got tired of always having to run to the store when she wanted to do a parent/ child activity.

Joan's product was exceptionally good, but she wasn't selling many units. Her problem was that her market was fragmented. Because most educational toy stores are individually owned, she couldn't reach them by calling on a few buyers for large chains. Educational toy stores are a relatively new segment, and there are no established distributors or manufacturers' sales agents. Joan had to have her own sales force call on each store. Maintaining a sales force creates high product-support expense.

Joan's other options were to sell her product to mail-order catalogs, to send a sales flyer to the names on a purchased mailing list of parents of young children, or to advertise in magazines. Joan didn't feel mail-order catalogs would generate enough sales, and she couldn't afford a large mailing or magazine advertising. There was no inexpensive way for Joan to put her product on the market.

Every market has a variety of distribution networks. You need to choose a network that you can afford and can penetrate. As an example, let's look at exercise equipment. The potential distribution networks include: mail-order catalogs; health clubs; medical equipment (for physical therapy) distributors; order blanks in magazine ads; sporting goods stores; discount or department stores; and other manufacturers.

Let's take a quick look at the promotional cost for each network.

- **Mail-order catalogs.** If you sell to a mail-order catalog company, your only promotional expense may be the cost of providing a color picture and a short explanation of the product. The problem with mail-order catalogs is that a product can be overlooked in the middle of name-brand, low-priced, and discounted items. A mail-order catalog might work well for an inexpensive consumer item, but high-priced equipment from an unknown manufacturer probably won't sell in a catalog unless it's endorsed by an athlete or famous personality. Celebrities don't endorse products for free. They usually charge a minimum of $10,000, or they require a percentage of the product's profit.

- **Health clubs.** Promotional costs will be high. At a minimum, you will need to demonstrate a product before a health club will consider it. You may be required to leave it at the clubs for a free trial period. To demonstrate health equipment, you'll need either a salesperson or a sales agent. Product creators typically prefer a sales agent working on a 15 to 20 percent commission, but very few sales agents handle health club exercise equipment. The market is dominated by just a few large companies, such as Nautilus, that carry a wide variety of products. The advantage of selling to health clubs is that products established in the clubs will sell more easily in other markets. Word-of-mouth advertising works well in a small market like health clubs because many of the buyers know each other.

- **Medical equipment distributors.** Like health clubs, these distributors will have service and demonstration requirements. An endorsement from a medical expert may also be needed. An advantage of this market is that there are established distributors and sales agents for medical products. Sales agents usually won't sell a product that has extensive service and demonstration requirements, unless they get a minimum $300–$500 commission per sale.

- **Order blanks in magazine ads.** NordicTrack (exercise equipment) is an example of a manufacturer that sells most, if not all, of its products through magazine ads. Placing ads in magazines has several advantages. A key benefit is that you can have more control of your business. Retailers and distributors may decide to stop carrying a product, but magazines always take ads. If sales fall off, you can run more ads. Another plus is that, as the manufacturer, you receive the total retail price. The big disadvantages of magazine ads are that they take a huge upfront investment and they are rarely effective until people see them at least three or four times. Some ads don't produce a positive return for six to nine months. Over that time period, an investment in ads could approach $50,000, with no guarantees of success. An ad campaign can flop completely, no matter how many times the ads are run.

- **Sporting goods stores.** Chains like Herman's, and numerous independent sporting goods stores, are found in virtually every medium-size and large city in America. Sports product creators will run into stiff competition from major manufacturers, especially at large chains. The chains will request an advertising campaign to support the product's sales. Independent stores can be a better outlet for a product creator. When counted together, independent stores make up a good share of the market, but each store's small size prevents it from getting a large discount. By offering a large discount, a product creator can give a retailer a chance to make more money per unit sold. The network of distributors and manufacturers' sales agents that already serves this market can be contacted by attending regional trade shows for sporting goods retailers.

- **Discount or department stores.** Selling to K mart, Wal-Mart, or Target is the dream of every new entrepreneur. The lure of the potentially large orders is irresistible, but these orders can be difficult for an entrepreneur to obtain. Most discount stores prefer products with well-known brand names, an ad campaign, or a huge promotional discount. During the 1990 Christmas season, I saw the Atomizer, a small piece of plastic that people sit on while doing sit-ups, in both Target and K mart. On the Atomizer's package, in bold letters, was the statement "as advertised on national TV." That's the type of product support this market often needs. Another problem for budding entrepreneurs is that most large stores don't look favorably upon small, one-line companies. Too often, the companies quickly go out of business.

- **Other manufacturers.** In this network, an inventor sells to another company, which then packages and sells the product under its own name. When I worked for the dental supply manufacturer, we sold a dental light that carried the company's name. The product was made for us by a tiny manufacturer in England. When the product was first created, the inventor didn't have a marketing department or a salesforce, so he offered the product to us. We had no dental light in our line, so we were happy to carry the product. Selling to another company is the quickest way for an entrepreneur to achieve a significant sales volume with minimal product support costs. A disadvantage of selling to another company is that profits can be hard to come by. Manufacturing companies typically have sales and marketing costs totaling 20 to 30 percent of their sales dollars. When another company, in effect, becomes your sales and marketing department, you need to offer a discount of 40 to 50 percent, which is the same as almost doubling your marketing and sales costs. Only products that can be sold for six to seven times their manufacturing cost can afford this discount.

Based on these evaluations, a poorly financed entrepreneur has only three viable options: mail-order catalogs, independent sporting goods stores, and other manufacturers (also referred to as private labeling).

If you're unsure about the promotional costs of a distribution network, find a manufacturer in the same market but with a product that won't compete with yours. For example, if an exercise equipment manufacturer makes a cross-country ski machine, then a noncompeting product could be a stationary bike. Call up one of the manufacturer's salespeople, or a manufacturers' representative (or sales agent), and ask what types of promotion the manufacturer uses and what expenses you can expect when you introduce a product.

How does a hopeful entrepreneur come up with the various ways to distribute a product? By following the guidelines on professionalism, given in Chapter 4. I can't emphasize enough how important it is to know the basic information about a market.

How Big Is the Market?

"The market" is not the total of all potential customers. The market is the customers that can be reached by the distribution networks you can afford. For example, for the exercise equipment market, an estimate of the size of each distribution network can usually be found in trade magazines. A typical statistic would indicate that about $20 million of equipment is sold through health clubs. If you can't find information in trade magazines, locate the industry's trade association in *The Book of Associations*, available in the reference section of most large libraries. Most associations will provide market size data directly, if requested. Another way of estimating the market is to research companies' annual reports to see whether they list a product line's sales dollars and market share. The sales number can be divided by the market share to calculate how big the market is. Independent statistics give the best profiles of market size. If necessary, fall back on the information from industry insiders or salespeople.

To calculate a risk/reward ratio, you need to be able to estimate your potential sales volume. Entrepreneurs like to say that they should be able to capture a certain percent of the market. One inventor told me that he had such a superior product that he would be able to capture at least 25 percent of the market. That's a totally wrong approach. Markets are not that predictable.

A much better way to estimate sales potential is to gather data on the market shares of companies in the market. Most markets have three types of competitors:

1. **The market leaders.** Usually one or two companies dominate a market. Their name recognition and promotional muscle make them tough to dislodge.

2. **The second-tier companies.** Three or four companies will usually have a market share that is about 25 to 50 percent of that of the market leaders.

3. **The small companies.** Several companies in a market will have
   small market shares.

Your highest potential market share can be expected to lie
somewhere between the share of the top small company and that of
the lowest second-tier company. As a rule, you'll find that this market share ranges between 5 and 8 percent.

If you have a completely new product, you can estimate your
potential sales by gathering data on another product in the same
industry. Terry P. created 18-inch-high posts that could be placed in
a garden in such a way that gardeners could run a soaker hose
through them. The benefit of Terry's product was that, by prevent-
ing plants from blocking the hose's spray, it allowed more even
watering.

When Terry couldn't find any products like his on the market,
he consulted *The Great American Catalog Guide* at his library. Terry
found the address for the Gardener's Supply catalog, which had the
slogan "Innovative Gardening Solutions." Terry ordered the catalog
and found in it a product called Hose Guides—little wheel-tracks
atop $10^{1}/_{2}$-inch steel spikes, for routing a hose around the outside of
a garden. This simple guide eliminates the problem of gardeners'
crushing flowers after accidentally pulling a hose into the garden.
Terry's next steps were to order the Hose Guides, see who the manufacturer was, and call that company for more information on potential sales volume. Most manufacturers will share a considerable
amount of information provided you send them a drawing or
product sample to reassure them that your product does not compete with theirs.

Product creators are disappointed when they find that a similar
product has a relatively low sales base. Market share is based on
more than how good a product is: a company's promotional muscle
and distribution network are key factors, and most inventors don't
have them.

Entrepreneurs are not wrong in looking at the total size of a
potential market; that large market could make an idea worth a million dollars. However, to penetrate an entire market takes five to ten

years. Dollar volume and risk/reward ratios should be predicted only for the market size served by the distribution network selected for initial sales efforts.

How Long Will It Take to Collect Receivables?

Manufacturers would like to think that once they ship a product, payment immediately follows. Sales don't work that way. Payment in 30 days ("net 30") is common, but, in some markets, distributors or stores pay only after 60 days. A one-product company that is not a regular supplier is always paid last. Because you won't have much cash, how long it takes to get paid is a big consideration. You might receive money immediately from someone ordering off a magazine ad, but you might not be paid until after 90 days if you sell to sporting goods stores through manufacturers' representatives.

Operating cash is an inventor's responsibility. Six months may go by between the time supplies are purchased and the time payment is received. Calculate carefully how much operating cash you will need to make your projected shipments. As a safety precaution, add an extra 30 to 60 days' operating cash to your projections.

Lack of operating cash causes a lot of inventors to fail. They line up some distributors, their product is placed on store shelves, and then, because of cash problems, they are unable to ship additional orders. The distributors then lose interest in the product.

I had operating cash considerations when I introduced a lottery pen, a novelty item for picking lottery numbers for Lotto America. The pen's top compartment held 48 white and 6 blue balls. On the side of the pen were 2 long slots. To pick lottery numbers, the user tipped the pen upside down to bring all the balls into the top compartment, and then tipped the pen down so that the balls would run down into the slots. Next to where each ball stopped was a number from 1 to 54. A lottery player would use the numbers next to the blue balls for his or her lottery ticket.

I introduced the pen in October. My two partners and I thought that timing was ideal. Before starting sales, we had to figure out our operating requirements. Our key target market was convenience stores that were lottery locations. About three-fourths of the convenience stores were chain stores; the rest were independents. To sell to the chains, we had to go through rack jobbers. We could sell directly to the independent stores through salespeople.

Rack jobbers are important in many distribution networks. In addition to convenience stores, they sell to drugstores, variety stores, and some large department stores such as Target. A rack jobber obtains a verbal or written agreement to supply all of a certain type of product to a store. For example, a drugstore might use a hair products jobber as the supplier of all of its brushes, barrettes, ponytail holders, and so on. A convenience store might have all its stationery products and toys furnished by a jobber. Typically, the jobber provides the initial merchandise at no charge to the retailer, and invoices the store for only the merchandise the jobber replaces. This is a great service for the retailer, who receives an inventory loan, a weekly or biweekly restocking of merchandise, and an ability to stock small quantities of products at a reasonable cost.

Jobbers are difficult for an entrepreneur to deal with. They are an extra step in the distribution process, and they usually require a 30–45 percent discount. More important for our lottery pen, jobbers are almost always low on cash because they have to put merchandise in stores without charging for it. The jobbers don't get paid for 60 to 90 days, and it's very tough for a new entrepreneur, with just one product, to have to wait 120 days to be paid.

Sales to independent stores, through a salesperson, could be made directly for cash on delivery. Our problem was recruiting salespeople for a 3- to 6-month job when a box of pens sold for $34 and we paid only a $9 commission.

There were roughly 1,500 locations in our area that sold Lotto America tickets. About 1,000 of them were convenience stores. On our supply side, we had a $1,500 line of credit from the manufacturer and 30-day terms. Our price was $18 per box. The manufacturer would not ship us product if we were over the credit limit. Figure 5.1 shows our operating cash analysis. An important point to note is that we didn't want to have more than 60 boxes in inventory at any one time, to minimize our risk if the product didn't meet expectations.

Sales Goals: Sell 250 boxes of pens between October and December, and 300 boxes between January and March, with 25 percent of the sales being cash sales.

Comments: You need a sales goal to determine how much operating cash is needed. Otherwise, you won't know how many units to buy. Set your goals modestly. If your goals are too high, you might not be able to come up with enough money. If sales are much higher than you expect, you should be able to use those orders to borrow money from a bank. Our goal was based on selling 2 boxes each to 125 stores; we were expecting to sell to about 12 percent of the lottery locations.

Cash Flow Analysis

	Sept.	Oct.	Nov.	Dec.	Jan.	Feb.	Mar.
Units ordered	18	126	54	54	130	85	85
Cash outlay ($)	—	(324)	(2,266)	(972)	(972)	(2,340)	(1,530)
Cash sales (units)	—	20	20	20	30	30	30
Cash received ($)	—	500	500	500	750	750	750
Credit sales (boxes)	—	90	35	30	72	72	72
Cash received ($)	—	—	—	—	—	2,250	875
Total cash received	—	500	500	500	750	3,000	1,525
Change in cash position	—	176	(1,766)	(472)	(222)	660	(5)
Ending cash position	—	176	(1,590)	(2,062)	(2,284)	(1,624)	(1,629)
Ending inventory (units)	18	34	33	37	60	43	26

Notes:
1. We expected payment on credit sales in 120 days. Our actual terms were 60 days, but we anticipated late payments.
2. We paid for the products received from our supplier in 30 to 45 days. Most new entrepreneurs will have to pay cash to their suppliers and should factor in immediate payment on their part.
3. We could afford to make only one big (90-unit) sale to a convenience store, in order to hold our operating cash requirements to less than $3,000. Notice how we projected another big sale in January, one month before we expected payment on the first big order. Most entrepreneurs have to watch carefully how they take big orders, to avoid a cash crunch.
4. Chapter 11 (p. 226) has an operating cash statement for an entrepreneur/manufacturer of a product.

Figure 5.1   Operating Cash Analysis—Lottery Pen Sales

Some people take a shortcut to calculate their operating cash. They take the average units ordered per month (in this case, 100 boxes) and multiply it by the difference in time between when the customers pay and when supplies have to be paid for (in this case, 4 months minus 1 month, or 3 months). The operating cash is then that number (300) times the cost from the manufacturer ($18). Using this method, our operating cash requirement was $5,400 plus a contingency of $900, or $6,300. I prefer the more detailed method, which provides a more accurate amount. A thorough approach helps you to set sales goals and sales patterns based on their impact on operating cash.

We sold the lottery pen for only 3 months. We put about 300 boxes on the market, but each box took 30 to 60 days to sell out in a convenience store. That turnover wasn't fast enough to generate the repeat sales we needed to have a profitable product. We made money on the project, but not enough to justify our time and effort.

How Should the Product Be Designed?

Most products can be made in a variety of ways. For instance, exercise equipment can be made from chrome-plated steel and sold for a premium price, or it can be made from painted plastic parts and sold for a low price. Each distribution network sells a slightly different type of product. A health club, for example, wants a sturdy, premium-priced unit. A sporting goods store looks for midpriced products. Discount stores want to buy only low-priced products.

Suppose you are manufacturing toys and you decide to sell them through distributors, then rack jobbers, and then convenience stores. You know from your market research that rack jobbers won't handle a product with a retail price over $10. You also know that the required discounts are 40 to 50 percent for convenience stores and another 40 to 50 percent for rack jobbers. That means the rack jobbers will buy the product from you for about $2.50, and the convenience stores will buy it from the rack jobbers for about $5. You have to make the product for $1.25 if you want to make any money. As an example of how the discounts affect a manufacturer, our lottery pen sold for a retail price of $2.99. The retailer paid $1.55 per pen and the rack jobber paid $1.05.

What your product needs to be like is not a distribution go/no-go decision. But the cost of the product will be important when you decide on how to manufacture it. (Manufacturing issues are discussed in Chapter 7.)

Your first three go/no-go decisions revolve around the costs of doing business within a distribution network:

1. Does a network exist where you can afford the product support required?
2. Is the market size of that network large enough to justify your initial investment for developing the product as you envision it?
3. Can you afford the operating cash requirements for your chosen method of distribution?

When Is a Product Easy to Distribute?

I have four criteria to help me determine whether a product will be easy to place on the market:

1. Is the market small?
2. Are consumers easy to target?
3. Is the distribution network concentrated?
4. Is the market open?

If you can't answer yes to at least three of the four criteria, you'll have trouble and you'll need a lot of money to introduce your new product idea.

Is the Market Small?

I consider any market less than $5 million to be small. I believe the ideal market size for a product creator is $3 million to $5 million. Some of you are probably surprised to see this limited recommendation because a big market is where you can really make money. However, an inventor has several advantages when approaching a small market.

1. **Better market information.** Insiders in a small market will be able to predict, fairly accurately, whether a product will succeed. They will also be able to offer you a detailed introduction plan. These insiders are knowledgeable because there aren't many companies in the market.

In big markets, companies with new products come and go quickly. A wide variety of consumers support big markets, for different and sometimes changing reasons. Product creators will always have trouble predicting how their products will do in big markets.

2. **Larger profit margins.** A profit margin is calculated by dividing profit, after all expenses, by total sales dollars. If a company had a $10,000 profit on total sales of $100,000, its profit margin would be 10 percent. Large markets are crowded with competitors and generally have lower profit margins than small markets. The margins can be especially low for entrepreneurs who don't have a low-cost manufacturing method.

In a small market, usually none of the manufacturers has a low production cost. Most small-market companies are saddled with high overhead, which allows inventors to enter the market in a favorable cost position. As a result, inventors can often make a 20 percent (or higher) margin in a small market.

3. **Minimum competition.** Large companies don't like small markets. A company's costs for maintaining product support, which include manufacturing documentation, engineering time, quality control, and purchasing, are almost the same for a low-volume product as for a high-volume one. This fact discourages large companies from entering small markets.

4. **Stability of small markets.** The same products can sell for years in a small market. The primary reason for the inertia is that the market size is too small to justify the expense of a steady stream of new products. This is a tremendous advantage for product creators. With a market that is slow to change, once they can understand it and succeed in it, entrepreneurs may keep a market position for a long time.

5. **Diversity of small markets.** Many industrial products have small markets. Semiconductor wafer handling equipment and a device that simplifies the installation of fire sprinklers are examples. Some consumer markets are also small. A device that alerts homeowners in southern regions when their external water pipes are about to freeze during a rare cold wave, and a blizzard survival kit to carry in a car during northern winters have specialized and quite different markets.

Actually, the total potential market for the blizzard survival kit is fairly large, but the product is sold exclusively through automobile clubs—another reminder that a market's size is determined, in part, by the size of the distribution network.

Are Consumers Easy to Target?

Fred J. created a product that allowed a motorcycle to be towed without a trailer. All a motorcyclist had to do was take off the front tire, lock the wheel so it wouldn't turn, and then attach the wheel to the product, which linked up with an ordinary trailer hitch. The product had a nice benefit and was reasonably priced at $70. What gave the product a chance to succeed was that motorcyclists who travel are easy to reach. Fred needed only to purchase a booth at some of the big summer motorcycle events, or purchase a list of motorcycle owners with incomes over $30,000, or both.

How can you tell whether your product's consumers will be easy to target? Your product's users must be clearly defined and easy to locate. Motorcyclists who travel have both characteristics.

In contrast, consider a product that protects paint brushes for reuse. How can you identify the people who will want this product?

If they own paint brushes, they may have already solved the reuse problem. Even if you could identify potential users, how could you find them? There is no reliable source of names of people who would want this product.

A product like the paint brush protector would need to be placed in a retail store or mail-order catalog. Don't look down on this type of distribution network; many products are sold successfully this way. However, in this type of network, a product creator won't have control of how the product sells; the retail outlets will control its success. There isn't much that can be done if stores or catalogs won't carry the product.

The motorcycle device's inventor, however, had several options, if retailers wouldn't carry his product. He could run an ad in a motorcyclists' magazine, buy a mailing list from a magazine or from another manufacturer, or display and sell the product at motorcycle shows.

You might wonder why I'm not recommending advertising the paint brush protector. In most advertising campaigns, you pay on the basis of the number of people who will potentially read, hear, or see the ad. When your market is unclear, as it is for the paint brush protector, you end up advertising to a broad audience, such as homeowners, even though only a few of those you reach might want to purchase the product. That spread of advertising doesn't pay off. The motorcycle product's ads will reach a much higher percentage of potential buyers, the key factor in having an advertising program that has a chance to be cost-effective.

Is the Distribution System Concentrated?

When I first investigated the market for my tire cutter (see Chapter 1), I was happy to learn that there were only about 45 key distributors throughout the country. That meant I only had 45 customers to call on.

A concentrated market allows you to better estimate your chances of success. With the tire cutter, when I talked to 5 distributors, I had surveyed over 10 percent of the market. If I had had a gift item, which could have been bought by thousands of shops, talking to five stores wouldn't have helped much at all. With only 45 tire cutter distributors, I was able to obtain accurate market research without spending any money. On a gift item, I'd never have been able to conduct any reliable inexpensive research.

A concentrated market has two other advantages:

1. Promotional expenses will be lower;
2. Inside contacts will be extremely helpful because they will know most, if not all, of the people who control the market.

Rarely will you find a market as nicely concentrated as the market for tire equipment. The entrepreneur's job is to find ways to make a market smaller. For example, let's consider several ways in which a product creator can concentrate the gift market, which is extremely fragmented:

- Sell the product as an executive gift, through advertising specialty companies. These companies call on large and medium-size corporations to sell products suitable for sales and other incentive awards or customer gifts. Typically, any city has only a few large advertising specialty companies.
- Sign an exclusive distribution agreement with one of the large department store chains in your area. Department stores like having an exclusive offering. If your product sells well, you can expand to stores in other cities.
- Set up your distribution through one or two mail-order catalogs. You may need to offer an exclusive contract.
- Offer your line, on an exclusive basis, to a large gift distributor. You may have to offer an introductory price or a promotional program to sign up a distributor, but once you have one, its promotional muscle will help sell your product.

Many inventors are reluctant to give anyone an exclusive distribution agreement because they believe an exclusive agreement will limit sales volume. Potentially, it can eventually be limiting. However, an exclusive agreement is often the only way you can start to sell a product.

When you talk to possible sales outlets, remember their desire to be different from their competitors. Sales outlets don't want their merchandise to be like everyone else's, because then sales are governed by which outlet has the lowest price. Stores want products that are unique and different.

Concentrating your market will also help your sales efforts. You'll be able to customize your product, your sales literature, and your sales approach to the needs of a specific market.

Is the Market Open?

Martha M. was a great cook, and she made a cheesecake that all her friends loved. They persuaded her that she should market her cakes. Martha started selling her cakes first to a local family restaurant. After her product was selling there, she purchased a booth at a small trade show for restaurant owners and food buyers and received a tremendous amount of interest from several restaurants and some food stores. Martha soon received an order to supply cheesecakes to a chain of 30 family restaurants.

Martha's friends were ready to invest in her cheesecake and put it into every grocery store in America. But their enthusiasm immediately ran into a dead end: the food distributors that supply grocery stores typically place orders for 250,000-case lots from manufacturers. They didn't want to buy in smaller quantities, because of the cost involved in processing small orders.

When the friends went to talk directly to supermarkets, they got a negative response toward purchases of small quantities from an individual manufacturer. The supermarkets wanted a slotting allowance, which is a payment made in return for shelf space. Martha M. discovered that supermarkets are not an open market.

This didn't mean the cheesecakes couldn't be sold. It meant that they couldn't be sold through a distribution network that included supermarkets. When Susan Schwartz ran into the same problem with her Dakota Seasonings product line, she started to sell the product, packaged as a gift item, in gift shops in North Dakota. Susan started to attend gift shows and found a distributor to sell her product across the country. Gift stores don't sell the same volume as supermarkets do, but their sales level is more than enough for a profitable business.

Besides supermarkets, closed or restricted markets can occur when there are too many similar products being offered and when two or three manufacturers dominate the market.

1. **Too many similar products.** Buyers, whether industrial buyers, store owners, or consumers, don't like too many choices; they get confused. Most people respond to a market that has too many choices by buying the best known brand. How do you react when you're shopping for a toaster, coffee maker, car wax, shaver, or any other product that has a multitude of brands? You're probably not willing to carefully evaluate each choice. You buy the brand you know best, the brand that's the cheapest, or, for some products, the brand that's most expensive. An entrepreneur faces tremendous resistance when introducing a product into a crowded market.

James S. created a cutting board that had a three-inch-high vertical board on one end. People could hold tomatoes, cucumbers, apples, sausage, and other foods against the vertical board for fast, precise slicing. I thought the product had a great benefit, especially for people like me who know only how to cut thick slices. The product sold briskly at home shows and fairs, where Jim demonstrated it, but retailers didn't want to carry it. They were already selling cutting boards and saw no advantage in carrying a new board. When Jim succeeded in placing the product on the shelves of a store, consumers wouldn't buy it. There were too many cutting boards to choose from. The cutting board needed an advertising program, which was an expense Jim couldn't afford.

2. **Major players' control of the market.** The power tool market is controlled by Black & Decker and Sears. In some industrial markets, one or two major suppliers control 60 to 75 percent of a market. Heinz and Hunt's dominate the ketchup market, Campbell's

outdistances all competitors in the soup market, and Nike, Reebok and L.A. Gear control the sports shoe market.

Markets dominated by one or two companies are difficult for new entrepreneurs to penetrate. The companies' promotional programs encourage retailers to buy as many products as possible from them, and they have been known to use subtle pressure to keep new products from getting shelf space. Marketing can be a power game. In markets that have many competitors, the power lies with the retailer. In markets that have only a few dominant manufacturers, the power belongs to those manufacturers.

I once introduced to metallurgical laboratories an industrial product that measured very thin layers of industrial coatings. The product was a variation of a traditional product line that was purchased primarily from two companies. Our product was superior in applications where the coatings were less than two microns thick, which is much thinner than a piece of paper. The traditional product line worked better for thicker coatings. Our product cost $8,000, a small percentage of the $200,000 to $500,000 that a new laboratory had to spend on traditional equipment. But the two traditional suppliers didn't want us in anyone's laboratory. Metallurgical labs were regarded as their own personal markets, not to be invaded by anyone who might get even a small share of sales. The companies disputed some of our technical findings and tried to discourage potential customers from contacting us. Their resistance turned what should have been a simple introduction into a difficult one.

Even if dominant manufacturers don't offer active resistance, they still can present problems to a new entrepreneur. Retailers and other customers often enjoy the simplicity of ordering from a large product line. Sales call frequency is another advantage of dominant companies. They might call on larger retailers weekly or biweekly, but an entrepreneur can only call every few months. Dominant manufacturers' promotional programs, which offer retailers a discount based on purchase volume, tend to prevent product creators from establishing their products. For example, a retailer might be able to obtain a 10 percent discount by buying $15,000 worth of products.

Retailers don't want to lose that discount, and their sales might drop if they bring in another, less proven product line.

Ease of distribution is a crucial go/no-go decision, but it is not the final answer. The next section explains ways to overcome distribution problems. My key advice here is to keep expenses to an absolute minimum until you're confident that you've found a way to put a product onto the market.

Tactics for Resolving Distribution Problems

Dave S. discovered a new process for impregnating air freshener chemicals into a variety of materials. He created a line of products for homes, autos, and lockers. Although his product line was appreciably better than other air fresheners on the market, he wasn't able to penetrate the distribution network. The market wasn't concentrated, and there were already too many air fresheners on the market.

Dave decided to change tactics. He approached a sports shoe manufacturer, offered a special air freshener for shoes, and persuaded the manufacturer to buy his product as a sales premium for its shoe customers. The company ran a six-month promotion that included the freshener, and the product was a hit with shoe customers. When consumers started returning to buy more freshener, some shoe stores started to carry Dave's product.

Dave was resourceful; he kept looking for a distribution outlet for his product. Product creators often end up with good products that they can't launch into the market. Some of the tactics you can use for market launch are:

- Sell your product as a promotional item.
- Use another manufacturer as your distributor.
- Drive your business through distributors.

- Combine your sales efforts with those of other inventors.
- Initiate another distribution channel.

Typically, at a minimum, you'll need a model and some market research to use these tactics successfully. You might have to invest a limited production run to secure an order. If at all possible, try to have exploratory talks with potential customers before you spend too much money.

Sell a Promotional Item

Dave S.'s air freshener was sold originally as a promotional or premium item. Dave sold the product to a company that then gave it away, or sold it at a large discount, to a purchaser of one of its products. Premium items are constantly sold through soft drink, cereal, food, and sporting goods companies, as well as fast-food restaurants. Virtually every company is a candidate to buy a promotional item if it can be persuaded that the item will increase its sales.

The advantages of selling your product first as a promotional item are:

- The marketing power of a large company helps to establish your product;
- A large order may be obtained before you make a significant investment.

The disadvantages are:

- A steep discount has to be offered;
- Large companies can be very slow deciding whether to use your idea;
- Competition for promotional items is fierce; 20 to 30 items may be involved.

I like this tactic because an entrepreneur needs only a few models and can then approach a manufacturer or other company. If the idea doesn't sell, only a minimal investment has been made. If the idea does sell, a lot of the ground toward success has been covered for very little money.

Use Another Manufacturer for Distribution

The cheesecake venture I mentioned earlier had a tough time getting its product into supermarket freezers, primarily because its volume was too low. The company arranged to sell its cakes through a frozen-pie manufacturer. Distributors started to carry the product because the combined volume of pies and cheesecakes was acceptable.

Manufacturers are often willing to buy and then resell a product that fits into their product line. They receive several benefits, including an expanded product line with little or no risk, more commission opportunities for their sales force, and extra income.

Entrepreneurs who have inexpensive products that complement costlier items should consider private labeling their products through other manufacturers. For example, Susan Anderson developed an antistatic kit for computers. Her product was inexpensive and her potential customers—primarily computer users at companies—were easy to identify. The users were easily reached through a host of computer magazines and computer sales outlets. Susan's problem was that most sales methods, such as placing magazine ads or having a sales force call on stores, cost more money than Susan could generate with her inexpensive antistatic kits. Rather than trying to sell the product directly to end-users, she sold the kits to computer manufacturers. They had Susan put their own names on the kits they ordered, and then sold them as part of their product line. By selling through established companies, Susan was able to quickly penetrate the market.

An inventor benefits when he or she can utilize a larger company's distribution network. There are disadvantages. You'll have to give a large percentage of your profit margin to the manufacturer, you won't be able to control your business, and you run the risk that the manufacturer will develop its own product and drop yours.

Still, this is another tactic that I like, primarily because the marketing arrangement can be set up with a minimal investment; often, only a few models are needed.

Drive Your Business Through Distributors

Richard Worth, the founder of R. W. Frookies cookies, wanted to develop a healthier cookie. He created a cookie that had no cholesterol and was sweetened with fruit juice, but he wasn't able to get food distributors to carry his line. Richard attended the 1988 Fancy Food trade show. When he received some orders, rather than deliver the product himself, he took the orders to a distributor. Not wanting to turn down a guaranteed sale, the distributor agreed to handle the product.

The dental supply company that I worked for started the same way. The founder, John Naughton, invented the first reclining dental chair, a product that is now used in virtually every dental office in the country. When John started out, dental distributors would not handle his product. They already had dental chair suppliers and they weren't interested in buying a product from an underfinanced inventor who was producing the chair in his garage. John went from office to office, selling his chair directly to dentists. When he got enough orders, he gave them to distributors that would agree to carry the product.

Most product creators fill orders themselves, rather than pay a distributor a percentage on sales they have generated. Although they make more money filling the orders themselves, these entrepreneurs are really losing out. Having a distributor might increase their sales five to ten times. You should use whatever orders you get to gain distributors.

The big drawback of this tactic is that you have to start production and incur marketing expenses before you can find and obtain customers. This means you need to invest a substantial amount of money before you know whether you're going to succeed. I'd recommend using this tactic only if you're already producing your product or if you can make an initial run for a minimal investment.

Combine Your Sales Efforts

One-product companies are under tremendous pressure. They run into resistance from stores or end-users who prefer to buy from companies with broad product lines. The costs of selling their one product to a store or company are so high that they often can't sell enough units to cover the costs they incur.

One solution to these two problems is to combine efforts with several other one-line entrepreneurs, to be able to promote a broader product line. There are two ways to combine: have each entrepreneur pay the others a sales commission for crossover items that they sell, or have the inventors join their resources to form a company.

This is a good tactic if you can find two or three other people offering similar products. Whenever you start a project, be sure to look for other inventors. You can find them by attending flea markets, fairs, trade shows, and inventors' conventions, and by watching for product ads in local magazines. Another way to locate inventors is to look through the *Patent Gazette* at a large library. The *Patent Gazette* lists all the patents issued each week and has an index that lists inventions by state as well as by category. By looking through back issues, you should be able to find local inventors with similar products. Some of those inventors might still be trying to take their idea to market.

Be sure that any inventors you consider combining with have a professional approach and are willing to work as hard as you are. You'll become frustrated if you continually work with an inventor who refuses to take a realistic approach toward marketing a product. If you're willing to spend 40 hours a week trying to promote everyone's ideas, be sure your partners aren't planning on spending only 10.

Initiate Another Distribution Channel

Interplak developed a rechargeable electric toothbrush. Its main feature was a series of small rotating brushes that not only cleaned the teeth but also massaged the gums, a benefit that can minimize periodontal disease. Interplak's problem was that the toothbrush's initial price was $149, a price so high that it scared retailers.

The company sold the product through dentists, with a multi-level marketing program. The company lined up a core group of dentists who supported the product, and then had those dentists recruit other dentists. After the product started to sell throughout the country, stores were willing to stock it.

Another entrepreneur, Terry Sachetti, created a bedspread with fluorescent strips that emitted a low-level light. The idea was targeted at children who are afraid of the dark. When Terry couldn't get any stores to stock the product, he started selling it at kiosks in malls, in the hope of eventually selling franchises of his kiosk concept.

I don't recommend this method. You have to spend too much money before you know whether your product will sell. Typically, you need both a marketing plan and a production plan before attempting an alternative distribution system, which requires a considerable investment. I'm mentioning this method because readers may at some point have a substantial inventory that they need to sell. An alternative distribution channel may resolve their overstock problem.

The Importance of Proper Timing

There are three reasons for establishing a distribution network *before* you invest in a project:

1. You must know your market potential. Remember, total market size is not relevant to you at the start. The only market that matters is the one your distribution network will reach. You may be able to expand later to reach the entire market, but that might take years. Confine your investment to a level that's justified by your immediate distribution plans.

2. You have to know how best to package and promote your product. Each distribution network may require different types of packaging and promotion.

3. You need to know what margins to incorporate into your product costs. Each distribution network requires a varying percentage for the people or companies selling a product. Be sure your product has enough built-in profit to cover your distribution costs.

Distribution Go/No-Go Decisions

1. If a distribution network exists, does it have product support costs that you can afford?
2. Is the market size of the existing network large enough to justify your initial investment?
3. Can you afford the cash investment required by the network's payment schedule?
4. Is the product easy to distribute?

6

Product Appeal: Will Customers Buy?

"I know my product will sell. It's a brain teaser that has two parts that will come apart when twisted just right. I leave it on my coffee table and everyone who comes over picks it up to play with." Over 50 percent of the product creators I talk to will go ahead and invest in their ideas with little more than this amount of input. These people aren't careless; they just don't know how to conduct market research.

Jim T., the creator of the puzzle, made several research mistakes, but his biggest error was not simulating the selling situation. Customers don't buy puzzles off a coffee table. They select them in stores from among dozens of similar products. Jim needed to know whether people would buy his product instead of one of the other twist-apart puzzles.

In the movie *Big*, a toy company is doing market research with a group of children. A room is full of toys—theirs, competitors', and the new toys being tested. The marketers want to see whether kids will play with the new toys. If the kids pick up a new toy and then put it down after a minute or two, the marketers know that the product won't sell. If the kids pick up a new toy and play with it for an extended time, the marketers know that the product could be a winner. That's the type of research an inventor needs to do.

Jim should have had six or seven other brain-teaser puzzles alongside his puzzle on his coffee table. If his product fared well, then he should have placed the products on the table unopened, to test reactions to their packages. The research would have improved a little more if his friends didn't know which product was his.

The market research cycle has two steps:

1. Initial research, to see whether a product concept has merit;
2. Research with a model or prototype, to determine whether people will buy the actual product.

These steps follow the preliminary research that precedes the start of any project: compiling all available background information regarding competitors, pricing, distribution networks, and manufacturing techniques. As noted in Chapter 4, entrepreneurs who act professionally pull these data together. That preliminary research is the only research you should consider having someone else do for you. All the research that follows it concerns how people react to your product. I believe it's crucial for a product creator to hear this input first-hand.

Marketing research is important not only because it helps you make the go/no-go decisions, but also because people's reaction to your product may lead to design, marketing, and packaging changes that might make the difference between success and failure.

Preliminary Marketing Go/No-Go Decisions

Product entrepreneurs need to decide early, before they invest any money, whether their product can survive in today's self-service environment. Consumers' shopping habits are dominated by quick glances. Whether they're walking down a department store aisle,

scanning a mail-order catalog, or skimming a direct mail piece, consumers give a product entrepreneur only a few seconds to convey a
message. Inventors trying to reach industrial buyers often get about
as much time. The buyers quickly scan trade magazines and product
literature before deciding which one or two companies they'll talk to.

The self-service environment places considerable pressure on
product entrepreneurs. Not only do they need to fight off competition from other entrepreneurs, but they also have to reach consumers who are overexposed to advertising, promotion, direct mail,
telemarketing, and other marketing messages.

You should carefully choose product ideas that meet three preliminary marketing criteria:

1. The product's benefit can be shown quickly;
2. The product is clearly different from others in the market;
3. The product has a significantly benefit.

The Benefit Can Be Shown Quickly

You have, at most, 5 to 10 seconds to communicate a product's
benefit. For some products and packages, you will have just 2 to 3
seconds to persuade a potential buyer to pick it up. If your product's
benefit can't be communicated quickly, you'll need an extensive advertising campaign, which most product entrepreneurs can't afford.

Communication problems are compounded because, besides
telling people a product's benefit, you have to convince them the
benefit really exists. Sam R. and Jeff L. created a handle that attached to the middle of the shaft of rakes, hoes, shovels, and similar
garden tools. Sam and Jeff came up with their idea because they felt
people would have fewer back injuries if they didn't have to bend
over as far as they did when using conventional garden tools. The
product's package was adequate: it clearly indicated that the product
reduced back strain while gardening. Sam and Jeff's problem was
that people couldn't understand why an extra handle on a garden
tool would reduce back strain. The product failed.

Chip Clips have been a big seller. Their initial package simply showed how an opened bag of snacks was sealed with a Chip Clip. Consumers quickly grasped the product's intended use and its benefit. Compact disks, on the other hand, succeeded only after a great deal of promotional publicity from major electronics companies. Consumers couldn't initially understand a compact disk's benefits.

The products that succeed grab consumers' attention immediately. You must have a way to show people a benefit. When we developed our tire cutter, we didn't show the cutter itself, because people wouldn't understand what it did. Instead, we showed a cut-up tire, a benefit customers immediately recognized.

Don't try to market a consumer product unless people can understand its benefit in less than 5 to 10 seconds. Don't try to market a nonconsumer product unless customers can understand in less than 15 seconds how you're solving a problem.

The Product Is Clearly Different

Everywhere I went in the summer of 1990, I noticed covers for soda and beer cans in point-of-purchase displays. This product snaps over the entire top of a beverage can. It has a reclosable snap flap that can be opened when the user wants a drink. The product's benefits are that it keeps an open can of soda or beer from going stale too quickly and it stops bees from going into an open can. Why did the product end up on so many countertops? Because it was different.

In the fall of 1990, two hot-selling products were the slap bracelets I mentioned earlier, and orange garbage bags with a black pumpkin face printed on them. Both products were successful because they were unique. Another new product that did well recently was the Balloon Wrap, the vacuum-chamber balloon machines that put teddy bears and other furry-creature toys inside of big balloons. Again, the fact that the product was clearly different gave it a chance to succeed.

Products can be clearly different in many ways. For example, a cordless drill, a rechargeable flashlight, a fishing reel that doesn't

get tangles, or a T shirt with a new slogan can all be different because they're innovative. But a clear difference can also be introduced in a product's operation, size, or weight. For example, a faster
running drill with more torque, a lighter, smoother functioning
hedge trimmer, or an easier-to-apply car wax could all be products
that are clearly different. How do you know when a product is
clearly different? When a potential customer can look at it and recognize within 1 to 2 seconds, that the product is unique. If consumers can't make that snap judgment, then a product doesn't pass
this go/no-go decision test.

A product entrepreneur needs a distinctly different idea, to
have a chance of selling a product to a distribution network. As an
example, consider Phil Q., who created a new walleye fishing lure
that combined the benefits of a jig and a slip sinker. Walleyes can't
be caught on the surface, so bait must be placed near lake bottom,
which requires a weight of some sort. A jig is a weighted hook, usually partly made of plastic, with some feathers or other appetizing-
looking material on it. Besides the advantage of being weighted, the
jig can be jiggled around to attract a fish's attention. The jig's only
drawback is that walleyes will often spit out the bait when they feel
the jig's weight. The slip sinker, which corrects this problem, is attached a short distance from the hook. When the walleye takes the
bait and starts to swim away, the line slips through the sinker so that
the fish doesn't feel the weight. The problem with a slip sinker is
that the person fishing can't put any action or jiggle on the bait.
Phil's product was the first one on the market to combine the features of a jig and a slip sinker.

Even though Phil's product was different, he ran into heavy
resistance from fishing retail stores. They weren't anxious to take on
a new product from an unknown supplier: they were already buying
from two or three major lure manufacturers and didn't want the
paper work of adding another. The stores were also afraid of losing
their promotional allowances. Typically, manufacturers of seasonal
items (like fishing lures) offer promotional discounts that are pro-
rated for the volume purchased by a store. For example, a retailer
might receive a 10 percent discount for a $15,000 purchase. A store

will be reluctant to take on an item from a new product entrepreneur if its promotional discount will be jeopardized.

Finally, the stores wanted to see an advertising program to support the lure. Retailers don't like to give up shelf space to an unknown product. A retailer can minimize the chances of a rejection by being sure that a new product is advertised. Phil was undercapitalized and couldn't afford advertising.

Although Phil has been able to overcome all of this resistance and place his lure in several stores, it's too soon to know whether the product will succeed. A product creator's idea must be clearly different if it is to overcome the built-in inertia that prevails in most distribution networks.

The Product Has a Significantly Better Benefit

Mosquitoes are a constant hot-weather problem. Just outside my front door in summer, I often have anywhere from 20 to 100 mosquitoes hovering, waiting for their next meal. When a company introduced a small electronic device that repelled mosquitoes, I bought one for $5.95. The product's benefit was very appealing to me.

Another inventor had devised an innovative spice rack that was designed to be pulled in and out of a kitchen cabinet. The product was an improvement, but because its benefit wasn't important to most people, the product failed.

When consumers look at a product's benefit, what matters is how much better that benefit is than the benefits of competing products. The mosquito repeller's competitors were bug sprays. By comparison, the repeller didn't smell, lasted forever, and was environmentally safe. The spice rack's 10 to 20 percent improvement wasn't enough to attract consumers.

Product creators often become confused over this issue because companies repeatedly introduce products that offer only minimal improvements. Those companies' position is completely different from that of product entrepreneurs. The companies often replace their own products on store shelves. The retailer isn't faced with making supplier changes. If a company has a strong brand name, stores will want to stock its products. Most hardware stores will carry any new product introduced by Black & Decker. Finally, companies have established distribution networks and promotional programs. They have contacts in place to help introduce a product. Product entrepreneurs don't have these advantages. They must rely on having a product with superior benefits.

The soda and beer can covers I mentioned earlier had two important benefits: they kept the drinks from going flat, and they kept bees out of the cans—pretty good benefits for a 99-cent product. As for the slap bracelet and the halloween garbage bags, their benefit was that they were fun. American consumers place a high premium on any product that adds some inexpensive fun to their lives.

How do you know when a product has a significantly better benefit? When consumers say they'd really like to have it or exclaim: "That's fantastic! Why didn't anyone think of that before?"

Conducting Initial Marketing Research

You should do the initial marketing research in two steps. Decide whether your idea meets the three criteria we've been discussing. If you feel it does, then confirm your decision with input from potential customers, using the market research tactics listed in the chapter's next section.

During your initial research, you won't necessarily have a model or prototype. You might have only a drawing or a crude model, which won't yield perfect input from potential customers. You can still get valuable input by using two simple tactics.

The first tactic is to verify your premises. Suppose you have a product that kills flies. Your premise—that consumers need a better way to kill flies—is the reason you developed the product. You want to be sure that people agree with your premise. The best way to verify consumers' needs is to show people products that are currently being sold and ask them:

1. Have they used the products;
2. Do they feel the products work effectively;
3. In what way the products should be improved.

People will give you a wide variety of answers, but you should be able to tell, for example, whether or not people feel there is a need for a better way of killing flies.

If your product doesn't have competitors, then you should ask people how they currently meet the need you've identified, and whether they would like an alternate solution to the need. Charlie R. designed, for condominium owners, a bed that could double as a locked storage space. The inventor needed to ask whether owners who sublet their units still kept items such as golf clubs, tennis rackets, and other valuables in their units; and whether the owner/landlords were interested in having a secure way to store their valuables.

A premise doesn't have to be as dull as a better way to kill flies. Do-it-yourselfers might want an inexpensive power tool; bike riders, tired of ten-speed bikes, might want a more comfortable bike, like a mountain bike; people of all ages might find a novelty item a lot of fun.

The second tactic is to verify that potential customers can see how your product will meet the preliminary go/no-go marketing decisions. Show people the idea, have them compare it to competitive products, and then ask how long it took them to understand your product's benefit, how different it seems in comparison to other products, and how important the new product's benefit would be to them. If competitive products don't exist, show your product and ask people how long it takes to see the benefit and how important the benefit is.

You're asking the same question twice when you ask someone to verify a premise and then to tell you how important a product's benefit is. I like to do that because people won't always realize how important a product's benefit is if they see only a drawing. They need to see the product. Asking them to verify a premise is a double-check to see whether a product will have an important benefit. Another reason to check twice is that people sometimes get confused by a drawing and, rather than tell you they're confused, they'll give you an answer without thinking. People usually don't have any problem explaining why they think a premise is valid or invalid. Ask both questions just to improve your research's accuracy.

Free or Low-Cost Market Research

Product creators tend to think that market research is something that only big companies can afford to do. In fact, most individuals can gather almost as much quality information relative to their potential markets as large companies do, without spending a fortune.

Most of the tactics listed here can be used for both the initial and final market research steps. I recommend using as many tactics as possible in the initial research; your first research efforts occur *before* you spend much money. Do the best job you can when you gather initial research, to avoid spending money on a product that can't be marketed.

Gather Input from Friends

I don't recommend investing any money based on friends' input, but there is nothing wrong with doing some preliminary research with them when you're deciding whether you should even start a project. Don't tell your friends that you have a great idea and then ask them whether they agree. Instead, use your friends as a research panel. They can provide you with an initial response to the validity of your product premise, and further proof that a product meets the preliminary go/no-go decision criteria.

Set Up an Impartial Research Panel

If you're developing a consumer item, you can pass out to your neighbors a flier offering $10 to anyone willing to participate in a market research study. Explain on the flier that you've created an exciting new product and you need people to evaluate it. You can even list on the flier the type of people you're looking for: fishing enthusiasts, women who have jobs, people who like to do home woodworking, and so on. You'll pique people's curiosity with the flier, and some calls will start to come in.

Among other tactics you can use to find people for a research panel are: join any relevant clubs in the area, such as a woodworking or a garden club; post a flier in a store that sells products in your category of research; and ask friends to give you names to contact. To research nonconsumer products, you can attend trade association meetings and set up appointments with appropriate engineers and marketers from companies in the market you hope to penetrate.

Use Industry Insiders as Paid Consultants

An industry insider is someone who is already involved, as a manufacturer, distributor, or retailer, in the market you're trying to enter. Insiders don't have much free time during the course of a day. If you get to talk to one of them, the conversation will be held to about 15 minutes. One way to get around this is to offer to hire the insider for a couple of evening hours. Some people are flattered to be asked to consult, and they'll give you a tremendous amount of input. Usually, you can find someone to help you for a fee of about $100. Chapter 8 covers how to find and use insiders.

Run Ads

Sometimes, research will show that a product has potential, but will leave you unsure whether people will quickly grasp the idea's benefit and then buy. A good tactic to use in this situation is to run an ad and measure the response.

As an example, Gary O. developed a smelter system that attached to a wood stove. His product could be used to melt down aluminum and metal cans. Once the metal was liquid, it could be poured into a mold to produce a metal ingot, which is a large bar that can be sold to a foundry. The product was primarily targeted at people living in rural areas, who had no convenient way of recycling food and beverage cans. Gary's product was difficult to research because only a small percentage of people were potential customers.

Gary ran a classified ad in the magazine *Mother Earth News*. The ad offered, for $12, plans for the smelter. He received enough orders from the ad to convince him that his product might succeed.

Another example is a fly trap that I worked on. The product competed with electronic bug killers and fly strips. Everyone told me the product was great, but I was worried that people wouldn't be willing to go to the trouble of setting up and then emptying the trap. I ran ads in small local papers in Georgia, offering two traps in a kit for $4.95. The ad response was pitiful and I dropped the product.

Newspaper ads are generally too expensive to be used for research. Magazine ads tend to be much cheaper and you can usually find a magazine that is specifically targeted at your potential customers. For example, NordicTrack manufactures a cross-country skiing version of a treadmill. Its primary customers are affluent people who can afford to spend $500 and more for home exercise equipment. Its initial advertising appeared in airline magazines; most airline travelers/readers have incomes of over $40,000. You don't have to restrict your advertising to small local magazines. Many larger magazines will inexpensively run an ad in a small geographic area. *TV Guide*'s rate for an ad in a limited urban area is under $350. Your ad should invite people to either buy the product or request more information.

Incidentally, be careful if you decide to run an ad that asks for advance payment. After receiving an order, you only have 30 days to either ship the product or offer a refund. Otherwise, you might be violating postal regulations. Plan on sending out refunds, or offer only a free information package in the ad.

Interview Store Owners

Once you have a model or prototype, along with a product's packaging, you're in a position to talk to store owners, distributors, and other prospective sellers in a distribution network. If you have an industrial or other nonconsumer product, call on distributors or manufacturers' representatives who sell the product. You can also contact people in companies that might use your type of product.

It's imperative that you obtain some input from people who sell to your market. Their input is more reliable than consumers'. You can't be sure that consumers will buy a product, even when they tell you they will; people don't like to give other people negative feedback. Consumers won't always know what other products are available to buy instead of yours. People in a distribution network, besides being informed, are always evaluating objectively the ideas proposed by salespeople and employees. They won't feel guilty about telling you that they don't like an idea, and they're usually honest about the reasons they won't buy. Consumers often try to soften the impact of negative comments.

Another reason to talk to store owners or industrial buyers is that you can give them a sales presentation. When you deal with consumers, it's dangerous to try to sell them a product, because your presentation may influence them too much. People in a distribution network are not so easily swayed. Give them a presentation and you can find out not only whether they'll buy your product, but also whether your sales strategy is on target.

Attend Flea Markets or Trade Shows

The advantage of selling a product at these outlets is that you can contact a large number of potential buyers in a short time. Flea markets are handy because you don't need a polished product. Lou B., for example, created an improved wheelbarrow. Lou had several working but rugged-looking prototypes; he had made them by modifying existing wheelbarrows. Lou knew he could test the product at flea markets if he could also sell old wheelbarrows. He visited flea markets and garage sales for a couple of months, rounding up as many used wheelbarrows as he could find. Then he took them, along with two of his improved version, to a flea market. After a weekend of concentrated sales effort, Lou concluded that people didn't understand his product's benefit. (Flea markets or craft shows often rent table space for under $20.)

Trade shows are usually not open to the public; they are held for retailers, wholesalers, and distributors who are in a specific market such as gifts, toys, or sporting goods. You can rent a small booth at a trade show, and you will receive valuable input by showing the product to both buyers and sellers. Trade shows cost more than flea markets, but you can hold down your expenses if you attend small regional shows.

You can find out what trade shows are coming to your area by checking with your city, county, or state convention/tourist bureau; talking to retailers; reading your area's business magazines; or checking the industry's trade magazines.

Don't go to an industry's largest trade show. It will cost too much, and your product concept may need some refinements before it can be shown to a large audience.

Final Marketing Go/No-Go Decisions

Start a marketing evaluation with the three preliminary go/no-go decision criteria (see page 96). You can do this, most often, with a drawing or a rough model. Once you're confident that your idea meets those criteria, make a model that's representative of what the final product will be like. As a last step, check your idea against the final go/no-go decisions given below.

The final go/no-go decisions help a product creator to determine whether, with limited resources, he or she can introduce a product. The criteria will *not* determine whether a product could be introduced by a large, well-funded company. A product like compact disks wouldn't pass these go/no-go decisions because the benefits of the disks weren't obvious. Compact disks were a great product for a company that could afford an extensive promotional program.

Is the Product's Benefit Obvious?

The first three final go/no-go decisions are the same as the preliminary decisions. You should check these three points again, after you have a model. The model allows you to show the product to people, who will then be able to give you a more reliable response than could be gained from only looking at a drawing.

Is the Product Clearly Different?

Ask people to look at a group of similar products that includes your representative model, and to state which ones they've seen before. Then ask the research respondents to rate the products, from highest to lowest, by how unique they are. If people respond that they've seen your product before, or give the product a poor ranking for uniqueness, you'll know the product is not clearly different.

Asking people to determine which products they've seen before also gives you some feedback on how aware of the target market your respondents are. If a person has never seen a product that has been on the market for years, you should note that fact when you review the respondents' comments.

Is the Benefit Significantly Better?

This is an important point to recheck. In your initial research, you told people what your benefit would be, and then asked how important that benefit was to them. Most people respond with the belief that a product would completely meet the need. In reality, few products are that perfect. You need to know:

• Does the prototype meet the need people thought it would?
• Does the way the product works provide an important benefit?

For example, the benefit of the tire cutter I introduced (see Chapter 1) was that discarded tires would take up less space at a garage or dump. Preliminary research indicated that this was a big benefit. When we had a model, people could see how much space the cut-up tires required. The tires used less space than some people had imagined, and more space than others had thought was needed.

When people see a product and the job it performs, they can decide again how much better the benefit is.

Does the Product Have Emotional Appeal?

I have two sons, eight and five years old. They saw the Teenage Mutant Ninja Turtles in a toy store long before the turtles were popular or even advertised. The minute my sons saw the characters, they wanted one. The Ninja Turtles were the only items in the store they wanted to buy. That's the type of appeal that helps a product sell.

A consumer product can have emotional appeal because it's "neat," like the Ninja Turtles; or it solves a problem, like a rechargeable flashlight; or is cute, like a Pet Rock or Halloween garbage bags; or helps a consumer project an image.

Wayne C. and John M. created a product that appeals to people because it creates an image. They developed a storage container for fishing gear that could be permanently locked into a boat. Their idea was that the gear could be stored overnight, and the container's location allowed a person fishing from a chair to easily grab anything that was needed.

I'm not a fisherman; the product looked dull to me. But others who fish thought it was fabulous—a perfect product for fishing enthusiasts who had everything. Why did the product have appeal? Because it was new, different, and convenient to use? I don't know why people like it; I just know they did.

Wayne and John failed to put their product on the market. The initial market research was done with the product priced at $29.95, but Wayne and John couldn't keep costs down low enough to charge that price. Instead, the product ended up costing $59.95. The product's appeal vanished at that price. Emotional appeal is a combination of looks, features, benefits, and price. Changing the price changed the product's combination and destroyed its appeal.

Inventors have trouble measuring emotional appeal. They're excited about their product, and they're anxious to have people praise it. The best method I've found to gauge a product's appeal is to have people rank a group of five or six similar products, one of which is your product. Pick three types of products for the group—some with strong appeal; some with less appeal; and some with no appeal. You'll get a better idea of what category your product is in.

Can the Product Be Packaged Effectively?

Some products, especially midsize ones, are difficult to package. Tom S. created a new camping grill that hung down from a tripod so that it could be used over a wood fire. The product was targeted at boaters, hikers, hunters, and backpackers, who aren't always able to stay at a structured campground. The grill came in a cardboard box that measured 18 by 24 by 2 inches.

Tom's package posed several problems. The box was an awkward size that took up too much space on a retailer's floor. Sales volume was too low for retailers to set up a display model. The grill failed because, without a model, consumers weren't able to see and touch the product.

Packaging possibilities can add real spark to a product. Dale McGinnis came up with an idea to prevent crayons from breaking. He called the product Boo-Boo Toobs: fluorescent-color tubes, the same size as a crayon, which slipped over crayons to protect them. Dale packaged the product in sharp-looking little containers that resembled the top of a crayon, and put the product in a point-of-purchase display that had some cute pictures of a kid using the Boo-Boo Toobs. I believe Dale's package is the most important reason that his product is in over 500 stores.

Does the Product Have an Acceptable Price/Value Relationship?

When people look at a product, they decide either consciously or subconsciously what the product is worth. For example, you might look at a toy figure and decide that it's worth $5. If the product is priced above $5, you probably won't buy it, no matter how much you or your kids like it.

To check a product's perceived value, place it again in a group of similar products, and ask people to list the products by the order of their value. Because you know what the other products sell for, you can estimate your product's perceived value. For you to make money, your price normally has to be at least four times the manufacturing cost (as determined in Chapter 7).

You should experiment with a product's perceived value. Sometimes, minor product modifications can add a great deal to a product's value. Glen A. developed a plastic puzzle in which five solid rings could be linked together or taken apart. The puzzle's perceived value was only $5, primarily because it was made of plastic. If Glen had made his puzzle out of stainless steel, the puzzle would have had a perceived value of about $8.

As you work on your project, start a price/value chart of similar products. The chart can show you how to change a product to bring its price/value ratio in line. A chart for Glen's puzzle is:

Features	Typical Price
1. Plastic	$5
2. Steel	7
3. Stainless steel	8
4. Steel with rubber handles	10
5. Upscale packaging	2 additional

Is the Product in an Established Category?

Rhonda L. developed a new, inexpensive alarm to let people know when someone was breaking into an apartment or home. The alarm slipped over a door. A 3-inch pole extended from the top of the alarm. When the alarm was on the door, the door jam pushed the rod back against a switch and the alarm was quiet. If the door was opened, the pole moved forward, activating the alarm.

At first glance, the alarm seemed like a great product to sell through discount stores. The problem was that discount stores didn't have a place for this type of product. If it were stocked with locks, only people looking to buy locks would see it. Rhonda couldn't afford to advertise enough to make people ask for the product, and the product wasn't suited for a point-of-purchase display. The product had potential, but there was no place to put it. Product entrepreneurs have a very tough time marketing products that fall out of established product categories.

Does the Product Have a Great Name or Other Promotional Possibilities?

"The Pet Rock" was a great name. Large, fold-up windshield shades and soda or beer can huggies (coolers that fit over aluminum cans) sold because they are great ways for companies like Coca-Cola, or stores like 7-Eleven, to promote their names.

Slim-Fast and Ultra Slim-Fast have easy-to-promote names. Closet organizers show up well in pictures. Products that are in "hot" neon pink or blue are promotable because they look good in a photograph.

Other products don't adapt well to promotion. Clyde S. came out with a dart board that included a game called Chicago. In this dart game, the players try to try to hit numbers 1 and 6. Each player throws 5 darts. A 1 is worth 100 points, a 6 is worth 60 points, and all other numbers are counted at face their value; for example, a 5 is worth 5 points. The game's benefit was hard to show both on the product's package and in an advertising program.

I once saw a novelty product that featured clock components that rocked back and forth. The only way the product's feature could be shown was in a demonstration, which made it hard to package the product effectively.

Going Forward

I don't think you should try to market a product unless it meets at least 6 of the 8 marketing go/no-go decision criteria—and I don't mean *barely* meets. You should display your product with 6 others, to allow you to see not only whether your product has a selling point, but also how strong that point is.

Some readers may feel that my criteria are too tight. Other manufacturers are certainly introducing products that don't meet every point. One of the book's main points is that product creators have to introduce products when they have a fraction of the marketing power of a large company. They must compensate for their deficit by choosing ideal products.

Brian P. came into my office with fashion sports shoes that everyone else thought would be an enormous hit with teenagers. I didn't. I have trouble getting excited about a product before comparing it to the competition. I gathered a few brochures showing shoes that were coming out in the next season (a manufacturers' representative who had attended the last major shoe trade show loaned them to me), along with a few comparable products that were already in stores. People lost much of their enthusiasm after they saw what other shoes were available.

The moral of the story is to take one step at a time. One of your most important steps is to carefully check whether people will buy your product.

7

Manufacturing: Not Every Product Can Make Money

I met Jim E. at a boat show. Jim had created a small wheel device that fit underneath the front of a boat's hull and made it easier to pull the boat up onto a beach. Jim only sold his product at boat shows. When I asked him why he didn't sell through distributors, he told me he couldn't afford to sell the product at wholesale because his manufacturing cost was higher than the product's wholesale price.

Where did Jim go wrong? He had to know the perceived value of his product because he was a boat owner. What he didn't know was that, to make money, his manufacturing cost couldn't exceed 25 percent of the product's retail price. Jim used high-quality materials, and one of his friends was his contract manufacturer. His production costs were 75 percent of his retail price.

Manufacturing is an area where you must be a hard-nosed negotiator. If a cost should be no more than $3, then it *must not be* any higher. If you look again at the cost flow-through chart in Chapter 4 (page 52), you can see that there's no margin for errors in costing. Errors will make an already slim profit margin disappear.

In addition to final manufacturing costs, a substantial investment will be needed to put your product on the market. Models,
prototypes, tooling, set-up charges, and packaging are all areas that
can consume a tremendous amount of money. I've talked to many
product entrepreneurs who've spent over $50,000 just to get ready
to produce a product.

You should concentrate on three manufacturing concerns:

1. Can you hold a product's manufacturing cost down to less than
   25 percent of its perceived value?
2. Can you hold the model, prototype, and first production costs at
   a level you can afford?
3. Can you afford, or get a contract manufacturer to absorb, the
   tooling and start-up costs of putting your product into production?

The Preliminary Evaluation

The two major product cost components are manufacturing and
packaging. The two minor cost components are product liability insurance, which typically runs about 1.5 to 2.0 percent of sales, and
scrap/product returns/shrinkage, and so on, which usually total
about 5 percent of sales. All four cost components added together
equal a product's total cost.

Before you start spending money on a project, be sure that you
can make your product at a cost that's less than 25 percent of the
proposed retail price. You won't have a product or a prototype to
cost out, but you can utilize comparison products and estimating
techniques to decide whether an idea can make money.

Estimating Manufacturing Costs

Your first step is to find a product that is about the same size, is
made out of the same materials, and has about the same complexity

as your projected product. You'll receive more accurate cost quotes from manufacturers if you can give them a clear idea of what the product will be like.

If at all possible, try to find a product that is handled in the distribution network you hope to use, and that has a sales volume similar to the volume you expect your idea to achieve. You can find a similar product in a mail-order catalog, magazine, or retail store, or at a trade show. Be sure to purchase the product. You won't be able to get by with just showing the manufacturer a picture.

The next step is to make a mockup (a crude model of an idea). You can use cardboard, papier mâché, wood, or other inexpensive materials. The first thing you need to do when you're making your mockup is to list every feature the product will have. If possible, include all those features in the mockup. If that's not possible, then make a model, or another mockup, that shows only what that feature will look like and how it will work. For example, when I was working for the dental supply company mentioned earlier, we developed a new dental chair with a feature we called compensating traverse. This feature kept a patient's head in the same vertical plane, as the rest of the chair was being reclined. Our mockup of the chair represented what the chair would look like, but it couldn't simulate compensating traverse. We constructed a small wooden model, about 6 inches high, that demonstrated how that feature would work. If your product includes a feature of another product, such as a nozzle from a spray paint can, be sure to obtain a sample of that part. The manufacturer must understand every detail of your product before offering a quote.

A model or prototype will generate more accurate quotes than a mockup, but I don't believe the quotes will improve enough in your favor to justify investing in a prototype just to obtain price quotes. On the other hand, I've always been disappointed with price quotes based on drawings. The problem sometimes lies with the manufacturer, who may leave off, or may not understand, features that are shown in a drawing. More often, though, the problem lies with product entrepreneurs who forget, or don't explain, important features. A mockup forces you to explain all the details of the idea.

The last step is to obtain price quotes from several manufacturers for both your product and a similar product. To obtain these price quotes, you'll need to approach manufacturers that make the same type of product as yours. For example, if you have a plastic product that measures 4 inches high, 3 inches wide, and 2 inches deep, approach manufacturers that make a similar size product.

Tell the manufacturers that you may be introducing a new product and that you need two price quotes, one from a mockup of your idea, and one from a finished, active product. When you receive the quotes, be sure to ask why the quote for your product is different from the quote for the established product. You might find that one or two features cost too much or that the low-cost material you've chosen has left you free to consider a higher-grade option and still stay within budget. At the very least, you'll learn quite a bit about how to convert an idea into a manufacturing process. When I first received quotes on my tire cutter, the estimates were too high. But I found out from the manufacturer that one feature of the product, a handle that attached at a 90-degree angle, was difficult to manufacture. I was able to cut the quote by $4 per unit by switching to a differently angled handle.

There are many ways to find manufacturers that can give you a cost quote:

- Ask some of your contacts in the industry.
- Look in the Yellow Pages, or in a business-to-business telephone book.
- Look in your state's industrial directory, available at your library. The directory will list manufacturers by the type of products they produce.
- Keep copies of want ads published in your city. Often, the ads tell what type of products a company makes. Ads for salespeople are especially informative.
- Use *Thomas Register of American Manufacturers* at your library, to find local companies that manufacture products similar to your idea.

Should you get quotes even if you're planning on making the product in your basement? Yes. When you do your initial production runs, you may not make any money on your sales. That's OK; your initial production run should be used only to prove that your product can be sold. Sooner or later, you'll have to go into full production in order to succeed. You must be sure that you'll be able to make money when you reach a normal production level.

What if the quotes come in considerably higher than 25 percent of your projected retail price? For instance, if a hardware product brings in quotes that average $4.05, or about 45 percent of the planned $8.95 retail price, the production costs would appear to be prohibitively high. I wouldn't worry too much about that, as long as the comparison product also receives quotes of about 45 percent of its retail price. At this preliminary stage, you'll almost always get high quotes. Once you can show that an idea has sales potential, you'll be able to receive more favorable pricing. Later on, you can investigate some possibilities for lowering the manufacturing costs.

Estimating Packaging Costs

This is the second of a product's two major cost components. For some products, especially those in lower-priced ranges, packaging will be 25 to 30 percent of total costs.

Packaging costs are dependent on a product's sales volume. A small consumer product in a blister pack might have a packaging cost of 8 cents at high volume, or a cost of 25 cents if volume is low. In Chapter 5, I discussed how to estimate a product's sales volume. Be sure to check your volume estimates carefully before you talk to packaging suppliers. You can find suppliers through your contacts, the phone book, state industrial directories, or *Thomas Register.*

Packaging costs have two components: upfront costs for tooling and artwork, and a per-piece packaging cost. Your estimate might list a cost of 25 cents to package each product, plus set-up charges of $1,000 for color artwork and $1,500 for a blister-pack mold. Keep these charges separate. The 25 cents will be a part of the product's ongoing cost. The artwork and mold charges will be one-time start-up expenses.

Calculating a Preliminary Manufacturing Cost

After obtaining the first two estimates, you'll have a packaging cost, which should be reasonably accurate, and a manufacturing quote, which will normally be higher than you had expected to pay. You still don't have enough information to make a wise decision. You need to utilize the comparison product to evaluate your product's cost. The comparison procedure has four steps. In the first two, you'll calculate the manufacturing cost of the comparison product; in the last two, you'll estimate your product's total cost. Note that this procedure omits product liability insurance and scrap costs, but the omission will not affect the preliminary estimates because these elements make up only a small part of the overall costs.

Product Comparison Procedure

1. Multiply the retail price of the similar product by 25 percent. This figure should be close to the product's total cost.
2. Subtract the average packaging estimate you received for the similar product. The number you obtain is the estimated manufacturing cost of the similar product.

   Example: To determine the manufacturing cost for an existing hardware product that has a retail price of $8.95 and a wholesale cost of $4.47 (wholesale cost is typically approximately half the retail price):

   1. Multiply the product's retail price by 25 percent
      to obtain total product costs ($8.95 × .25) $2.24
   2. Subtract packaging costs   − .42

      Similar product's manufacturing costs $1.82

   Now you're ready to calculate your product's costs.

3. Calculate your projected manufacturing cost. Take the cost from step 2 and multiply it by the cost ratio that results from the two manufacturing quotes. To get the ratio, if your product's average quote was $2.75, for example, and the similar product's average quote was $1.96, the cost ratio is $2.75/$1.96, or 1.4.

4. Add on the projected packaging costs to determine your product's total cost.

Example: To determine your product's total cost based on the similar product analyzed in steps 1 and 2:

3. Calculate your manufacturing costs by multiplying
   the similar product's manufacturing cost of $1.82
   by the cost ratio of 1.4 $2.55
4. Add packaging costs   + .52

   Total product cost $3.07

This is the cost you should use in your preliminary evaluation of whether your product can make money. Your initial production costs will probably be quite a bit higher, but you can't expect to make money with low-volume production. Your goal here is to be sure that you can make money once you reach *normal* production levels. The total cost gives you a target amount to shoot for. Keep searching until you find a contract manufacturer that can hit the required price for your projected production levels.

Comparing Costs to Perceived Value

In Chapter 6, I explained how to estimate a product's perceived value. Take that value and compare it to your manufacturing costs multiplied by 4. For example, for the hardware product in the example, multiply $3.07 by 4 to arrive at a minimum final retail price of $12.28. The product can make money as long as its perceived value is more than $12.28.

After your preliminary evaluation, you must make your go/ no-go decision: can your product be made for less than 25 percent of its perceived value? If the product's perceived value is too low, review the price feature chart shown on page 110. Is there any way to add value to the product?

At least 50 percent of the time, product entrepreneurs need to adjust their product's value. It's important to keep track of what features add value, and what features add costs. Always ask manufacturers for a detailed explanation of their price quotes.

Building a Model or Prototype

If a preliminary evaluation indicates that a product can potentially make money, the next step is to decide whether you can afford the necessary models and prototypes. Most of these costs have to be borne by the product creator. Won't all the research you've done to date help to persuade investors that your idea has potential? Your research has only told you to continue with your project; you still don't have any convincing proof that the idea will sell. That proof comes, I feel, only after an idea has had some initial sales in the market.

A prototype looks and functions exactly like a finished production unit. A model may be slightly different in size and function than a production unit. You'd have a model if you bolted two plastic pieces together to represent a one-piece production unit. Use a model for a complex part, or for a product that has very high tooling costs. Some models show only one or two functions of a product— the improvements the idea has introduced for existing technology. A model may be made of a different material, such as wood, when the finished product will be metal or plastic.

As I mentioned earlier, you should always make a model or prototype before investing in production tooling. You can't do your final market research accurately without prototypes, and you'll often learn from them that your product has a few flaws that need correcting. It's not unusual for a product to have three or four different prototypes before the final version is ready to be introduced.

Unfortunately, many first-time product creators skip the prototype stage. They are positive their idea will sell and/or they don't know how to make a prototype inexpensively. They decide the investment for a prototype is unnecessary and proceed to buy expensive tooling and go straight into a production run. This mistake often leaves people, after an investment of $10,000 to $50,000, with a garage full of unsalable inventory.

Underfinanced inventors can't afford to skip the prototype stage. Not only do they lose an opportunity to perfect their products, but they lose the advantage of market research data that might convince a contract manufacturer to pick up their tooling costs.

I believe that prototypes for at least 95 percent of all products can be made in a person's garage or basement. I rarely even consider the expense of a prototype to be a go/no-go decision. I've included models in this chapter because so many product creators look at prototypes as an expense that only big companies can afford.

Did I really mean that you can make virtually any prototype in your basement, perhaps with just a little help from a machine shop? You have a plastic product that needs to be injection-molded, or a metal product that needs an investment casting, or an intricate piece of machinery that has 15 to 20 parts. *You can make all of these in your basement.* You may need to spend two weeks working out all the details, but that alternative is a lot better than spending $10,000 to $25,000 to have a manufacturer make a prototype.

How should you go about making models and prototypes? I can't offer you complete details for every type of product, but, when you get to the prototype stage, you should find information for your type of product available. I've listed in my "Helpful Sources" section (page 289) several books and magazines you can consult. My favorite book on prototypes, by far, is *The Modelmaker's Handbook* by Albert Jackson and David Day (Knopf, 1981). The book is written for hobbyists, but it contains most of the information you'll need. Its best feature is that it demonstrates how you can make virtually anything.

A magazine I highly recommend is *Fine Scale Modeler.* In addition to informative articles, the magazine has ads from companies that sell the supplies and equipment you need to make prototypes. Visit hobby shops, book stores, and your library to find other books and magazines that might be helpful.

The materials you need to make prototypes are not always readily available. I list several sources in this chapter; more are at the end of the book. I've found the best source for information to be the specialty trade magazines—*Fine Scale Modeler*, for example, or similar magazines listed in *Gale's Source of Publications*. Both sources can be found in large libraries.

Builders of model airplanes are great contacts. At any model display, look for modelers who've used your technology, or ask around until you get the names of people who know how to make a good model. These people can be of great help. If you're a klutz who isn't handy with tools, these hobbyists might make your prototype for a very low price.

Wood Models

These models are useful for a variety of applications: to simulate plastic or metal parts; as reference parts that can be used by a machine shop to manufacture a prototype; as models for molds for injection-molded parts; and as actual molds of vacuum formed prototypes.

Balsa wood, which is readily available in hobby stores, is the best wood to use if you have to bend or curve parts. Otherwise, you can use almost any wood that is available. You'll find an ample supply of woodworking books at any library, and most cities have several woodworking shops. Any model airplane hobbyist will have a sizable amount of woodworking equipment. If you don't want to make the model yourself, ask at a woodworking shop for the names of people who have large home shops. They might enjoy working on your project for a nominal fee and perhaps even at no charge.

Clay Models

If you're going to make a mold for a plastic or metal model, you will usually start with a clay model. Use the modeling clay sold in art supply stores. Its soft pliability allows you to add all the intricate features you'd like. The model should be as smooth as possible because every feature will come out in the final mold. Be sure to sand out any imperfections after the clay dries. Clay models make useful guides if parts have to be machined.

Plastic Models

You can make plastic parts out of a plastic mold (usually used for small parts); from temporary tooling (the best method for intricate parts); with a vacuum forming process (the easiest way for doing larger parts); by simply bending the parts (the cheapest and simplest way to make uncomplicated parts); and with fiberglass lay-up (typically used for very large parts).

1. **Using a plastic mold.** Hysol Electronic Chemicals has a line of plastic tooling materials, all of which cure at room temperatures. You can use the chemicals to make either a one-part or a two-part mold. A one-part mold is used when product features are on only one side of the product and the other side is flat. A two-part mold is used when features are on both sides of the product; each part of the mold has half of a product's features. To use the mold, you clamp the two parts of the mold together and leave a plug, which is a small hole through which you pour the molten plastic. After the part is molded, you can cut off any excess plastic from the plug.

To make a plastic mold, start out with a clay, wood, or machined (made from metal) model. Next, make a wood box that is about 40 percent bigger than the model. For a one-part mold, fill about 25 percent of the box with mold-making plastic, such as Hysol's TE6345NA. Place a mold release compound on your model, and then place the model in the box so that it is about a half-inch from the bottom of the box. Add molding plastic until it comes even with the back of the part. After the plastic cures, you will have a mold. You can use the mold while it is still in the box.

A two-part mold is made almost the same way. The only difference is that you'll use two boxes, and each mold will handle half of the part. After you do the first half, turn the product upside-down, place it in a box 25 percent full of molding resin, and bring the plastic mold material up to the same spot where the first mold stopped. Once the molding compound cures, clamp the two parts together, drill a small plug through the bottom, and you are ready to start making parts. After the mold is ready, coat it with a layer of nonsilicone wax, and then pour in plastic that you've heated over a Bunsen burner or stove. You can use this procedure with a silicone rubber compound from a company like Castolite. Hysol's plastic products are handy because you can machine the plastic mold to correct imperfections or to add features.

Your plastic mold can be used for a prototype and for your initial production run. Hysol's catalog *Plastic Tooling Materials* (#TG-15, 5/88) is very informative. The best plastic to use is polystyrene, which you can get from a hobby shop or virtually any chemical distributor.

2. **Temporary tooling.** Some parts need a lot of pressure to force the plastic into all the crevices; an injection molding machine is required, but an expensive mold is not. Instead, use temporary tooling. When you make a mold, you start out with a metal molding form, which functions as the wooden box does when you're making a plastic mold. Instead of buying brand new forms, look for used molding forms that are slightly bigger than your product. You usually can buy these from distributors of molding machines. Next, you need a metal or plastic model. For temporary tooling, aluminum is used instead of molding plastic as an insert in the used mold. A temporary mold may cost only 10 to 20 percent as much as a permanent mold. You'll need to find a small plastics manufacturer, or a company specializing in prototypes, to make the aluminum insert. The best sources for finding these companies are local distributors of plastic molding equipment. You should be able to find their names in a phone book or an industrial directory.

Some plastic products are too large for temporary tooling but need more strength than a vacuum formed part can provide. An example of this type of part is a 6-inch-long scoop, with a 4-inch handle, that can be used to throw and catch a ball. Prototypes for this type of product are best made with a temporary rubber mold. To do this, make a model of wood or sheet metal, and then cover the model with a silicone rubber mold material from a company like Castolite (see Helpful Sources, on page 289).

3. **Vacuum formed products.** Parts that are vacuum formed are usually larger and simpler than plastic molded parts. A mold for a vacuum formed part is different from a mold you would use with a plastic or temporary mold. For those methods, your model would be exactly like your product. In vacuum forming, the plastic wraps around the top and sides of the mold, and the part looks like a thin shell that would cover the mold. For example, a plastic canopy, or tray, or box could all be vacuum formed. The mold would look like the inside of the part.

The easiest way to make a vacuum formed part is to complete a wooden mold in your basement and then take the mold to a vacuum forming shop to have it made into your prototype. As long as you have a mold, the cost will be reasonable. Buy a sheet of ABS plastic for making the parts. ABS is readily available at any plastics distributor, or you can buy it from the vacuum forming shop.

Another option is to buy a small vacuum forming machine. Some cost less than $1,000. You can use the machine for models and prototypes, as well as for an initial production run.

4. **Bending plastic.** Plastic is fairly easy to bend and reshape. You need only wrap the plastic in aluminum foil and hold it over an electric stove until it softens. (An electric stove's heating area is less uneven than a gas stove's.) Be sure to wear insulating gloves. Bend the soft plastic around a block, or can, or other surface, to form the plastic into the shape you want. Once the plastic cools down it will hold its new shape.

Bending plastic and then machining it or reworking it is one of the fastest ways to make a model or prototype. You can successfully bend plastics into models without any experience. Buy acrylic and acetate sheets or rods from a plastics distributor, or bend an already existing part.

5. **Fiberglass lay-up.** This process, which is used in making boats and other very large shapes, is really a layering process.

Start with a wooden (or even cardboard) mold or base that looks like the outside of the part. Put down a coat of polyester resin, a layer of fiberglass, a layer of resin, and so on, until you build up enough strength for the product. Let the resin dry thoroughly between applications.

Fiberglass has very high strength and can be used in models in place of metal. On a dental chair, a large back portion required tooling that cost $45,000. The part could have been made from fiberglass, and then painted. It wouldn't have been as strong as metal, but it would still have been acceptable for a model. Small chemical distributors often carry fiberglass resin. It can also be found at some hobby shops.

Machined Parts

Machining refers to modifying or working a model by machine. Drilling, punching, turning, shaping, planing, and other operations are all machining processes. Most models require at least some machining. You can do it yourself if you have the proper equipment, or you can take your model to a machine shop or hobbyist for completion.

One of the easiest ways to make a model is to find similar parts or products, and then contact the manufacturer to see whether any old or discontinued molds are available. If they are, you may be able to have a mold machined so that it will make your part. This requires less work than starting from scratch, and you'll often get a better looking model. Occasionally, you might pick up a free mold. Charlie R. had a new applicator for floor wax. He found a medical supply company that made a part similar to the one for which he needed a mold. He talked to the company, and was given a mold from a discontinued product. Charlie had the mold machined into the shape he needed, for $250.

Most machine shops work off engineering drawings, which are expensive. But I've found that many smaller shops will duplicate a part from a model. This approach has several advantages: it saves on expensive engineering time, it minimizes the effect of drawing mistakes, and it provides the machine shop with a better idea of what the product will be like.

You might want to consider buying the machines you need to make your model. If you need only one or two machines, the expense won't be terrible. You'll actually save money by owning them, if you have to make three or four models before you create one that sells. You might then be able to make the initial production run yourself. Look for sources of small machining equipment, listed in modeling magazines. (Another good source is Micromark Corporation.)

Sheet Metal Models

Sheet metal is economical to work with and can be substituted for plastic in some large parts. A drain tray designed to go under washing machines will probably eventually be made of plastic, but the product's features can be demonstrated from a sheet metal model.

As mentioned earlier, the best way to obtain a model is to make a crude mockup out of cardboard or papier mâché. Take the mockup to a sheet metal fabricator who can make the final prototype. For most parts, you can obtain the model for under $300.

Fabric Models

Most fabric or vinyl models can be made either with a home sewing machine or through a contract manufacturer. If the fabric is heavy or if the item is fairly complex, I'd try to have the model made by a manufacturer. It won't cost any extra money because there won't be any tooling and set-up charges, and the manufacturer will have the equipment to make a professional-looking prototype.

Metal Models

Some metal parts can't be machined or bent; they must be cast. This process is similar to making a plastic mold, except that you use a cold curing silicon rubber as a mold, and a metal casting alloy as the molten material. Castolite Corporation has a large line of casting compounds and molds, as well as a very informative catalog. The company sells an introductory kit that can help you become familiar with the metal casting process. Another product for making a temporary metal mold is General Electric's Construction 1200 glazing compound.

Cannibalized Products

You can take apart already existing products and use their parts to make a new product. Donna K. created a new stationery product that helps people budget their income. She bought two products at K mart and two at a stationery store, and she ordered another from a catalog company. She then combined parts of each product to make her product.

Cannibalizing products won't always work, but it can be an excellent tactic. Combinations of cannibalized parts can create new working models. For example, if your new product requires an electronic switching mechanism, you might be able to remove one from a product you already have at home or can buy at a flea market or discount store.

Packaging

For some market research, you'll need to show the product in its package, to help you decide whether consumers can quickly grasp the purpose and benefit of a product. I recommend that you make several packaging models and then evaluate which one—or which combination of packaging—will work best for you.

Choice of packaging can affect cost. I once made a packaging evaluation for presenting an improved clothespin design, which was easier to use and caused fewer wrinkles than a standard clothespin. The product (a set of 12 clothespins) was suitable for a blister pack (a plastic molded piece glued onto a cardboard backing). Another possibility was placing the product on a piece of cardboard, and then shrink-wrapping both the card and the product. (Many packaging houses will shrink-wrap a product for a minimal fee.) A third alternative was to attach the product to a thin cardboard with metal clips. The comparative costs per sales unit were: blister pack, 55 cents; shrink-wrap, 20 cents; metal clip, 12 cents. That's quite a price spread for 12 clothespins with a manufacturing cost of only 40 cents per clothespin. The 12-cent package worked best, saving the product creator a tremendous amount of money.

Package models can usually be made from standard packages, close to the size you might eventually use, that are available from packaging suppliers.

When testing the packaging models, be sure to include graphics, which includes both pictures and copy (the words on the package).

Graphics is an area where costs can get out-of-hand. Color artwork can cost $2,000 to $3,000, an expense you shouldn't incur during your research phase. Be prepared to improvise. Choose a black-and-white or a color photograph, clip art, or a picture from a magazine as your artwork. Add copy to the package, displaying prominently the product's name and benefits. If you don't have an artistic touch, take your artwork and copy to a freelance artist or art student. You should be able to get final package graphics done for less than $100.

Take the completed package graphics to a copy center that has a color copier and have one or two copies made. Glue the color copies to the packaging's cardboard backing or to a point-of-purchase display. If you intend to use the display, make it last longer by having it laminated. Keep the original artist's version of the graphics for possible future use.

Budgeting

Once you've sorted through all of your options and all the steps of building your model, determine what your model costs will be. The second manufacturing go/no-go decision is: can you afford to produce the models and prototypes required for your project? Plan on having to pay for them from your own financial resources, and try to hold model costs below 25 percent of your available money. Holding model costs down will leave you with the money needed for an initial production run. If the model cost is too high, you need to find either a contract manufacturer who will absorb the cost, or a lower-cost method of building the model.

Contract Manufacturers

A manufacturer that agrees to make a product for another company, or for a product entrepreneur, is acting as a contract manufacturer. Any manufacturer can be a contract manufacturer, even if it makes and sells several products of its own. Most underfinanced entrepreneurs have to rely on a contract manufacturer to put a product on the market. Setting up a manufacturing operation is too expensive and complicated for most inventors. I recommend that you try to find a contract manufacturer after you finish conducting your market research with a model or prototype.

Finding the right contract manufacturer provides tremendous benefits to a product entrepreneur. The manufacturer might have a prototype lab or machine shop capable of making revised models or prototypes as well as the initial production run. Besides helping to find ways to economically produce the product, a contract manufacturer might agree to amortize tooling and final engineering costs over the product's manufacturing run. The entrepreneur would then pay back the tooling costs through a per-unit surcharge. For example, the manufacturer might charge $15,000 to cover start-up expenses. The product entrepreneur would pay an extra 56 cents per unit until the manufacturer recoups the $15,000.

If a manufacturer is not fully utilizing a plant, a contract arrangement can be lucrative. The arrangement provides profit on new production; helps cover overhead expenses; improves plant productivity; and increases production without incurring the financial risks of developing a new product.

Don't try to find a contract manufacturer at the start of your project; you'll be wasting your time. Manufacturers need proof that a product has potential, and you won't have proof until you've done at least some market research with an initial model or prototype.

Contract manufacturers prefer to invest in an idea after the end of the first sales period. However, sometimes the models or prototypes are too difficult or complicated or expensive for you to make. Then another manufacturing go/no-go decision becomes: can you find a contract manufacturer that will help defray some of the cost for any required prototypes?

Does it sound like the manufacturer is giving everything away? If the product succeeds, the manufacturer will recover all its costs from a per-unit amortization charge. If the product fails, the failure will cost a lot less than if the manufacturer had tried to develop and market a new product on its own. New product failures are a part of business that companies learn to accept.

Not all manufacturers are good candidates for a contract manufacturing agreement. Some may already have high production; others may be introducing their own new products. Some manufacturers feel that contract arrangements are big headaches. To a manufacturer looking for more production, however, your product might represent the difference between making and losing money.

To be successful with a contract manufacturing agreement, you have to find a manufacturer with the right attitude and circumstances, and you must be able to show that your product has a reasonable chance of success.

To find the right manufacturer, first go through your files and find friends of friends or any persons who might have manufacturing contacts. If they aren't in a position to help, they may know someone who is. Another approach is to look through trade magazines and find ads for companies that supply raw materials for products. Call the companies' headquarters and ask what salesperson, distributor, or manufacturers' representative covers your area. Call up those contacts and tell them that you're an entrepreneur with a new product and that you're looking for a contract manufacturer that might be willing to amortize tooling costs. You may have to call several contacts, but you'll get a list of manufacturers that might work with you.

You can also pick up contacts at trade shows. Some manufacturers attend shows to promote their contract services. The phone book is another source. If nothing else works, go to the library and find potential manufacturers in your state's industrial directory.

Check out small-town manufacturers up to 200 miles away. They'll have lower labor costs and, on occasion, they can get financial aid from their communities to pay for new molds, as long as a product will increase employment.

You must show that your product has a good chance to succeed. Manufacturers are constantly approached by entrepreneurs, and they also have products of their own to introduce. Show that your product has the best chance to make money.

In Chapter 4, I told you to record every contact you made and to follow up each contact with a letter. Most readers may have thought I was crazy to suggest such a time-consuming task. But when you try to convince a manufacturer that your product will sell, you'll have proof of whom you have contacted and what each person said. In Chapter 4, I also covered how to package an idea. My advice will help you to convince a manufacturer to support your product.

When you find an interested manufacturer, be honest about any problems you're facing. Most manufacturers have experience in introducing new products, and their people may be able to resolve puzzling situations. An important point: make the manufacturer responsible for the quality of your production units. Frank Q. had a room full of defective manufactured units of a hardware product. The manufacturer said the defect was the fault of the supplier; the supplier blamed the manufacturer. Frank didn't have enough experience or know-how to solve the dispute, and he ended up paying for products he couldn't sell.

There are three areas where you might have conflicts with a contract manufacturer:

1. Simplifying your product, to cut both tooling and production costs. Sometimes, simple changes can reduce costs without impacting a product's perceived value. Other changes might have

a negative impact on how customers respond to your idea. Resist any negative changes.

2. Finding the best technology for your product. One inventor I talked to had lined up a manufacturer with vacuum-forming equipment for a product that should have been injection-molded instead. Keep informed on technology through trade magazines and various manufacturing contacts.

3. Getting a lower per-unit price from another manufacturer. When this happens, conflicts can arise because entrepreneurs resent paying more than necessary to a manufacturer. Keep in mind that your contract manufacturer may have absorbed tooling and other costs that have been added to your per-unit price. Be loyal to any manufacturer that helps you get started, and be sure that a price from another manufacturer includes all charges, including initial set-up.

Firm Price Quotes

After you finish conducting your market research with a model, get a firm quote for the actual manufacturing cost. Can the product be sold for four times its cost? Whether you would make money on the project was a go/no-go decision in the preliminary manufacturing evaluation. You must review your decision again, after your model has been built and tested.

You can develop a firm price quote yourself, or you can use a contract manufacturer's quote. I strongly recommend that you base your product's cost on a quote from a manufacturer, even if you are planning on making the product yourself. People who have no manufacturing experience have a very tough time generating a manufacturing cost. I spent 10 years working on new products in companies that had established manufacturing cost systems, and I thought I understood the systems quite well. I never once was able to estimate a final manufacturing cost with an error of less than 50 percent.

Why is it so tough to estimate a cost? Doesn't a product creator know what raw materials are required and how long each product will take to make? Unfortunately, an estimate is not that simple. A key question is: how many units a day will a person be able to make? Suppose you know that you can make 25 units per hour. But a worker won't produce constantly at peak efficiency. Time must be given to breaks, lunch hours, holidays, stocking materials on the line, cleaning up, packaging, delivering, reworking, and rejecting parts, all of which affect a worker's output. There are many hidden expenses: supplies, freight on incoming orders, unemployment taxes, social security taxes, and phone bills. The list of areas where a product entrepreneur might make costing mistakes is virtually endless. Your best bet is to get a quote from a manufacturer that's used to dealing with total costing.

The Initial Production Run

The initial sales period is only designed to prove that a product can be sold. A small production run of somewhere between 25 and 200 units will do this. This is *not* the time to invest heavily in tooling and other expenses, because many products never make it past the initial sales period. Instead, build or manufacture the number of units that represents the smallest possible investment. Holding down tooling costs will raise your unit cost to a high—and sometimes extremely high—level. That's OK, as long as your initial production run is small. Your go/no-go decision at this stage is: can you afford whatever investment is required to produce a small number of units?

Bob D. created a ski bag that had a number of special pouches for virtually every item a skier would need. Bob had a sewing machine in his basement and his "production" runs came out of his "factory" every Saturday morning. Bob's costs were high because he was buying all his supplies at retail prices. His manufacturing cost was $24, and his wholesale price was only $22, a price that guaranteed Bob would lose money. Bob could have had lower costs working with a sewing manufacturer, but he would have had to produce patterns, drawings, production specifications, samples, and instructions for the inspection department. Bob found it much more practical and inexpensive to produce his product at home.

If you're forced to use a manufacturer, the burden of finding a low-cost production method will still fall on you. Some of the best ways to hold down manufacturing costs in the initial sales period include modifying other products, making the product out of another material, or using temporary tooling. All of these tactics require finishing work such as sanding, drilling, and polishing. Manufacturers don't like to work on a product twice; they prefer straight-line production of a unit.

To benefit from the up-front cost savings of temporary tooling and other low-investment production techniques, be prepared to "volunteer" to do all the finishing work yourself. Your willingness to help will be appreciated by the contract manufacturer and might prod the manufacturer into picking up the costs of temporary tooling.

Watch for alternate manufacturing methods during the entire time you work on a project. Read every trade magazine you can—both the articles and the ads. Get on the mailing lists of appropriate catalogs that you see advertised in magazines. Often, your ability to hold down costs will be directly related to how much you know about alternate manufacturing techniques.

Modifying an Existing Part

Nick T. and Andy S. were going nowhere with a plastic tool that attached to a roller and prevented paint from splattering. A quote of $25,000 for tooling stopped them cold on their idea. No manufacturer would absorb the tooling cost without a firm order from either a retailer or a wholesaler. Nick and Andy shouldn't have been moping about their lost opportunity; they could have easily solved their problem.

Their product had a one-piece design, but it had two parts: a top and a side. Those parts could have been made separately out of readily available parts. Only a small amount of machining would have been needed to allow the parts to be snapped together with a small plastic clip. The initial-run product would have cost $2 to make, compared to a retail price of $1.50, but this cost difference would have been all right during the time when Nick and Andy's only goal was to show their product could be sold.

Making the Product from Another Material

Nick and Andy could have made their painting product out of aluminum and dipped it in a plastic coating compound like Plasti Dip, or they could have painted it. Another option was to make the product out of fiberglass. A successful inventor of a plastic spice rack made his initial production model out of wood. I don't normally like to use different materials; I prefer to sell a product that's exactly representative of the final product. However, using alternate materials is a viable option if you're having trouble getting a contract manufacturer to invest in tooling, or if you need some sales momentum to generate financial support from your family.

Using Temporary Tooling

Most plastic products and all metal products can be made using temporary tooling. For plastic parts, the temporary tooling could be an aluminum insert in a used mold, or a plastic or rubber mold; for metal parts, it could be a silicone rubber mold or a sand casting. Temporary tooling usually costs only 10 to 20 percent of the cost of permanent tooling. The biggest drawback to temporary tooling is that no one knows how long "temporary" will be. The tooling might last a week, or it might last several years. No matter how long it lasts, you should be able to get enough initial production to know whether your product will sell.

Temporary tooling is a good option when you have a contract manufacturer. Alternatively, have your initial production run made by a prototype shop. These shops put together prototypes and small production runs for established companies. They have a lot of experience with temporary tooling and short runs. You can locate prototype shops in the Yellow Pages, by contacting manufacturers' representatives of production equipment, or by calling the purchasing departments of larger companies and asking them for names of any prototype companies in your area.

Again, your go/no-go decision here is: can you afford the cost of your initial production run? You don't want to spend all your money on your initial run. You'll still need money to help finance the transitional sales period.

Start-Up Manufacturing Costs

After you've completed your initial sales period, you enter the transitional sales period, when you start producing larger quantities of units. You may be forced at this time to make the tooling investments you've avoided. You face the last manufacturing go/no-go decision: can you raise the money to cover the start-up costs?

Manufacturing costs involve more than tooling costs; they also include engineering documentation, inventory, labor, packaging, instruction manuals, and consignment units. Remember, as you add up these projected costs, that you may be able to persuade a contract manufacturer to absorb some of them. The advice in Chapter 8 will help you find insider investors. You might also be able to find investors among friends and family.

This last go/no-go decision is difficult to make until you've completed your first sales period. Only then will you know how well your product is accepted and how much help you can expect from contract manufacturers and investors. Knowing the start-up manufacturing costs before starting the first sales period can help you decide whether your research is positive enough to justify entering the first sales period. If start-up costs are high, you'll want to be sure your product does very well in its initial research. You'll also want to be sure of help from several insiders. If your costs are lower, you might proceed with a little less positive input.

Most start-up manufacturing costs are fairly high. Along with your start-up marketing expenses, they may be more than you can afford. Don't worry about that just yet. Before you incur these costs, you'll have some limited sales history, you'll have a product that has survived several rounds of market testing, and you'll have a fairly well-defined manufacturing process. These factors might be all you'll need to line up investments from family, friends, or insiders.

Let's examine start-up costs category by category.

Tooling Costs

Gather estimates from several manufacturers to determine these costs. Try to get a contract manufacturer to pick up some of them, or look for discarded tools that you can modify. You'll be responsible for raising the money to cover this expense.

Temporary tooling has a negative connotation to many product entrepreneurs, but I've been involved with products that have been marketed for over 5 years with "temporary" tooling. Try to wait until the product is selling well before purchasing permanent tooling.

Engineering Documentation

Before a product goes into standard production, a package of information is needed so that other people can produce the product. This package is referred to as engineering (or manufacturing) documentation. It includes drawings, a bill of materials, assembly instructions, specifications, inspection requirements, and assembly times. The package is not easy to put together. You might be able to prepare the initial sketches, but you'll need a professional draftsperson to do the drawings and an engineer to rework your initial wording into the proper format and language. If your product is not complicated, your contract manufacturer may do the documentation package at no charge.

If your product is complicated, you'll probably need to cover at least some of the cost of preparing the package. Professional drafting charges range from $25 to $50 an hour, and 20 to 100 hours may be needed to complete the drawings. The total costs can be quite high.

On complicated products, find an engineer who will be one of your inside advisers. Ask him or her how long it will take to prepare the engineering drawings for your product. Add about 30 percent to that estimate (to cover unexpected cost overruns) and then call up engineering drafting firms, as well as temporary help agencies that offer drafting, and ask for their hourly rates. Ask friends if they know of any draftsperson who might work on the project in the evenings for about $20 per hour. On some products, documentation costs might be as high as $10,000 to $20,000. A manufacturer might share the expense with you if your product has strong sales potential. However, because most complicated products are geared toward small markets, many inventors of complicated parts end up making the products themselves. Labor costs stay low, and the need for a documentation package is reduced.

Inventory

You probably will have inventory costs for both supplies and finished goods. You need to buy supplies in order to start production, and you will have to pay the contract manufacturer for the units produced.

Try to work with your suppliers to keep your inventory costs low. Most suppliers want payment within 30 days. If you are an unproven product entrepreneur, they may want full payment in advance, or they may require a 25 to 50 percent deposit with your order. Rather than paying in advance, your goal is to have 60 to 90 days to pay for inventory. You should try to work on payment terms early, because only a few suppliers will offer 60- to 90-day terms. Even with long payment terms, you will have trouble generating sales *and* collecting money before 90 days have passed. You should include in your start-up costs the inventory costs of both the raw materials and the finished products for one production run.

Labor Costs

If you're not going to use a contract manufacturer, you may need to hire a few people. You should have six months of their salaries on hand before you hire them. Incidentally, labor costs are another reason for my recommending that you use a contract manufacturer. During your first year, when sales are low, you'll probably need only occasional help. If you hire workers, you'll have to pay them regularly. With a contract manufacturer, you'll only pay for labor when you need it.

Packaging Costs

These costs can be considerable, yet they are often overlooked by entrepreneurs. The product creator almost always has to pay all packaging costs. Artwork, the biggest cost, includes the initial drawings or photographs, the color separations, and the printing. The drawings, photographs, and color separations could easily cost $5,000. For black-and-white or two-color artwork (black and one other color, on a white background), costs will still run $1,000 to $2,000. Most printers won't do a run of less than 1,000 pieces, so your minimum printing cost will be $400 to $500 for two-color artwork, and $1,000 to $2,000 for full-color artwork.

You'll also have to pay for the package itself. A mold for a blister pack can run a minimum of $500 to $2,000, depending on the size; special cardboard packaging costs at least $500 to $1,000.

A contract manufacturer won't pick up the packaging cost because it won't be doing the work. Your artist, color separator, printer, and packaging supplier will be completing the work. Contract manufacturers might pick up their own costs, such as for inventory or labor, but they won't pick up costs paid to someone else.

Instruction Manuals

Any costs for instructions, whether assembly or operational, are paid by the product creator. Most creators do a poor job of writing instructions. The result is product returns, the major reason that retailers or distributors drop products. Tom L. created a board game that I put into seven stores. I got all the games back after three people returned them because they couldn't understand the instructions.

Instructions require printing and preparation. The printing cost can be estimated by finding similar instructions and getting a price quote. A local print shop can do most instruction manuals.

Preparation refers to the pictures or drawings and the written descriptions in a manual. If you are using pictures, have them done by a professional photographer. Lighting has to be just right if a picture is to print well. Professionals have that know-how, and a good-quality photo is important. Expect to pay $75 to $125 per picture.

Because most entrepreneurs write their own instructions, they're usually terrible. Part of the problem is that entrepreneurs aren't experienced writers; in addition, they don't spend enough time on instructions. I've taken as long as two weeks to write instructions that were only two pages long. The secret to writing good instructions is to give them to people who don't understand the product, and test whether they can follow them, with good results. If they can't, the instructions need work.

Consignment and Demonstration Units

If you sell through manufacturers' representatives or distributors, you may need consignment units—units you loan to distributors so that they can promote a product. You may also want to loan or give products to potentially large customers. You won't be getting paid for these units. Include their costs in your start-up expenses.

Manufacturing Go/No-Go Decisions

1. Do the preliminary cost estimates indicate that the product's perceived value is four times the product's projected manufacturing cost?
2. Will the model and prototype cost be less than 25 percent of the money you have to invest?
3. Can you find a contract manufacturer that will work with you on favorable terms?
4. Can you afford the investment required to produce a small initial production run?
5. Will you be able to raise the money to cover the start-up manufacturing costs?

8

Inside Help: Everyone Needs Key Contacts

When I worked for an industrial equipment supplier, we developed what we thought was a great new product for assembling large, low-volume, surface-mounted, printed circuit boards. The product was unique and cost-effective, and appeared to answer a large, unmet need. Our main stumbling block was that a working model would cost $50,000 to $60,000, which was more money than we wanted to risk.

We moved ahead with the project, for less than $30,000, with help from key inside people. I located two people who were responsible for specifying this type of equipment for their companies. We hired each one (for about $200 apiece) as a consultant for an evening. They provided us with the following:

- An evaluation of our product's features and benefits;
- A list of features they felt we could drop;
- The names of contacts at several manufacturers that might field-test the product;

- Local distributors (again, with the names of contacts) that would probably be willing to sell the product;
- Estimates of our potential sales volume.

When my partner and I were introducing the tire cutter, we weren't sure whether we should try to license the product or try to start a business. We didn't know whether we could sell the product for $70, or whether we could set up a distribution system without an advertising program. We talked to key people at a distributor that sold tire-mounting equipment and to a store manager for a tire dealership. We found out that: our idea had merit, the cutter had to work when tires were on or off a wheel rim, and the companies would help us with our initial market research.

This inside advice steered us in the right direction, not only for product design, but also in our subsequent efforts to set up a sales network. On other occasions, inside advice convinced me to drop products, but at least I dropped them early, before spending too much time and money.

Another important reason to use inside contacts is that they can become investors, partners, or future employees. Most people dream about being involved someday in their own business, and the ideal business for them is one they know a great deal about. Most product entrepreneurs hate to give up a part of their company, but I think it makes sense for an entrepreneur to take on an insider as an investor. The company gets involvement from a knowledgeable source, an impressive management team for future loan applications, and additional capital to fund the business.

I once took a new inspection microscope to Digital Computer. The product had a 3-inch by 4-inch viewing lens, rather than the traditional two eyepieces. The product greatly reduced operators' back and neck strain, which resulted from bending over the traditional eyepieces. When I first showed the product, two of the people who specified microscope equipment immediately asked to invest. That type of insider can help a product by contributing both market data and money. Unfortunately, the inventor of the microscope couldn't consistently put enough light on the screen. Operator eye-strain resulted and the product failed.

This chapter has only one go/no-go decision: can you find the inside help you need to introduce your product?

Inside Contacts: Why You Need Them

Inside contacts have the experience, connections, and knowledge that can help put a product on the market. They can offer many pieces of valuable information.

Sometimes you won't be able to find an insider in your specific market. You still have to have an insider, even if the person works in another market. Dennis Courtier created a new cider drink. It's not easy to find a helpful insider in the beverage market, which is ruthless and dominated by large companies; insiders are too busy to help a new entrepreneur. Instead, Dennis found help from a radio station contact. The station used the cider drink as a promotional item. The exposure helped Dennis to set up a small distribution system.

History

What similar products have been successfully introduced? How long does it take for a product to become established? What percentage of users will buy a new product in its first years? What mistakes have caused other products to fail? What is a typical first-year sales volume for a new product? What companies have been able to continually introduce successful new products? Every answer to these questions can give you key insights into the steps you'll have to take to introduce a product.

Product Review

Most product categories have several nuances that aren't apparent to everyone. For example, a hedge clipper might need a grease fitting to lubricate the gear case. Product entrepreneurs often overlook little points, much to the detriment of their product. Insiders will usually spot design defects, primarily because they've seen them cause other new products to fail.

Besides noticing product nuances, insiders can offer a fairly accurate review of your product's main features and benefits, including how well they work, how important they are, and what their perceived value is. Getting insiders to evaluate a product while it's still in the mockup stage can minimize the number of product changes you might have to make later on.

Manufacturing Help

Insiders can give you names of companies that might make a product on a contract basis, tell you what manufacturing process the market likes for a certain type of product, and generate negotiating leverage. You'll probably obtain more help from a contract manufacturer if you can show that you've received input from both the general manager of a major distributor and the merchandise buyer of a large retailer.

Distribution Hints

Insiders often know which distribution networks are easiest to enter; what networks are most likely to take on a product from a small, one-line company; the best price point for a product; how much marketing a product needs; and what type of payment terms you should expect.

Connections

Insiders know the people and companies in the market. The names of new contacts will help expand your potential sales base, and you'll have much better luck approaching those contacts when you can say that the insider suggested the call.

Promotional Help

There may be certain trade magazines that generate high numbers of ad responses. Particular trade shows may be crucial for you to attend. The market may respond to only certain types of promotions. Your product literature and price lists may lack essential information. There may be certain mailing lists that are very effective, or an ad format that has always worked well. All of this information may be available from insiders.

Help during Initial and Transitional Sales Periods

Finding your first few sales outlets, before you have any sales momentum, is difficult. Often, insiders become your first customers, or they help you find your first customers. Once insiders help you to start sales, you'll be able to build on your initial momentum and line up additional distribution outlets. Without insiders' help, you might not even be able to place a product in front of customers.

Finding the Right Insiders

I've talked throughout the book about how to find manufacturers' representatives or salespeople. Their help is valuable, but they don't qualify as key insiders. They probably only know how a portion of the market works, they don't always carry enough clout in the market to help during the initial sales period, and their backgrounds usually aren't strong enough to provide the management experience needed on future loan documents.

Your goal is not necessarily to work with the best known person in the market. He or she is probably too busy to help you, will cost more than you can afford, and will be too difficult to contact. But you should try to find someone who is significant in your local market. For example, if you have a hardware product, your insider might be a buyer for a local chain of hardware stores, the president of a large distributor, a key executive in the local hardware association, or the marketing manager of a local hardware products manufacturer. Any of these people will have enough contacts in the local market to help get a product established.

John Naughton is an example of an entrepreneur who knew how to take advantage of inside help. When he created the first reclining dental chair, John had the initial support of a core group of several well-known dentists. With their help, John started selling chairs one at a time throughout the Midwest. Through the dentists, John contacted the most successful district sales manager in the industry. John made an attractive offer to him. Within two or three years after the offer was accepted, the company was selling well over $1 million per year.

Scott Turner developed a new product to measure diffusion depths in silicone wafers, a crucial test in the early production of semiconductors. One of the reasons Scott succeeded was that he had, at one time, worked for a key semiconductor production manager in the Philadelphia area. That contact helped Scott to sell some initial machines and gave him the names of people to call at other prospective customers. I worked with Scott for two years, and he taught me the value of the question: Do you know anyone else I should talk to? This question will help broaden your base of insiders.

Graham Lovelady, a California dental equipment servicer, put together a vacuum pump specifically designed to provide all the needed suction during dental procedures. Graham enlisted the aid of the western regional manager of the industry's largest distributor to generate his pump's initial sales. His company's sales quickly rose to over $5 million per year.

These key people are harder to find than manufacturers' representatives or salespeople, but you should be able to meet them if you learn to use your initial contacts and if you make a dedicated effort to become involved in the activities of your chosen industry.

Using Initial Contacts

I was trying to help Craig N. conduct some California market research on a new bracelet for kids. The research was important because California is by far the biggest market for fad products. Dave Butts, whom I work with, has a sister who sells products to California convenience stores. She got a few stores interested in the bracelet, and she had the store managers mention the product to a rack jobber distributor that sold them cheap costume jewelry. The store managers also mentioned my name to the jobber's merchandise buyer. Finally, I talked to the buyer, who liked the product, wanted just one change in its packaging, and agreed to sell it at a suggested retail of $1.99—provided he could buy it for 70 cents. Craig is still trying to find a way to make the product in volume for 35 to 40 cents, but the important point is that Craig got all this information for a minimal price. He has a potentially valuable contact if he can find a low-cost production method.

If initial contacts give you insiders' names, you can either have the contacts arrange a meeting, as in the previous example, or call the insider yourself. I usually prefer to call the insider, unless an initial contact can provide leverage because he or she is a customer or an important supplier of the insider. When you meet or talk to the insider, explain that you're working on a new product. Describe what benefit the product offers: why you feel the product is marketable; what response you received in your initial research; and how you've heard from several people in the industry that the insider is an important person to talk to. I recommend that you offer to pay the insider to be a consultant.

This approach tells several things about you:

1. You're serious; you're taking a professional approach.
2. You have a chance to succeed because you're seeking out expert help early in the project.
3. You probably only have a rough mockup.

Trade Associations

Drugstore owners, toy manufacturers, industrial distributors, and countless other groups have associations that meet regularly to discuss common problems or opportunities. Many of these associations have local chapters; one may meet in your state. If a local chapter doesn't exist, attend any local trade show and find out whether any associations will run meetings in conjunction with the show.

Trade associations are great places to meet insiders. Not only are members of the association knowledgeable, but they have more than the typical number of connections.

Chambers of Commerce

Chambers exist to promote business growth. They do this primarily by lobbying for business interests, but they also are supportive of new business ventures. By attending their meetings, you might meet some key people. Tell the Chamber what you're doing and ask whether they know anyone who would be able to help you. Chambers often have important business leaders as members, and their help can be valuable. A woman I know went to a Minneapolis Chamber of Commerce meeting and met Harvey McKay, the owner of his own envelope company, a key Minnesota businessman, and the author of *Swim with the Sharks without Getting Eaten Alive.* Harvey suggested several contacts that helped the woman expand her business.

Magazine Articles

When I needed technical insiders to evaluate equipment for a surface-mounted assembly, I found them by looking through a year's back issues of trade magazines. Two people had written lengthy articles regarding equipment similar to the new product I was researching. I called the people and set up appointments. I started both conversations by mentioning that I had read the magazine articles. About half of all the people I've found through magazine articles have been cooperative.

Many product creators are not experienced in business. They're apprehensive about calling up and talking to a businessperson. Their fears are groundless. Some people will be rude and others won't have the time to talk, but many more people will not only talk but will offer their help and advice.

Speakers

Another tactic is to check trade magazines for speakers at local association meetings or trade shows. You can also obtain speakers' names from the trade association itself or from Chambers of Commerce. Other sources of speakers' names are newspapers and magazines, where experts in a market are frequently quoted.

When to Use Insiders

You should use insiders on every project, but you must be careful to use them sparingly. Don't make them feel you're taking advantage of them, even if you reimburse them for their time. There are critical times during a project when you *must* consult insiders, either because you're about to invest a considerable sum of money, or because you need their help in selling the product. Save your consulting requests for those times.

When You're Starting Out

After you have a mockup or a drawing of an idea, you should consult with one or two insiders. You won't have spent much, if any, money, and you don't want to make an investment if there's a reason the product will probably fail. This is also an ideal time to gather as much market information as possible.

Some product entrepreneurs are reluctant to show an idea when it's still in its initial, rough stage. They're afraid people won't understand the idea or won't like it because of its crude appearance. These points are valid. I've found, though, that insiders will still offer valuable advice if they're informed in advance that they'll see a rough product. See an insider after you've received positive input from your initial market testing.

After You Have a Model

With a model, for the first time you'll have something concrete to evaluate. Until you have a model, people's evaluations are based on what you say—or what they imagine—your product will be like. People won't need to speculate after you have a model; they'll be able to see, touch, and use it.

Insiders will be able to tell whether your product provides its expected benefit, to identify any drawbacks the product might have, to estimate the product's perceived value, and to know whether its benefit is obvious.

Before the Initial Sales Period

Insiders can steer you to stores, distributors, and companies that may buy a product. If at all possible, you'll want to use these contacts to set up an initial distribution network. This momentum will help future sales because the product will look like a winner to potential sales outlets and distributors.

When You Enter the Transitional Sales Period

In this phase of an introduction, a product moves from having just a few isolated sales to having a solid sales base in a small part of a market. For example, a hardware product might have its initial sales in eight regional hardware stores. The transitional period would be marked by expansion of sales throughout half of the company's home state.

This is a difficult period. You can do almost everything yourself in the first sales period; in the transitional period, you'll need to rely on other people to sell a product. Insiders can help you make contacts with key distributors or manufacturers' representatives. They might even know of a recently retired salesperson who could help your sales efforts on a part-time basis.

The transitional sales period is almost impossible to survive without insiders' help. Some product entrepreneurs succeed because an insider happens to notice their product and decides to help them. For example, Lynn Gordon of French Meadow Bakeries, who made bread from a fermented mix of grains and water, happened to call on a grocery store buyer who was on a special diet that didn't allow oil, honey, or dairy products. Lynn's bread was just what the buyer needed. You shouldn't make your future dependent on luck. Find your insiders early in a project, and use them during the introduction process.

Asking Insiders to Invest

The two times to ask insiders to invest are: before starting the transitional sales period, and when expanding sales into a larger market area.

To quickly review, the stages of a project are: initial conception, first sales period, transitional sales period, and sales expansion period. Almost every product entrepreneur needs financial help in the latter two stages. At those times, insiders' investments can provide not only needed capital but also the cash leverage required to obtain additional loans from banks or finance companies.

Why Wait Till the Transitional Period?

Most product creators ask: "Why shouldn't I get insiders to invest right away?" If you are going to keep control of a product, you must provide more than just a good idea. If an idea is all you have to offer, and insiders think it's a great idea, they might move to take over the idea and give you a 5 or 6 percent royalty. Instead, you should postpone asking for money until you can prove you have management capabilities and an established sales pattern.

Most new product entrepreneurs don't have extensive management experience. The one way they can show they're capable of handling a project is to complete the initial stage of the introduction cycle. Survival through the first sales period shows insiders that a product entrepreneur has devoted the time and effort required to put a product on the market and is resourceful enough to find ways around the numerous introduction problems everyone encounters.

You should be able to show that a product is actually selling before asking insiders to invest. Even if the product is in only four stores, at least you will have evidence that people are buying it. A product becomes more and more attractive to investors as its sales level rises.

Lloyd G. created a lure retriever, a fishing product that retrieves lures when they get caught in weeds or among rocks. Lloyd had sold about 500 units for $9.95 at trade shows and flea markets. Then Lloyd got tired of attending the shows and allowed a friend to try to sell the product to stores and distributors. The friend was unable to deliver any sales, and Lloyd went two years without selling any product.

Lloyd decided to try to sell his product to a manufacturer. He had invested $30,000 in the idea and felt it had "million-dollar" potential, so he decided to ask for $100,000. The manufacturer's president told Lloyd that, without ongoing sales, he would consider offering only $5,000 plus a royalty. Maybe, when Lloyd was selling the product throughout a few states, he'd offer $20,000. Unless the product had nationwide distribution in place, $100,000 was out of the picture.

The key to establishing a company's or a product's worth is potential sales volume—what it will sell in the next year. Where does that leave you, if you're trying to raise money in a project's initial phase? In trouble. Insiders like to see some proven sales history before they invest.

What's a Product Worth?

There's no firm formula for determining a product's or company's value. For two similar products, the value can vary tremendously. Still, I think product entrepreneurs can say that an established product is worth its annual sales volume. If a product is new and its sales are steadily increasing, the product is worth about twice its expected next year's sales. As an example, if you've completed your initial sales period with sales of $5,000, and you project, based on distributor commitments, to sell $30,000 in the transitional period, then the company would be worth about $60,000. A product's worth can change if it has a high margin, a large capital requirement, or an explosive growth potential.

Every time you put a price tag on a product, you must start with a sales projection. This isn't a problem if a product has been sold for several years. However, a sales estimate is very difficult when you dramatically increase sales in the first year of the transitional sales period and again in the early part of the sales expansion period.

There are three methods to estimate sales during sales growth:

1. Average the sales estimates you received from industry insiders and sales representatives.
2. Analyze the sales of one or two similar products in the targeted market.
3. Use the actual sales per outlet or per salesperson that were achieved during the initial sales period.

As an example of the third method, suppose you approached 50 convenience stores in your initial sales period, and you were able to persuade 10 of them to carry your product. After four months, each store averages 10 units sold per month. If the transitional period's target market has 800 stores, and you can call on them with the same success rate (20 percent) as with the 50 stores, you could expect to sell to 800 stores times 20 percent, or 160 stores. Each store could sell about 120 units per year (10 units per month times 12 months per year), for an estimated annual sales volume of 19,200 units.

Product entrepreneurs often like to estimate sales using the first two methods, primarily because they're a lot easier than the third method. Estimates under those methods, however, are almost always too high. A new entrepreneur doesn't have the promotional muscle of an established company, and he or she won't be able to achieve the same market penetration. The third method, using actual sales results, is most reliable. When you obtain an estimate based on past experience, divide the number by two to estimate the next year's sales potential. Dividing the sales level in half is important; you will need time to sell to the larger market.

Compare your estimate based on actual sales to the estimate based on input from insiders and salespeople, and to estimates based on sales of similar products. If the sales level is lower, that's OK; you can expect it to be lower. If the estimate is higher, go back and lower your estimate. Sometimes, higher estimates from actual sales are the result of initial sales at some friendly outlets that provided premium shelf space. You probably won't get favored treatment in the rest of the market; use lower estimates.

How to Ask for Investments

If you've been working with insiders all along, you'll find that they're easy to approach for an investment if you do it properly. The secrets to success are: approaching them at the right time, having a presentation package, and asking for a modest investment.

When approaching potential investors, tell them that you're looking for people who'd like to invest $5,000 (or another appropriate amount) in the company. Explain that you've prepared an information package and ask if they'd like to look it over. You should receive a fairly positive response if your contacts like the product, and if they have some money available to invest.

What's in a Presentation Package?

Your presentation document doesn't have to be an extensive business plan. Your insiders have been working with you all along and should know the product fairly well. The following topics are essential.

1. **A brief history.** Provide a short summary of why you came up with the idea, what made you think of your particular product design, and why you think it will sell. Include a list of any insiders you've been working with.

2. **A competitive products chart.** Analyze the products that are already on the market, what they cost, and what their strong and weak points are. Include your product in the chart.

3. **Current sales efforts.** Provide a listing of where the product has been sold and a summary of the sales results at each location.

4. **A transitional sales plan.** Explain how you're planning to expand to a larger market. For example, you might have decided to take on three more distributors or three more salespeople, or to attend two trade shows to line up manufacturers' representatives. Chapter 11 contains additional information about the transitional sales plan.

5. **The product's profitability.** Include the product's expected margin, which is the net profit (after all expenses) divided by the sales volume. If you expect to make $10,000 after expenses, on sales of $100,000, the product's margin is $10,000/$100,000, or 10 percent. Include a profile of what happens to the dollars generated by a retail sale. The profile should look like the hardware product's breakout chart in Chapter 4 (page 52).

6. **The product's value.** Use the methods discussed earlier (see pages 152–154) to determine a product's value.

7. **An orderly financial plan.** Show how you're going to finance the business's growth. You don't need an operating pro forma that lists your projected cash flow; you won't have enough information to create one. First, detail how much money will be

raised in the transitional period, what percentage of the business will be sold, and how the money will be used. For example, if you project sales of $100,000 per year, you might have a goal of raising $40,000: $20,000 from investors, to whom you're offering a 20 percent share of the business, and $20,000 from a commercial finance company, to fund an initial marketing program of ads, product literature, and promotional support materials.

Next, explain what expenses you'll personally be handling in this period—for example, certain manufacturing and packaging start-up expenses. Show that you're covering certain costs, either out of your own pocket or, preferably, by having them absorbed by a contract manufacturer.

Finally, show how you'll finance future growth. For example, after the product is established in the transitional market, you might plan to raise an additional $200,000, half by selling another 20 percent of the company and half from a bank loan.

Two points are important when considering a financial plan: (a) Try not to sell more than 20 percent of the company in the transitional period. You may need to be able to offer additional shares of the company at a later time. Another advantage of limiting sales to 20 percent is that your early investors will realize they're buying shares at a much lower price than will be offered to investors who will buy later. (b) Always show that you realize additional money will be required to fund the sales expansion period. Businesspeople expect that you'll need additional financing, and they expect you to realize it too.

8. **The size investment you're looking for.** I know that entrepreneurs do a tremendous amount of work to get through the first phase of a product introduction. But most insiders will still view a project as an iffy proposition. Try not to ask for an investment that's greater than $5,000 to $10,000 in return for a small share of the business. As an example, you could offer 5 percent ownership in return for a $5,000 investment. People can always ask to buy a bigger share later, but try to make their initial investment an easy step. Remember, you're interested in the insiders' help as much as in their money.

Part II Summary:
The 12 Key Go/No-Go Decisions

In Chapter 1, I listed the basic criteria that determine whether an individual product creator can successfully take a product to market:

1. Is the product easy to distribute?
2. Is the technology simple?
3. Is the product perceived to be unique?
4. Is the benefit obvious?
5. Can the product be sold for three to five times its manufacturing cost?

The go/no-go decisions are designed to help you know when your product meets these criteria. In some cases, the relationship between the criteria and the decisions may not be obvious; for example, one reason you need insiders is so that your product will be easy to distribute. Other decisions, such as whether the product is perceived to be unique, are directly related to the criteria.

I've covered quite a few decisions in Part II, but I feel you must answer yes to all of the following 12 questions, in order to continue moving forward on a project:

1. Can potential customers quickly understand your product's benefit?
2. Is your product clearly different from others in the market?
3. Does your product have a benefit people want?
4. Can the product be packaged effectively?
5. Is the market open?
6. Does a distribution network exist with product support costs you can afford?
7. Are your customers easy to target?
8. Can you afford to make your models, prototypes, and initial production runs?
9. Can you find a contract manufacturer that's willing to absorb some of the start-up manufacturing costs?
10. Can you find market insiders to help you?

11. Does your product have a perceived value that's at least four times its manufacturing cost?
12. Is the market size of the distribution network large enough to justify your time and expense?

Entrepreneurs often overlook the last question. If you're going to sell through two or three catalogs, and the average sales for products sold that way is $200,000 per year, you're likely to make about 10 percent of your sales dollars, or $20,000. Is that amount enough to justify your effort? It all depends on you. One product might not require that much effort on your part, and $20,000 might be a nice annual return. Another product might require a full-time effort on your part, along with a large investment, and not be worth the effort. That's a decision only you can make. The important point is that you make it. Too many hopeful entrepreneurs keep spending money and time on their ideas when their projects have only a small profit potential.

Part III

Selling Product

If your product idea earns a yes on all the go/no-go decisions, you may be so excited that you can't sleep at night. You can't wait to take your product out to where customers can buy it. You probably feel like your project is a freight train running at top speed, ready to burst through any barrier. Right?

Wrong. You've climbed the first 30 feet of a 50-foot cliff. You've made a lot of progress and your future looks bright, but you still have a long way to go before you can call yourself successful.

Gary F., along with three partners, tried without success to introduce a hairbrush that untangled hair. The partners had rushed their product into production, assuming that it would sell. Gary told me that he had recently watched a TV show that covered all the preliminary work the marketers had performed for the Teenage Mutant Ninja Turtle toys. Gary's reaction was: "Who did we think we were, expecting the brush's introduction to be such a snap?"

Don't run headlong into the market and then find out you can't sell a product. Continue with the step-by-step approach I've been advocating all along. Part III explains the actual process of selling a product, which is really the heart of a winning introduction. Your idea won't succeed unless you can sell it.

Be prepared for a great deal of rejection when you start to sell a product. You might have only one sale after making ten calls—or maybe even twenty. That's normal. Every company runs into sales resistance from customers. Don't let it discourage you as long as some people are buying your product.

9

The First Sales Period: Proving a Product Will Sell

After a product has passed the go/no-go decisions, the next step is to prove that it can be sold. This is not the time to gear up production and try to saturate a market. At this stage, you produce as few as 100 to 200 units and then see whether customers will buy them.

Manufacturers almost always take a product to a small test market before they launch it nationally. Product entrepreneurs often think a testing cycle is unnecessary. Unfortunately, bypassing this key step is usually disastrous.

When I worked at the dental supply company, we introduced a product for cleaning out root canals. The product's benefit was that it minimized the problem of files breaking in canals—an important benefit because a dentist might need an hour or longer to extract a broken file. We invested $25,000 in market research studies; the results were so positive that we were afraid we couldn't make enough units. We introduced the product with a double-page ad that drew a response from 8,000 out of 120,000 dentists, by far the highest response rate we had ever heard of. We couldn't even supply literature to every interested dentist.

In four months, with 25 salespeople and 400 dealers, we were able to sell only $150,000 worth of product, which was less than 20 percent of what we felt was a very conservative budget. Dentists weren't buying the product, despite its tremendous benefit, because the product sold for $995. Another product of ours, similar in appearance, sold for $495. The new product's technology was different, but the dentists didn't care; the products looked the same. Our mistake was that we hadn't had a first sales period to see what problems we would encounter.

During the first sales period, product entrepreneurs are better off if they're undercapitalized rather than well-funded. Someone who is short on funds doesn't have money to waste. Keep your expenses low. You don't know whether your product will sell, what price consumers will pay for it, and how many units need to be produced.

Goals of the First Sales Period

Business Area	Stated Goal
Financial	To break even.
Manufacturing	To make a product for the lowest possible total cost.
Sales	To sell a minimum of 50 to 250 units, through the targeted distribution network.
Market research	To establish the ideal price point, the packaging required, the best name, the most important features, an effective distribution network.
Scheduling	To complete the preceding goals in 3 to 15 months.

Financial

I'm discussing the financial area first because many product creators mistakenly try to make money in the first sales period. Cliff

L. had an ice-fishing product that both skimmed ice out of a fishing hole and grabbed a fish on the line after boring below an ice hole. Cliff didn't want to invest in expensive tooling—a smart move on his part—but he made another mistake. He spent all the money he had ($3,000) to buy material for 1,000 units. By buying that much inventory, he got a 40 percent discount. At the discounted price, he could make and sell his product for a profit.

Cliff placed the product in six stores on a consignment basis. The product didn't sell. Customers apparently weren't able to understand the product's benefits, primarily because of the product's poor packaging. Unfortunately, Cliff didn't have any money left to modify his package.

Cliff should have made up only 20 to 30 units. When it became obvious that he needed a new package, he could have taken one or two photographs that demonstrated the product's benefit, made 30 copies, attached them to the package, and tried to sell the product again. Twenty or 30 new packages could have been made for $50 or $60.

A friend of mine, who is a small entrepreneur, likes to say: "Now is the time to show intestinal fortitude and put your money on the line." A lot of product entrepreneurs would agree. I don't. Ninety percent of all products fail within three years. No one knows for sure whether a product will sell until someone buys it.

Manufacturing

You should make your product for the lowest possible *total* cost. You must include tooling, set-up charges, packaging, manufacturing, reworking scrap, and everything else. Most entrepreneurs tend to look at the final product costs, not the total cost. For example, an entrepreneur might be able to make 1,000 units for $4 each, or 30 units for $9.50 each. Many people would choose to make 1,000 units. But 1,000 units will cost $4,000, and packaging and set-up charges can run another $750. The total cost for 30 units will be $285 plus packaging and set-up charges of $175. Per-unit costs are high for limited production runs, especially when temporary tooling is used, but your goal is to spend as little money as possible.

Sales

Your sales goal at this stage is to prove that your product will sell. You don't have to sell a carload of units to get that proof. As a rule, 50 to 250 units are enough. Be sure that they're sold in a situation that simulates actual selling circumstances as closely as possible.

Greg H., the creator of a new type of bracelet, asked my help in placing the item at convenience store and drugstore checkout counters. Greg produced 200 units. I made four point-of-purchase displays out of bakery boxes. Photographs of teenagers wearing the jewelry communicated the product's benefit, and I used press type for a few lines of copy. I put the displays into two convenience stores and two drugstores, and then watched to see whether the product sold.

Rarely is advertising worthwhile during the first sales period, primarily because advertising results are very limited on a short-run ad campaign, and because any demand created by advertising might be lost if buyers can't find the product. Instead, the focus should be on creating demand with clever point-of-purchase displays and on placing the product in stores where it can be bought.

If you feel your product won't get a fair trial without advertising support, run a specific store promotion. One inventor placed an antifungal product in a local drugstore, and then ran ads that featured the drugstore's name in the local paper.

Market Research

A product doesn't rest—or sell—on its merits alone. Its total package of features, which includes its price, packaging, name, unique benefits, and marketing campaign, contributes to its success. Try to gather as much research as you can on your product's total package during your initial sales period.

1. **Price.**   Try out two or three prices, even if you lose money on the lowest one. When we were introducing the tire cutter, we found that a similar product had been introduced earlier for $149. No one bought the product because it looked like it had a manufacturing cost of about $15. At $60, our product could sell; after a product redesign, it could sell for $100. Tom R. developed a writing board that slipped over a steering wheel. It could be used by delivery drivers, law enforcement officials, or service people. Tom's manufacturing cost was about $5, which meant the product should retail for about $20. When the product didn't sell at all at $20, Tom tested it at $14.95. It sold quite nicely at the lower price. Tom knew that he would have a viable product if he could lower his manufacturing cost to 25 percent of $14.95, or about $3.50.

Not every product sells more at a lower price. Some products sell at about the same volume at any price. Adult toys often fit into this category. For a while, I sold digital diaries at Macy's. Casio sold a model for $109; Selectronics sold a similar product for $79. Casio's diaries, at the higher price, always sold considerably more units than Selectronics' diaries. People bought what they thought was the best product, and they interpreted Casio's higher price to mean the Casio diary was better.

On some products, price doesn't significantly impact sales; a 10 percent price increase might cause only a 5 percent drop in sales. On these products, entrepreneurs are better off with a higher price. Car and truck accessories are good examples of products for which price will have only a small impact on sales volume. When I started to sell the lottery pen, I tested it at three prices: $1.99, $2.49, and $2.99. The sales volume per store changed only slightly as the price changed. People either liked the pen and bought it at any of the tested prices, or they didn't like it and wouldn't buy it at any price.

2. **Packaging.**   Your choice of package can be a major cost consideration. A blister pack with four-color artwork might cost 50 to 85 cents per unit; a two-color card with shrink-wrapping might cost 25 cents—a big difference when the product costs less than

$2. Still, a package must convey the message of a product; for that to happen, you may need the blister pack. The only way you can know which combination will produce the best results is to test several options.

3. **Name.**   A well-chosen name can add 30 to 50 percent, or even more, to a product's sales volume. For some markets, the name will dictate whether a product will succeed. Chip Clip is a great name; I doubt that the product would have sold without it. Hula Hoop is another product whose name clearly added to its sales appeal.

4. **Unique features.**   Some products have one or two features that add a disproportionate amount to their cost. Try to sell the product without the feature(s), to test their importance. Ray A. created a basketball game targeted at the adult market. One feature of the game was that its shooting positions could be rotated to allow bank shots. This feature represented 40 percent of the product's final cost.

Most product creators are tempted to skip any testing of product features. If you look back over your product's development, you might find that a feature is the result of input from only one or two people. Perhaps one friend told Ray that his game got boring after an hour or so, which inspired Ray to add the bank shot. Most products have one or two features that are responses to limited input, and a great deal of money could be saved if the features could be dropped.

5. **Stores/distribution.**   If possible, try to sell your product through a variety of stores or other sales outlets. A fishing product that kept leaders straight illustrated the benefits of trying new distribution outlets. A leader, a heavier piece of line that attaches to a hook, has two benefits: it minimizes the chances that a fish will bite the line in two, and it makes it easier to change hooks. Unfortunately, leaders can be easily tangled. The straight-leader product was initially sold through bait and tackle stores. A distributor took the product to a fishing trade show and found that charter fishing-boat captains would buy the leader holder. The new

market that opened up turned out to be much better than bait and tackle shops.

Not everyone can do all the testing I've outlined here, but each entrepreneur should do all the testing that's possible. It will pay off. I held marketing positions at the dental supply company for seven years and introduced one or two new products every year. I thought I knew the market about as well as anyone could, but there were always a few surprises in every introduction. To succeed, you need to be able to adjust to those surprises.

Scheduling

Product entrepreneurs like to look at the first sales period as a single effort that might take a month or two. Sometimes that happens, but more often the first sales period is a series of activities. Ted Z., who created a knife-sharpening device, started selling his product at flea markets, then moved up to rod-and-gun shows, and finally placed the product into four retail stores.

Manufacturing delays can stretch out a projected timetable. Delays can result from making a few units at a time or from a need to make product or package modifications. Art T. had a new face shield that was designed to keep construction workers warm in the winter. During his initial sales period, a new hardhat was introduced. A construction worker couldn't use Art's shield while wearing the new hardhat. Art solved that problem but then discovered that his shield didn't provide enough airflow. Each modification took time and money.

Most readers probably reacted with "No way!" when they saw a scheduling goal of 3 to 15 months. New entrepreneurs are anxious to bring their product to market and start making money. They must worry first about taking the right product, in the right package, at the right price, to the right distribution outlets. For product introductions, "slow and steady" usually wins the race and preserves enough cash to cross the finish line.

Preparing to Start

Incorporate

You open yourself up to tremendous legal liabilities when you sell a product. If it should injure someone, or if another type of calamity should occur, you could be personally liable. One way to protect yourself is to incorporate, which insulates your personal assets from business claims.

Numerous books on incorporating a business are available in libraries and bookstores. The Office of the Secretary of State in your home state will send necessary forms and filing instructions, when requested. *Entrepreneur* magazine sells booklets showing how to incorporate a business without a lawyer in each state. Most incorporations can be effected for under $200. If you're reluctant to incorporate on your own, contact a lawyer but be prepared to pay for his or her professional time and services.

Buy Liability Insurance

Product liability insurance protects you if someone claims your product caused an injury. Some stores and distributors will not carry a product unless it has insurance. Even if you can sell a product without insurance, you should obtain it if a product might cause an injury.

Liability insurance can be expensive: a typical insurance company will want a payment ranging from $2,500 to $10,000 to set up a policy. One way to avoid this steep expense is to attach an insurance rider to a contract manufacturer's policy. This tactic should be acceptable because your contract manufacturer will also be liable for damages if your product causes an injury. If a product that you're producing isn't dangerous, you can usually avoid any insurance problems by selling to smaller stores that don't require insurance.

Maintain an Active Contact File

Go back through your notebook and your previous contacts, and find people who could assist your sales efforts. These contacts will usually make it fairly easy for you to place a product in a few sales outlets. To place a new clothespin that could be opened at either end, Craig D. called up a variety store owner whom he knew. His call resulted in the product's placement in two stores. Another contact, a manufacturers' representative, placed the product in three drugstores.

Some of your earlier contacts should be willing to help. They know you and what you're trying to do, they may have already offered you input and advice, and they may enjoy contributing further to a product's success.

Seek Community Help

I've mentioned throughout the book that community groups can be helpful, especially Chambers of Commerce and trade groups. I highly recommend that you go back to these groups whenever you have a problem, such as finding a store to place your first product. Ask the Chamber for names of retailers who might be willing to help a new manufacturer.

Find Out Why People Don't Buy

Many people will not buy your product. Plan in advance to take advantage of information you can receive from surveying people, stores, or distributors that don't buy. Why don't certain customers buy? Why does the product sell better in a particular type of store? Why isn't the product selling through catalogs when it's selling at flea markets? The answers to questions like these will often tell you a great deal about a product. For example, if you fail to sell a product to a store owner, you can ask for an honest reaction to your sales pitch. The answers might be: "The product just doesn't look sturdy," or "I can't make any money at that price," or "I already have six products like yours on the shelves." These answers can steer you to a new course of action that might help the product sell later.

Compare the rejection answers to the reasons store owners give for buying a product. "I'm not sure why I bought it. I guess I just like it and I think it will sell," or "I think the product provides a unique benefit," or "I would like to use the product myself." These are helpful, but they don't define your market as well as the reasons why customers won't buy.

Product creators don't like to ask why people don't buy, primarily because they feel that someone who doesn't buy the product doesn't like it. Any one person doesn't buy most of the products on the market. Many of the answers you'll get to "Why didn't you . . . ?" questions won't reflect badly on your product. Statements such as "I'm trying to focus my sales on a different type of product," or "I prefer to carry products that have a higher price," or "I just don't have any money," or "I've committed my shelf space to another supplier" are all possible and legitimate reasons for someone's not taking your product.

Keep asking questions when people don't buy. You'll be able to find out:

- Is your sales approach working?
- Is the product's benefit obvious?
- Is the package appealing?
- Does the product have any major flaws?

Questioning why a product will sell at one outlet and not at another can tell you how quickly people perceive a product's benefit. At a fair, I watched Jason R. give a three-minute demonstration to sell a unique tool pouch with a better organizational system than that of a traditional pouch. When I asked Jason whether his product had been selling in stores, he gave me a litany of his rejections. I wasn't surprised that the product could be sold only at fairs. Its benefit wasn't obvious; the pouch needed a demonstration.

Where and How to Sell a Product

Entrepreneurs have a wide variety of possible places where they can sell a product. One of the goals in the first sales period is to sell the product to your target customers through the distribution chain you plan on eventually using. Some outlets, such as flea markets, can give you valuable market information, but you still have to simulate your eventual distribution network before you can declare the first sales period a success.

Fairs, Flea Markets, and Trade Shows

George T. attended a home show with a tool apron that, when laid over a five-gallon paint bucket, became a painter's bench. George sold 300 aprons at $15.95 each. Two days later, he received an order for 100 aprons from a chain of paint stores.

Trade shows offer major benefits:

- You're able to sell a product; you can then parlay your trade show sales to penetrate other sales outlets.
- You can meet valuable contacts.
- You receive immediate input about a product.
- You can adjust the product's price.
- You can sell a product with and without certain features and measure each group of sales.
- You can sell the product when you have only a few demonstration models.

The last benefit, taking orders without immediate delivery, is extremely helpful. George took 400 aprons to the show. I wouldn't have done that. I would have made, at most, 50 units. When I was selling out, I would have taken orders for later shipment. Taking orders allows you to invest in minimum inventory, in case the product doesn't sell.

Bob S. created an adjustable outdoor bench swing that could recline. He took five units to a state fair and took orders for 30 more units to be delivered in four weeks. Those orders helped his small business keep growing.

If you're going to take orders, try to arrange to accept Visa or MasterCard as payment. Because you're a small manufacturer, some people will be reluctant to give you a check (they might not get a refund). They can always get a refund by disputing a credit card charge. This added security will increase your sales. Apply to your bank for an imprinter (it will cost about $75).

Two approaches can help you get a booth at a show at a discounted price. Don't contact the show until about a month before it opens. Delay your actual buying decision until the last moment. If the show is not sold out, the promoter might offer you a booth at a 50, 60, or 70 percent savings. The risks of waiting until the last entry day are that you might get a poor location and you might get no booth at all. A second approach is to tell the show promoter that a full booth is too expensive, and to ask whether any potential exhibitors might be willing to share a booth.

When attending a show, as an exhibitor or an attendee, arrive a little early so that you can meet other exhibitors. Try to find out how often they've come to the show and how many units they usually sell. Talk to other exhibitors about their distributors, suppliers, and sales outlets.

Retail Stores

Owners of small retail stores are often operating on their own shoestrings; they're not always willing to take a product from a new entrepreneur. However, large stores can be even harder to get into because they often place restrictions on new companies, such as mandating a large inventory level, or requiring 60- to 90-day payment terms. I believe new entrepreneurs are better off starting with small stores.

Whenever you're dealing with stores or distributors, you'll find resistance to ordering a new, unproven product. You'll need to be creative in setting up an order pattern that is as risk-free as possible.

One tactic is to put the product in the store on consignment. The store owner won't pay you until the product is sold. There are advantages to this method: stores will take your product, and sometimes you can request a favorable shelf position. The disadvantage is that you're putting yourself in a weak position because you don't obtain an actual order. An order puts you into a business relationship with the store or distributor, and an order history will help you obtain loans.

Another way to structure an order is to offer 60-day billing with a guaranteed sales clause. Under this arrangement, you ship in inventory, and you come back to the stores after 55 days and count how many units have been sold. The store pays you for the goods sold, and you take back any unsold products. This tactic ends up netting you payment in about 60 days, which is as fast as you'll usually be paid from any source.

When you're starting out, offer extra discount. Give a 50 to 60 percent retail discount, instead of 40 to 50 percent, to retail stores. When you call on any potential customer, you'll be bucking an established set of distributors or manufacturers. An extra discount will make people more willing to interrupt their normal buying routine.

When you approach a retail store, take with you the product in its package or display, a layout of a sales brochure, and a selling sheet (a list of a few of the benefits of the product, along with the retailers' and suggested retail prices). Figure 9.1 shows a sample of a selling sheet. Create a sheet listing any positive results or endorsements you've obtained from market research or sales outlets. It would be helpful to be able to show a retailer that a product is averaging 10 units per month at a competing store.

Start by approaching any retail contacts you've made during the go/no-go decision process. Sales to these contacts should be relatively easy, and you can then use those sales to persuade other retailers to take the product. To know whether your product was a success in a store, be sure to ask the retailer how many units per month the product needs to sell to stay on the shelf. You should also, if at all possible, try to learn the approximate monthly volume of the products near yours in the store.

THE LUCKY LOTTO PEN™

Increase your profits from the lottery with a fast-selling impulse item

Use for both the Daily Pick 3 and Lotto America

Directions	A Sure Winner to more Lottery Profits	
1. Tip the pen over so balls go to the top of the pen.		
	Suggested Retail	$2.49
2. Turn the pen back over so the pen points down.	Retailer's Cost	$1.25
3. Roll the balls in your fingers so the balls roll into the lottery slots.	P.O.P. Box of 24 Pens	
	Suggested Retail	$59.76
4. Pick the numbers next to the blue balls.	Retailer's Cost	$30.00

PLACE YOUR ORDER TODAY   Mail to: **SLICK PIC CORP.**
5200 West 73rd Street
Edina, Minnesota 55439

Quantity	Description	Price	Extended Price
_____	Lucky Lotto Pens*	$30.00	_____

Store Name _____

Contact _____

Address _____

City, State, Zip _____

Make checks or money orders payable to *Slick Pic Corp.*

All prepaid orders shipped freight prepaid
All C.O.D. orders shipped freight paid by store

All orders shipped within seven (7) days

Figure 9.1   Sample Selling Sheet

Stop into the store every two weeks to see how the product is selling. Ask if there is anything you can do to encourage sales. Find out whether there has been any customer reaction. One simple tactic that can help establish a smooth relationship is to send in a friend to buy your product. An early sale will convey an impression that the product has appeal, which might encourage salesclerks to promote it.

Entrepreneur Salespeople

Industrial and other nonconsumer products aren't sold through retail stores; they're sold through salespeople who call on companies. This type of sale is a real asset to product entrepreneurs because the only inventory they'll need is a demonstration unit. As a result, entrepreneurs can handle fairly complicated products, because they'll have orders in hand before they have to produce the products.

I mentioned earlier that I worked for Scott Turner, who invented a piece of semiconductor inspection equipment. When he started his business, he took his product to Texas Instruments and landed an order for three units. He borrowed enough money off the order to produce the units in his basement before heading back on the sales trail. Often, early sales are all made by the entrepreneur.

Preparing a winning sales script is a challenge. I've sometimes developed three or four sales presentations before finding one that worked. Don't be discouraged if your first attempts fail. Instead, keep asking customers what they're looking for in your type of product. Vary your approach until customers perceive that the product meets their needs.

Mail Orders

The mail-order market has expanded rapidly during the past ten years, but it has not become an easy market for product creators. Some of the problems in dealing with mail-order companies are:

- They want a product with an established demand;
- They don't like to handle product introductions;

- They sometimes want discounts that could run as high as 70 percent;
- They worry that a small manufacturer won't be able to ship the orders they receive.

You can run your own mail-order ads in magazines and card packs. This tactic can be dangerous because the cost of an ad can easily be two to three times higher than the profit on sales you might generate. Before advertising in a magazine, find copies of the last 12 back issues. Count how many advertisers repeat their ads. Call up one or two advertisers to see how many sales their ads generated. I once sold a book through general-product card packs. Each issue of the packs contained about 20 book ads. When I called an advertiser, I learned that one company was promoting 80 percent of the books in the deck, and that it was receiving a 60 percent discount. My contact told me I'd need a similar discount before I would have a chance of making money.

If you want to try a magazine ad, *don't* start by advertising in the magazine with the largest circulation. Ask at your library for *Gale's Source of Publications.* Find your product category and pick out five or six magazines with small circulations. Compare the ad rates and select those that look least expensive. Don't be afraid of the high prices listed; ad rates are listed for full-page ads, but the magazines do sell smaller spaces. Call up the magazines and inquire whether they have a "first time" or "introductory" discount. Be sure to include a cut-out order coupon in your ad. Before running your ad, find ads for similar products. Imitate the format of the ad that has been running the longest.

You might try sending out a flyer on your product as an enclosure with another company's invoices or order acknowledgments. Most companies have trouble selling mail-order products unless they have a large line of products. The big profits in the mail-order business come when customers buy two, three, or more products. Companies that are short on products might be willing to work with you for a percentage of your sales. Save every piece of direct mail you receive that offers products that are anything like yours. Contact those companies before you are ready to start production. Be prepared to offer at least a 25 percent commission to entice the company to send out a flyer.

The main disadvantage to mail-order sales is that you won't receive any feedback. You know a customer didn't buy, but you don't know why. That missing information hurts your ability to adjust your marketing efforts.

Mail orders can be useful to generate sales momentum at retail stores. Showing a product advertised in a magazine, along with some proof that orders have come in, will sometimes help get an order from a retailer. Dennis Sperling is trying to use mail-order sales to generate orders from retailers for Solar Stat, an easy-to-apply vinyl window tinting. The expensive ads might not produce a profit, but they could help Dennis start to sell the product. I usually discourage people from running their own mail-order campaign because it's expensive and it may not work. Instead, try to sell a product to a catalog company to hold your costs down.

Distributors

I consider distributors or manufacturers' representatives to be the key to a successful product. You can only sell so many products yourself. To expand further, you need other people's sales help.

When approaching distributors, keep in mind that time and customers are their big concerns. A distributor's personnel have to utilize their time in a manner that will produce the highest possible sales volume. New customers are important to them. A new customer doesn't represent a one-time sale to a distributor; each new customer could be an ongoing customer who might conceivably add significantly to sales volume.

As with retailers, start with any inside contacts you might have and then expand to unknown distributors. Use the same sales tools as before: the product, the package, and, if appropriate, the point-of-purchase display. Include a retailer's price schedule (see page 176) and fill in the distributor's price below the retailer's cost. For the lottery pens, the distributor's price could be 75 cents per pen, or $18 per box. This schedule shows a distributor how much profit can be made per unit or per display.

The basic business points to make to a distributor are:

- The product has been selling well.
- The product is a natural fit into the distributor's line and will require only minimal time and effort.
- The product will generate inquiries from new customers.

Those points will start you off well, but to succeed you should make some or all of these offers:

- You'll travel with each salesperson, if necessary, to show how to promote the product.
- You'll turn over existing accounts to the distributor.
- You'll give the distributor a six-month exclusive in his or her geographic area.
- You'll run promotions over the next six months to support the product.
- You'll handle all product complaints and returns.

Work out all the kinks in your sales strategy before seeing distributors or manufacturers' representatives. If they don't generate immediate sales results, they'll drop your product or stop pushing it. During the entire initial sales period, you must continue to build on successes. Momentum is especially important when you're trying to persuade a distribution network to handle a product.

Product entrepreneurs are typically shocked when they realize how much their sales message is diluted before it reaches customers. An entrepreneur starts out with a passionate message. A distributor's selling pitch might be: "This product is selling; you ought to buy some." A store clerk's response usually is: "How do I know what the product does? I just work here." Take a proactive approach with the distributor. Provide a simple one-page selling card that highlights your product's key selling points.

"I'm on my way now, I've got a distributor!" crowed a proud entrepreneur. I asked: "How many units do you think the distributor will sell?" This question totally stumps most people. Distributors always talk about their contacts and the sales they can get you, but some of them only have small operations that they run out of their houses. A small distributor can be valuable and should not be overlooked, but you need an estimate of how many units the distributor will sell. Otherwise, you won't know whether your initial sales period will be a success or a failure.

When you first meet distributors or manufacturers' representatives, ask for their line card (a listing of the companies' products they carry). Call a few of these companies and try to obtain a ballpark figure on what the distributors can be expected to sell. Don't be disappointed if the number is small. You only need to know whether your distributor or manufacturers' representative is selling your product at a typical rate.

In Chapter 8, I described the importance of obtaining inside help from industry veterans. This help is crucial when dealing with distributors. Mention the names of your inside contacts to the distributors to broadcast your chances of success. Enlist your insiders' help in convincing distributors to choose your product for special sales efforts. Most distributors strongly promote only 15 to 20 percent of their product line. You want your product to be among those that are promoted.

A tactic that is especially applicable to nonconsumer items is to offer extensive sales support. For our tire cutter, my partner offered to accompany the local salesperson on sales calls to all of the local tire dealers. Our goal was to build up a history of success in our own town as leverage for sales outside our metro area. The distributor appreciated the support because it enabled the salespeople to spend time actively selling a product instead of merely servicing accounts.

Making Adjustments

If a product is not selling, don't drop it too quickly. The price might be out of line, the product or packaging might need some minor changes, or a new distribution network might be the solution.

Price

An instant coupon is a tactic for determining whether people think a price is too high. Offer, for one week only, a 40 percent discount. Place the coupon alongside the product, and make it clear when the discount will expire. If a big discount doesn't perk up sales, then customers either don't see or don't want the product's benefit. I tried selling wrap sunglasses at $2.99. Because of poor response, I dropped the price to $1.99 and finally to 99 cents. The product didn't sell at any price, and I discontinued it.

If you are having trouble signing up retailers or distributors, offer a special one-month sales incentive. For example, if you attend a trade show for giftware, you'll notice many manufacturers promoting a "show special," an offer of a 25 to 50 percent discount for any order placed at the show. This incentive generates a great deal of business. I've often offered distributors a first-order discount of 25 percent so that they could test how well a product would sell. A product has severe problems if you can't get distributors to handle it with a large discount, 60-day terms, and guaranteed sales.

Don't offer discounts too quickly or you'll defeat your goal of seeing whether your product will sell at a profitable price. But if you're running into sales resistance and your product won't get a fair trial, try a discount to get sales started.

Product and Packaging

This topic was discussed in detail in Chapter 6. I mention it here because most product entrepreneurs don't like to change their product, primarily because changes are usually expensive and causes manufacturing delays. A small change can make the difference between a product's succeeding or failing. If you visit a retailer or jobber that sells discontinued products, you'll see items that look pretty close to successfully marketed products. Take the time and effort to give your product the best possible chance of succeeding.

Distribution Networks

Sometimes, you'll be able to tell right away that your product isn't selling in a distribution network. Don't be afraid to try another distribution network. Jake S. created a variation of a grater that both grated and sliced food. Jake was a great showman, and he sold lots of his product at fairs. The product had several drawbacks. Its price of $29.95 was expensive for small hardware or variety stores. Big stores wouldn't take Jake's product until he had an established sales pattern. Because Jake had no early sales momentum, distributors and manufacturers' representatives weren't interested in carrying the product.

Jake decided to explore other distribution channels. He offered a limited quantity of his product free to a marketer of cleaning chamois who sold products through magazine ads and who had a network of salespeople selling products at state fairs. In return, he asked the marketer to test his product at three fairs. Jake then persuaded a small, independent TV station to run his commercials in exchange for a $15 commission on every sale. Jake lost money on both of these efforts, but he learned that his product would sell in certain sales outlets.

Selling is hard work. Don't switch distribution networks at the first sign of sales resistance. If a distributor places an established product into 20 percent of the stores it serves, then your product is doing well if it is placed in 10 percent of the stores. But if prolonged efforts are not turning up any sales, consider switching channels.

Keeping the Light Green

Everyone loves a winning product. One of your early strategies should be to always appear to have a product that has tremendous momentum. If you approach a store and the manager won't take your product, don't go back until you have some initial successes. Otherwise, the store will look at your product as a failure. One entrepreneur got this response: "Are you still trying to get that product off the ground? Isn't it time you just gave up?" Don't get caught in that position. Plan your efforts so you always appear to have ongoing momentum.

In the first sales period, you should let your sales drive your production. Don't overproduce the product with an expectation of selling it. Instead, be prepared to work weekends to replenish your inventory. You'll find that, 99 percent of the time, sales don't materialize as fast as you'd like. Be cautious and conserve your capital.

A dental product my former employer introduced sold sensationally in the first three months. Unfortunately, the product had an unanticipated characteristic that caused it to malfunction during repeated use. It took us six months to correct the mechanical problem, and we were never again able to regain our momentum. How we wished we had taken the time for a first sales period.

You have to be the driving force behind your product. This book should make you realize that a product creator doesn't operate like an established business owner. The creator of a new product has to be constantly searching for an angle, an advantage, or some imaginative way to make things happen.

10

Evaluation Time: Before You Spend Big Money

Dee K. created a new storytelling board game. She placed the game in five retail stores and received a large order from an insurance company that wanted to use the product as a promotional item. After that, nothing encouraging happened. Dee had hoped that someone else would stock the game, but nobody has yet.

To increase her sales, Dee needed to go into the transitional sales period, which would have required a sizable investment in promotional, manufacturing set-up, and sales costs. Dee was facing an investment five to ten times larger than the amount she had spent to make it into the first sales period.

Going into the transitional period is expensive and challenging. Before taking that step, product entrepreneurs need to reevaluate their idea. Dee's major problem was that she didn't realize she needed another introductory step. You'll know when you need the transitional period. You'll have to decide whether it's worthwhile to enter it.

Most entrepreneurs never stop to evaluate their ideas after they start to sell a product. That's not surprising; many of them have invested $50,000 to $100,000 before even starting their sales efforts. By following the action steps in this book, you will probably invest less than $5,000 to get into the first sales period. I certainly think that $5,000 is a worthwhile investment if you believe you might have a "million-dollar" idea. However, don't be afraid to drop an unsuccessful idea. You're better off cutting your losses rather than investing more money in a product that can't be marketed.

An X-ray screening device I worked with in the dental industry illustrates the importance of reevaluation. The product was originally designed as a small shield that attached to an X-ray head. The shield was to pick up scatter radiation that could potentially harm dental assistants.

Several leading dentists supported the concept, and we had a positive response from dentists during our initial market testing. In our research, we received some constructive advice regarding product improvements, and we incorporated those into our prototypes. We made a few additional changes to adjust for variations we discovered in different brands of X-ray equipment. After a year, we had a product that cost three times the original estimate and looked like a mechanical monster. We decided to drop the product and minimize our losses.

The Initial Analysis

Before reevaluating your go/no-go decisions, you should first do an initial analysis of your sales results. Most people, including product entrepreneurs, tend to hear only the information that supports their view. You can't afford to be swayed by what you *want* to hear. You have to force yourself to be objective by making a sales comparison, obtaining evaluations from people in the distribution network, and surveying customers. The topics covered in the following sections should get your careful, objective attention.

Sales Comparison

I've recommended several times that you find out the sales volume of products that are placed near yours in a store. To estimate the volume, you might have to count the products that are on the shelf every week. I know that's a nuisance but, as you'll read in this section, that information is essential.

To make a sales comparison, use a chart with the headings listed below:

Sales of Your Product	Competitive Product's Name	Competitive Product's Sales	Percentage Difference	Comments

The key to this chart is the comments column. There will be many reasons for your product's not selling the same volume as other products. The lower volume is to be expected, but you need to understand why there is a difference in order to determine what changes a product might need, whether the first sales period was a success, and what your product's potential sales volume is.

Packaging

A package has a tremendous number of jobs to do. It must catch consumers' attention, establish that a product is worth the price, explain the product's benefit, show how the product provides the benefit—and accomplish all of these tasks in about 10 seconds. A better package can account for a tremendous difference in sales volume. Critique your packaging first when you're trying to understand why products sell at different rates.

How well two packages catch consumers' attention is fairly easy to judge. Compare two packages and decide which one looks better. Or isolate two products and ask 5 to 10 people to point out the package that first catches their attention.

It's a little harder to evaluate whether a product is showing that it's worth its value. People like to see, touch, hold, and examine products before they buy them. That's why you see floor displays of products at K mart, department stores, and discount outlets. Other products require copy on the package to explain their worth. Packaging of camping equipment or sleeping bags will often list a series of features, such as down filling or special waterproofing. Camping products from major manufacturers sometimes state how a product was field-tested.

How well do two packages explain products' comparative benefits? Don't trust your own judgment on this point; you know your product's benefit too well to be able to judge how it is communicated. Three or four people who've never seen your product should be asked to compare the two packages.

A product entrepreneur once showed me a hair product that detangled hair—a great benefit, but the product didn't sell. The package didn't explain why the product worked, and nobody I knew could figure out how to use it.

The final packaging consideration is how much time is needed for a customer to look your package over and understand what your product is, what it does, and why he or she should buy it. This time should be as short as possible. Your sales will be appreciably lower if a competitor's product requires 5 seconds to be comprehended and your product requires 15 seconds.

Product Benefits

- Is the benefit easy to understand? Some products have easy-to-understand benefits; others do not. Compare, for example, a hair sculpturing/trim kit to a cordless mustache trimmer. The hair kit's benefit—putting stripes, or arrows, or Zs in a hairdo, usually along the scalp—isn't as apparent as the mustache trimmer's benefit, which is stated in the product's name.

  Having a benefit that's harder to understand is not bad, but it offers clues about sales potential. If the hair kit outsells the mustache trimmer, you can conclude that the product's benefit is more important to more people than the benefit of the mustache trimmer. If the hair kit sells slightly less than the mustache trimmer, the market for the two products is probably about the same because the product with the easier-to-understand benefit (the mustache trimmer) should sell more units. If the hair kit sells considerably fewer units, then customers might not understand the product's benefit, or the product might have a small market.

- Is the benefit different? To answer this question, you must compare your product to its competitors. For the hair kit, the product should be compared to sales of hair clippers to parents. Your product is favorably perceived by customers if your sales are equal to or greater than a competitive product. If your sales are much lower, then your product has only a small market or customers don't perceive that your product is unique.

   Some of you may be thinking: "If the hair kit isn't perceived to be unique, it should sell as much as the hair clippers." That's not the case: when in doubt, customers buy the product they are most familiar with, another obstacle that makes it difficult for a product entrepreneur to introduce a new product.

Price

What if the hair kit sells for $12.95, and the mustache trimmer for $19.95? Will the hair kit sell more units? Not necessarily. The products are for different markets. The hair kit is targeted at teenagers, and the mustache trimmer is a product for adults.

The price difference would be important if you were comparing two different types of hair kits. If one product were more expensive, I'd say it was outstanding if it sold as well as the cheaper product. I'd consider the expensive product to have a market if it sold half as well as the lower-priced product.

Initial analysis doesn't offer firm yes-or-no answers. Instead, you'll be compiling lists of trends, feelings, or observations that will help you decide whether your product meets the go/no-go decision criteria.

Advertising

Some product entrepreneurs feel that their products are outsold simply because another product is heavily advertised. Entrepreneurs tend not to be discouraged by this situation, and they proceed with their introduction. I become wary when a product loses sales to one that's advertised.

Most product creators need products that can sell with only minimal advertising, primarily because most entrepreneurs are underfinanced. If another product outsells yours because of advertising, your product needs advertising.

Aaron W. developed a home exercise machine. Impressed by the effectiveness of NordicTrack's ads for similar equipment, Aaron tried to duplicate NordicTrack's success with his own advertising campaign. Unfortunately, sales didn't come rolling in, and Aaron went broke.

This example points out two facts that entrepreneurs typically overlook. The first is that advertising programs fail—often. At least 25 percent of the programs I've run have produced minimal results, and most large companies have similar results. Product creators, especially those without a marketing or advertising background, are likely to have a much higher failure rate.

The second fact is that advertising has to be run repeatedly to generate favorable results; NordicTrack has run its ads for years. Repeated exposure increases the sales response to an ad. Unless you have a tremendous amount of money to invest, be leery of a product that requires advertising.

Competition

Entrepreneurs will inevitably lose sales to another product because that product's name is well-known. If their reaction is "That's to be expected," they have a dangerous attitude.

As I mentioned earlier, people faced with a confusing choice will usually buy the best known product. If a well-known, similar product outsells yours, you might have one of the following problems:

- People don't perceive that your product is different;
- People don't care about your product's benefits;
- The product requires an advertising campaign.

Information Evaluation

Marketing analysis usually involves sifting through a tremendous amount of subjective information. The information you receive from your sales comparison should be positive before you continue any introduction efforts.

Some readers may have noticed that I haven't mentioned using the sales comparison as a tool for estimating potential sales volume. Isn't it a reliable way to come up with a sales number? For example, if the mustache trimmer sells 200,000 units, then the hair kit's market should be 600,000, if it outsold the mustache trimmer by a three-to-one margin.

A sales comparison *is* an easy way to estimate potential sales, but I think it is the wrong approach for an entrepreneur to take. Sales levels are determined primarily by a product's distribution network. The sales comparison method of determining sales volume would only be valid if the hair kit were in as many stores as the mustache trimmer.

Distribution Network Evaluation

After you finish your sales comparison, you should go back and interview everyone who had anything to do with selling your product. Don't make the interview too long or too cumbersome, but be sure to ask the following questions.

- Did the product's sales level meet expectations? Most people in a distribution network will have an estimate, based on past experience, of a product's potential volume. It's a positive sign if your product's sales consistently meet their expectations.
- Was the sales level high enough? Every part of a distribution network has a sales threshold for a product to meet. For example, a

store might want to turn its inventory every two months. If your product doesn't sell out in two months, the store won't carry it. Be sure that your product has generated enough sales to stay on the stores' shelves. Turnover is also important for packaging and order-size decisions. Sell your product so that a store or distributor can order the right number of units. For example, if a store will sell five units of a product every month, be sure the store can order 10 units. You'll quickly be out of business if you insist on 25-unit orders.

- Was the product easy to sell? Product creators are most successful when their products sell themselves. If a product needs a demonstration, or potential customers ask a lot of questions, try to find out why the product was hard to sell. Make an effort to correct the problems. If you don't, you'll be in sales trouble. Stores, distributors, and manufacturers' representatives will usually drop a product that is too much work.

- What did potential customers think of the product? Everyone in a distribution network likes to keep customers happy. If a product does that, the network might keep the product even if it presents some problems. If customers are unhappy, the product will fail.

- What, if anything, can be done to increase sales? Don't be afraid to take advantage of the business experience of personnel in a distribution network. Some helpful suggestions will result, and the same suggestion may come from several people, such as: "Offer three products for $1.50 instead of one for 79 cents." Some of this input won't be given unless you specifically ask for suggestions.

- How clear is it that your product is different? An exclusive sales agreement is a powerful incentive, but it is only a sales point if distributors perceive a product to be unique. Before you push for an exclusive sales agreement, you must know whether retailers, distributors, and manufacturers' representatives consider your product novel.

- Will the network continue to support the product? Frequently, a distribution network will take on a product, sell it for a few months, and then drop it. The product may be seasonal, sales may not be high enough, or a new product may come along. This sequence can happen with virtually any type of product.

For a novelty item, like the slap bracelets, you should expect only a three- or four-month run. For a long-time product, such as a new fishing reel, you will hope that retailers keep selling it. Some entrepreneurs who have what they feel is a successful first sales period may find that their distribution network will no longer support their product. Find this out *before* you invest in the transitional period.

If distributors won't give you continued support, try to find out why. Distributors often drop products for reasons that have nothing to do with the product itself. Ordering or competitive factors can be influential. For instance, the network may feel that your product needs a bigger discount, or that your price schedule doesn't offer high enough discounts on small enough quantities. You may have the wrong size package, or your package may not fit into a space where retailers would like to put it. All of these problems may be correctable if you learn about them soon enough.

Your product could also be dropped because of competitive pressures. A major manufacturer might be introducing a new line of products that will take all the available shelf space; another manufacturer might be having a new promotion, or introducing five or six new seasonal products right before the start of a season. A distribution network will support products that are advertised and promoted. Your unadvertised product may be a casualty.

Customer Ratings

You should seek as much customer input as possible about a product. That's one of the reasons I recommend that you attend trade shows or fairs. Another way to get input is to include a warranty card with each unit. When you receive a warranty card back, call the customer and ask his or her opinion of your product. You can also place a 50-cent or $1 rebate coupon inside your package. Call the people who send in the rebate coupon.

Another tactic is to include a customer survey in each package. Offer customers $1 if they fill out and return the survey. This approach will save you the trouble of having to call people. Don't make the survey too long; ask a few pertinent questions that will help you gauge your product's future chances of success. If you don't understand some customers' answers, you still can call or write to those people for clarification. Listed below are some of the questions that should be on your survey.

- What features do you like about the product? You can list all the features and leave space for people to check off the features they like. Be sure to include an "other" category and space for comments.

- Is there anything you *don't* like about the product? People can check yes or no. Leave space for explanations of what customers don't like.

- Does the product work as you expected? Again, allow for yes or no and an explanation. If the product doesn't work as expected, the instructions may need revision, or users may not think the product works as well as you do.

- Are there any improvements you would like to suggest? Under the yes box, leave room for suggestions. Don't be discouraged if 25 to 50 percent of the respondents suggest some improvements. That rate is not unusual. Consider adopting any suggestions that are made by over 50 percent of those who reply.

- How did you learn about the product? Include boxes for: saw it in the store; heard about it from a friend; recommended by store personnel; and saw it in an ad. Include advertising even if you didn't advertise; you may have benefited from a similar product's advertising. If people see an ad and like that *type* of product, they may buy your product when they shop. It took me six months to realize that the little rabbit that keeps on drumming was in a commercial for Eveready batteries, not Duracell. You're in great shape when your product is clearly superior to one that's heavily advertised.

- Were you looking for this type of product, or was your purchase made on impulse? You'll have a better chance of long-term sales success if people are shopping for your type of product. For example, there is on the market a vinyl strip that replaces silicone sealant around the edges of a bathtub. People who buy that product should be out shopping for sealant. If the people who are buying the product are purchasing on impulse instead, the product is probably placed in the wrong part of the store. It's missing the people who are fixing their bathtubs on the same day they're shopping.

- Did you buy this product instead of another one? If so, what was the other product? You may be targeting to replace another product. If you get positive reinforcement from customers, you can use that as ammunition to place your product on the shelves right next to the targeted product.

- How satisfied were you with the product? Satisfied customers will spread the word about a product and possibly increase sales. If people aren't satisfied, your product may have a short sales life. Not only won't customers keep buying, but your distribution network will drop your product like a hot potato.

Re-Evaluating the Key Go/No-Go Decisions

As you go through the decisions this time, you need to be much tougher than you were the first time around. For instance, instead of an estimate that you can manufacture a product for a certain price, you'll need a firm price quote. You'll have to give reasons, based on your analysis, for each of your answers. Entrepreneurs usually don't like putting their product through a tough test, but a hard-nosed reevaluation is essential—not to look for reasons to drop a product, but to protect against failure and loss of money. Give solid business answers to the 12 key go/no-go decisions now. I've added some comments to help you with your evaluations.

1. Can potential customers quickly understand your product's benefit?

2. Is your product clearly different from other products in the market?

3. Does your product have a benefit people want? I like to compare the sales I've made myself with the sales made by other people. If my sales efforts produce a much better result, then customers aren't grasping the product's benefits. Compare your sales to similar products' sales in the same store or at other sales locations. For example, if your product is placed next to a product you've targeted, and your product is outsold three- or four-to-one, your product probably doesn't merit a yes answer for the first three go/no-go decisions.

4. Can your product be packaged effectively? Some products might not sell because of their package. This drawback should have shown up and been corrected in the first sales period. Or, you may have found that, even with your best efforts, your product couldn't be packaged so that it would communicate your message. Your package might run into other problems: it takes up too much room; it's too easy to steal; it doesn't conveniently fit on the racks. Your point-of-purchase display may have too many units. Packages and displays must fit into a distribution network's requirements, as well as providing the consumer with necessary information.

5. Is the market open?

6. Does a distribution network exist with promotion costs you can afford? Did you find a distribution network that requires only minimal promotion? Was that market open to you? A distribution network evaluation is important. These questions are hard to answer unless you ask people whether they will continue their support. Many answers will be hidden from you until the initial evaluation. For example, a store owner might have some open shelf space, allow you to put your product in for a test, and sell your product well. But the owner may prefer to promote

products that are advertised. Your product's stay on the shelf could be short-lived.

7. Are your customers easy to target? Your product should be in a store, catalog, direct mailer, magazine, or location where customers can easily find you. Targeting could become a problem if sales hover just above or just below a network's sales threshold. Terry M. had a device to stabilize a ladder on uneven terrain. When the product went into a hardware store, its sales were about the same as another product designed to stabilize a ladder. But neither product sold well, because the store wasn't targeted at people who owned homes built on uneven terrain. The store owner was willing to carry only one product for stabilizing ladders, and Terry's product was out. You can determine whether your sales outlets are targeting your customers by comparing average monthly sales. If most products in the store sell 10 to 15 units per month and your product only sells 2 to 3, you might have a targeting problem. I've often thought I should open a store that sells supplies for product creators—small parts, casting materials, low-cost molding equipment, and so on. But product entrepreneurs are hard to locate. Not only are they spread throughout the country, but every year new people join the ranks and others stop trying. The market is too scattered to make it practical to open a store for inventors. This same phenomenon can occur with a product: customers can be too hard to target.

8. Can you afford to make your models, prototypes, and initial production runs? If you can't, you won't make it through the initial sales period.

9. Can you find a contract manufacturer that's willing to absorb some of the start-up manufacturing costs? I wouldn't proceed to the transitional sales period without a firm agreement, backed up with either a contract or a letter. You need a firm price for start-up costs and for per-unit manufacturing costs. The first step in the transitional sales period is to prepare a budget, a detailed statement of how much money you need to raise. You can't prepare a budget without a firm manufacturing agreement.

10. Can you find insiders to help you? Change is the only constant factor in new-product introductions. Insiders are no different from anyone else. Some insiders will stay interested and excited about a project; others will lost interest. Their reactions may be a gauge of their expectations: have you exceeded or fallen well short of what an insider expected? Insiders' situations will change, and they may not be able to help you anymore. Keep in touch with your key contacts; know whether they're still willing to work with you.

11. Does your product have a perceived value that's at least four times its manufacturing cost? In the transitional period, you're no longer testing your product. Instead, you're taking the product onto the market to make money. You need a price equal to four times your manufacturing costs.

12. Is the market size of your distribution network large enough to justify your time and expense? Your initial sales period might have more narrowly defined your market. For example, your initial target market might have been all those who use a product. Now it may be those who use it 10 to 15 times per year. You might have also discovered that you don't have quite the same distribution outlets you expected. Estimate your potential earnings again. Then decide whether you should proceed into the transitional period.

Tactics for Correcting Problems

Suppose your product has not passed the go/no-go decisions. I know it's discouraging, but don't give up. You haven't spent much money, and you have plenty of time to correct your problems and reenter the first sales period. The evaluation isn't only to decide whether to drop a product; it's also to reveal whether you need to make adjustments before entering the transitional period. It's a rare product that doesn't need some adjustments. I said earlier that the first sales period could last from 3 to 15 months. Within that length of time, you can go back and start your sales over again. I also told you to prepare to sell only a limited number of units during the first sales period. That strategy pays off when you have to make adjustments, because you'll still have plenty of sales outlets to approach about taking your product.

Most of the problems entrepreneurs encounter are in one or more of the following areas: targeting, benefits, communication, costs, distribution, packaging, and promotion. Many of these problems can be resolved so that you can get your product back on track.

Targeting

Targeting the right audience is a problem not only for new entrepreneurs but for all marketers. Targeting refers to the tactic of identifying a specific type of market or customer for a product. For example, a new type of gardening tool might be targeted at gardeners who spend over 10 hours a week working in their flower gardens. That's a specific market, and only four or five stores in a city might cater to that market.

Most product creators and marketers are afraid to target a small market. They want to appeal to *all* users so that they can sell more units. But two things happen when they appeal to a larger market. They don't sell enough units to satisfy the distribution network, and their advertising fails to be cost-effective. The most discouraging result is that the product sells like a loser.

What would have happened if the gardening product had been targeted at the specialty market? The four gardening stores would have been happy with the sales volume. The inventor could have purchased a mailing list from a gardening magazine and announced, in a mailing, what the new product was and where it could be bought. The entrepreneur could have attended gardening association meetings and trade shows and contacted potential buyers.

I can't know for sure whether an entrepreneur will succeed in a targeted market. But I do know that the chances of success increase greatly when the focus narrows to a smaller market.

What is your target market? Most product creators answer teenagers, or housewives, or some equally general category. You'll fail if you don't target your market more precisely than that. Serving a small niche market doesn't prevent you from making enough money. Many small markets can produce several million dollars in annual sales. As an example, Arthur Engstrom and Howard Hawkins have built Park Tool Company into a $5-million-a-year business by making tools for repairing bicycles.

Benefits

A benefit is what a product does for a customer. Saving time, making better tasting coffee, or having easy-to-prepare dinners handy are all examples of benefits. Product creators have two problems with benefits: they don't tell people what their product's benefit is, and they don't find out what benefits their customers want.

Entrepreneurs don't clearly state their product's benefit because they wrongly assume that people will realize what it is. Michael D. created a product he called a toe jamb holder. The package stated: "Holds nails at a 45-degree angle." I asked what the benefit of the product was, and the answer was: "To get secure joints when putting up 2-by-4s at a 90-degree angle." Michael's product was helpful. When you're building a wall or a frame out of 2-by-4s, especially during remodeling projects, you sometimes can't hammer straight through one 2-by-4 into the end of another. When you are adding a new window to a house, for example, you need to frame in the top and bottom of the window. You can't hammer through the side of the vertical 2-by-4 into the horizontal 2-by-4 because a wall is in the way. Instead, a homeowner or carpenter has to hammer a nail in at a 45-degree angle to secure the frame. This job is somewhat difficult for a homeowner.

The product's benefit was that it simplified home repair by allowing any homeowner to make a secure toe jamb. I would have displayed on the package the product's name (toe jamb holder), the product's benefit statement (simplifies home repairs), and a picture of an application where the product was useful. This combination would have been more effective than Michael's package, which simply stated: toe jamb holder.

The second problem is that product creators don't find out what benefits customers want and then give them that benefit. In Chapter 6, I mentioned a product that reduces back strain when people rake or shovel. Does that benefit sound good to you? Maybe, at first glance. But do people with bad backs go out and shovel? Not often. People who use shovels want one benefit: make the job easier.

Communication

Many product creators simply don't communicate effectively to their target market. To remedy typical problems, I recommend telling potential customers what they want to know, and having short, informative messages that make it clear why the product will work.

- Tell customers what they want to know. Products require specific information. Is an item dishwasher-safe, microwave-safe, flammable, or toxic if taken internally? Does it need operating instructions or specifications? Your product won't sell without the proper information. Check all of your competitors' packages to be sure you are offering all the necessary data.

- Give short, informative messages. At least half the product entrepreneurs I've worked with make the mistake of not offering clear information. One reason for the problem is that entrepreneurs know their products too well. They often omit some very valuable information because they assume people already know it. Another source of poor communications is that entrepreneurs don't realize that their information is confusing.

To check whether a product's instructions are clear, I give the package and instructions to people who've never seen the product, and then watch to see whether they can understand them. I only let them have the package for 10 or 15 seconds before I take it away. I can't ever remember a time when I didn't have to make at least two or three changes in a product's information.

Joe S. created a new board game that was a lot of fun to play, as long as Joe was playing. No one could understand the directions without Joe. I was never able to get Joe to change the instructions. He thought they were clear enough, and the product is still sitting in his basement.

A last reason entrepreneurs don't have clear packaging and instructions is that they don't commit the necessary time. I've spent weeks trying to get one phrase that's exactly right for a package. Effective operating instructions can be particularly tough. I once worked for a month to develop instructions that a person could complete in less than a minute. The best method is to write out the instructions or message, then set a reasonable time for a person to understand them—10 seconds for a package, or 45 seconds for operating instructions. Ask people to read the package or instructions and see whether they can understand them within the time limit.

Writing something that's simple to understand is difficult. I recommend that you get help from a freelance writer or a technical writer if you can't make the information simple enough on your own.

Costs

At times, you won't be able to change the fact that a product's perceived value is not over four times its manufacturing cost. When that happens, I don't recommend that you proceed. Don't count on your costs coming down as your sales volume increases. That may happen; but your volume may never increase.

Instead, take corrective steps to get your costs down. Redesign your product so that it's cheaper to manufacture, look for another manufacturing source, or consider adding a feature or two to increase the product's value.

Another tactic is to transfer manufacturing overseas. This is a last-ditch strategy for a new entrepreneur. You'll need complete manufacturing documentation—engineering drawings, specifications, inspection standards, and so on—and they may have to be translated into another language.

To get low-cost products, you may also need to make a large down payment; overseas manufacturing may make low-cost production available to you. You can find overseas manufacturers by looking at trade magazines, reading want ads in your local paper's business section, or researching the business-to-business yellow pages of major cities such as New York, Los Angeles, or Chicago.

Another option is to look for domestic manufacturers out of your area and revisit some other local manufacturers. If you get a lower cost quote from another manufacturer, don't switch immediately. Moving a product from one manufacturer to another will cost you both time and money. Instead, take the new quote, along with evidence of your sales success, to your contract manufacturer. You may be able to negotiate a lower price.

You might want to consider adding a feature or two that will raise the perceived value of your product. A sunglasses manufacturer added a string so that the glasses wouldn't fall off and get lost or break when someone was participating in activities. The string probably cost 5 cents, but it raised the product's perceived value by $1 to $2. My son Eric is 8 and he is rough on his glasses. My wife found a pair of glasses with a spring that allows the bows to be pulled out, away from the ears, without breaking the glasses. The spring probably costs $2 or $3, but the glasses cost an extra $30.

Office supplies such as date books or appointment calendars are sometimes similar products inside but they have a big price difference because one has a fancier cover. Products such as jewelry or perfume offer a deluxe package to add value.

Distribution

If a product will sell and you can prove it, a distribution network should be willing to handle the product, right? Unfortunately, the statement is not true. There is an oversupply of products for a distribution network to sell. Unless your product is an incredible seller, the distribution channel can get along without you. The two areas to focus on are your sales efforts and your distribution mechanics.

A distribution channel always starts with the manufacturer's salesperson, which more than likely happens to be you, the new-product entrepreneur. The go/no-go decisions are designed to help you find a product that can be sold, but that doesn't mean you'll end up with a product that will sell itself. You still have to get out and sell the product. If your product isn't selling, answer the following questions honestly.

- Are you making a dedicated sales effort? You have to spend a lot of time to make sales. You must be prepared to spend the time needed to develop a sales presentation and then call on enough people. I wouldn't consider it unusual if an entrepreneur took a week to get one or two stores to handle a new product. Store own-ers will often be out or will be too busy to talk to an unknown salesperson. Probably only one out of every four or five owners that you talk to will buy.

- Do you have a sound sales strategy? Do your contacts include an experienced salesperson? Ask him or her to review your strategy and to make suggestions on how to improve it. I have sometimes spent two or three weeks preparing a sales strategy, along with the appropriate sales material, so don't expect to create an effec-tive strategy in an evening. If you have no sales experience, I sug-gest that you take a course on selling or buy a sales strategy book at your local bookstore and do some self-teaching.

- Do you have an effective follow-up system? I estimate that at least half of all sales are made with a follow-up call or letter. Again, ask for help from a contact who has sales experience, or find a good book.

Distribution mechanics deals with order size, payment terms, order schedule, number of units per carton, advertising and promo-tional support, and so on. These "little things," if done wrong, will kill your chances of selling a product. Because the mechanics of a distribution network are not always obvious, you need insiders, and you need to always ask people why they didn't buy.

Spearhead Industries of Eden Prairie, Minnesota, makes halloween and Easter merchandise. Spearhead has to know which trade shows to attend, when it needs to contact stores, the date by which it must receive orders, what dates to ship by, the type of payment terms it needs, what size cartons to ship in, the best minimum order size, and the correct policy on returned merchandise—an incredible number of details for a new entrepreneur to iron out.

Packaging

I've covered packaging thoroughly in Chapter 5 and have mentioned it frequently throughout the book. If you've tried quite a few packages, consider hiring a marketing consultant to review your efforts. Developing an effective package often requires marketing experience. An expert can't solve every packaging problem, but there may be times when an expert can find a solution that will turn your product into a winner.

Promotion

A product might need promotion or advertising. I've said repeatedly that new product entrepreneurs really can't afford to advertise their product; in fact, that's not always true. The one time you can afford to promote your product is when you have a small, targeted market that you can reach easily.

The secret of overcoming promotion problems is to shrink your target market until you can afford to reach it. You can expand to other markets after you have an established base. Andy Bonnette makes crosses and statues that can be either placed on poles for processions or hung on a wall of a church. His market was Catholic churches in Minnesota and Iowa. His family has had the business for 30 years and is quite happy with the business's small volume. When Andy's father started out, he envisioned a worldwide market. But he couldn't afford to promote to that market.

Targeting a smaller market is similar to shrinking a market. I mention them separately because targeting usually refers to defining customers by what they do. Shrinking a market means limiting the geographic area you're selling to.

Is It Go/Go-Go Time?

You won't be able to resolve every problem, but you should be able to resolve at least half of them. A normal pattern for most entrepreneurs, especially those who are introducing a product for the first time, will be to resolve at least two or three problems, and then reenter the first sales period before proceeding to the transitional period. Your evaluation should not be quick. Instead, take your time, and be sure that the considerable amount of money you're about to invest will be spent wisely.

11

The Transitional Period: Establishing the Business

Pepin Heights Sparkling Cider had revenues of about $250,000 in 1989. Its products are sold through bars, restaurants, delicatessens, and grocery stores in Minnesota. Pepin Heights is a good example of a company in the transitional sales period. It has a foothold in a regional market, its sales volume is large enough to give it stability and good credit, and it has a distribution network in place.

In the transitional period, a company moves from having a few sporadic sales to a steady, though small, ongoing business with an established distribution network and customer base. One key factor in this period is that the sales effort is no longer solely dependent on the product entrepreneur; instead, sales agents or stores generate sales volume.

I believe that this period is, by far, the most difficult time in the establishment of a business. I estimate that, out of ten entrepreneurs who start to sell a product, no more than one survives the transitional period. A typical example is Norm H., who created a cleaning cloth that looked similar to a wash rag but was capable of taking stains out of carpets, clothing, and furniture. The product sold for $3.99. Over a period of two years, Norm sold an impressive 5,000 units through drugstores. In addition to sales success, Norm received several testimonial letters from satisfied clients.

Norm appeared to be poised for a successful product introduction, but he couldn't persuade distributors to pick up the product and his idea died. What happened to Norm? Part of the problem was that he never appeared to have a company; he seemed to be someone making a product in his basement. Another part of the problem was that Norm didn't have a sales strategy that would convince a distributor to carry the product. Norm's major problem, however, was that he always figured distributors would be coming to him, if he could get his product into a few stores. Norm had no idea how to take his product through the transitional period.

Norm is not alone. Most product entrepreneurs don't even know that a transitional period is needed. That's not really surprising; every day, established companies are moving straight from market testing into nationwide distribution. Entrepreneurs feel they can do the same if they can get some investors or "one lucky break."

I sometimes ask entrepreneurs what they'd do if they found an investor. Typical answers are: "I'd put my product into production," "I'd be able to afford an advertising campaign," "I'd buy the tooling I need to lower my production cost," or "I'd hire a sales manager." The problem with all of these answers is that they don't address the total picture of what an entrepreneur has to do in the transitional period: advertising, promotion, distribution, manufacturing, administration, sales, customer service, and so on. Entrepreneurs need investors, and they can all use lucky breaks, but they also need an orderly plan for expanding their sales base.

The Transitional Plan

If you've followed the action steps I've outlined through the first 10 chapters, you'll have a fairly easy time with your transitional plan. Almost everything I've advocated is designed to prepare you for the transitional period. You have key insiders to help you set up a distribution network, and you know who your customers are, how they can be reached, and what benefits they want. You know how to package and promote your idea, and you know approximately how many units will sell in each sales outlet.

Why bother with a plan? There are three very good reasons:

1. The plan details a one- to two-year action plan. With a plan, you're more likely to do everything that's necessary, and you'll do it in the right order.
2. The plan provides the details you'll need for a budget. A product entrepreneur's plan will list all the costs of producing and selling a product, and these are the building blocks of budget numbers.
3. The plan forces you to channel all your thoughts into a coherent strategy. Product creators receive input from a thousand directions. Because they pick up bits of data from everyone they talk to, their information is often inconsistent and contradictory. A plan helps turn this maze of information into a purposeful pathway toward success.

The transitional plan doesn't have to be particularly long. The beginning text, which provides an overview, shouldn't be more than 6 to 8 pages. The action plan should cover in detail the steps you'll be following over the next 12 to 18 months.

Your transitional plan should contain the following items, preferably in the order shown:

1. Product description and benefits
2. Targeted customers
3. Targeted geographic market
4. Where the targeted customers buy
5. Market potential

6. Competition
7. Distribution plan
8. Current sales status
9. Detailed sales forecast
10. Promotional activities
11. Manufacturing overview
12. Start-up expenses
13. Action plan

In some respects, a transitional plan is simpler than a routine marketing plan: you don't have as much history or as many activities to detail. However, the detailed sales forecast is much harder, because you must explain where every sales dollar will come from. You can't say: "With the promotional program we have planned, we expect sales to increase 10 percent." Instead, you have to say: "I expect to gain three distributors [name them] next July. I have had initial talks with seven distributors in the area who indicated a strong interest in the product, and I expect purchase orders for 100 units from at least three of the seven." Note that you need to name the distributors, and you need to have had discussions. Backup like this is essential to having any hope that your sales forecast will be accurate.

Let's look at the plan's elements one-by-one.

Product Description and Benefits

State succinctly what the product is; why you decided to develop it; its features and benefits; its sales proposition; and any known deficiencies.

I've covered the first three points earlier. A sales proposition is a *SHORT*, clear description of why people should buy the product. Examples are: cuts weeding time 30 percent; cleans up bathroom clutter; reduces back strain by 50 percent; hot, new, fad item; improves testing accuracy by 80 percent; great conversation piece; totally new taste.

Pointing out product deficiencies is a task that product entrepreneurs don't enjoy doing. They don't like to acknowledge that their product may not be perfect. Every product has its flaws, and those flaws can have varying impact on your plan. Your product might have to be displayed on a counter or special apparatus because it doesn't package well enough to stand on a stock shelf. Or, you might want to sell through distributors because of service and installation requirements. Or, a product's benefit might be apparent only to an older audience. You can adjust for flaws if you know what they are. You should list not only what the flaws are but what you're doing to overcome them. For example, if you acknowledge that consumers need a product demonstration, your plan might call for demonstrators at stores every other weekend.

Targeted Customers: Who Are They?

To whom is your product going to be sold? As I've been telling you throughout the book, an entrepreneur has to focus on a small, easy-to-reach market.

In 1982, Len and Lisa Brown decided to go on a two-year horseback-riding adventure. Len and Lisa didn't last two years, but they learned that a traditional saddle gives a horse a very sore back. Len created his Ortho-flex saddle, which has a suspension made of sheet plastics and other synthetic materials. Len and Lisa's first sales efforts were directed to Western riders. The product didn't sell, primarily because the target market was too broad.

The couple decided to concentrate on the endurance rider market, which is composed of people who compete in 24-hour horse races. This market is focused and easy to reach. The riders could be contacted through lists of entries in endurance races, and the market had its own magazine, *Trail Blazer.* Five years after focusing on a small market, the Browns have branched out to Western riders and now have a million-dollar business.

Your transitional plan has to be specific, and it has to be able to make an impact on targeted customers. You need to list a series of activities that (1) can be accomplished and (2) will repeatedly reach target customers. For example, consider the Pepin Heights Cider Company, which I mentioned at the start of the chapter. Their plan could involve: sales through ten restaurants; a display card, promoting the cider, for each table; a point-of-purchase display listing the ten restaurants, to be used at participating delicatessens; and a promotional flier sent to each of the restaurants' mailing lists. These actions make sense because they connect directly to the targeted customers—people who frequent certain mid- to high-priced restaurants—and they communicate the same message to those people frequently enough to be effective. I feel strongly that entrepreneurs won't be able to reach their target audience unless it's small.

Targeted Geographic Market

In addition to limiting the type of customers you're going to appeal to, you should limit the area of the market you're trying to serve. The apple cider company's target market was Minneapolis.

Where the Targeted Customers Buy

Customers buy most products through a wide variety of outlets. Focus your efforts and choose only one or two outlets to work with.

Use a market analysis chart to support your choice of a certain distribution network. The chart reviews the market size, and various sales outlets and their distribution networks. It offers comments pertinent to the level of promotional support required, and it summarizes any previous discussions with the network. Figure 11.1 is a market analysis for a hair crimping iron.

After you present the chart, include a paragraph on why you chose a particular network. For example, an entrepreneur marketing the hair crimping iron might decide to sign an exclusive one-year sales agreement with a Metro-based department store because of the favorable sales publicity from a co-op advertising program.

Product category:	Hair styling	
Product description:	New type of crimping iron for introducing waves in women's hair	
Market size, U.S.:	Approximately 2 million units per year	
Market size, Metro:	1.5% of U.S. market or 30,000 units per year	
Unit sales distribution:	Drugstore chains	30%
	Independent drugstores	10
	Discount stores	30
	Mail order	5
	Department stores, Metro-based	15
	Department stores, non-Metro-based	10

Market Comments:

1. Drugstore chains. Sold direct or through rack jobbers. Chains prefer either a well-known or a well-advertised product. Required promotional support is too expensive at this time.
2. Independent drugstores. Sold through a buying cooperative or rack jobbers. Independents have expressed interest in the product, provided it has an appealing point-of-purchase display, primarily because they are not able to purchase the top-selling crimping products.
3. Discount stores. Can be sold either direct or through a distributor. Stores prefer a brand-name product, but they will handle a small manufacturer if its pricing is substantially lower than competitive products'. The chains prefer to purchase on a regional or national basis.
4. Mail order. Most catalogs are headquartered outside of Metro, which makes a sale difficult. In addition, mail order is just a small part of the market, and it's preferable to develop sales momentum at the retail level.
5. Department stores, Metro-based. Sold either direct or through distributors. Stores have expressed interest in an exclusive sales agreement, as long as a co-op advertising program is included. One store has promised to prominently display the product in return for the exclusive agreement.
6. Department stores, non-Metro-based. Sold either direct or through distributors. Meetings with buyers have been difficult because of the distance involved. Early talks indicate that the stores will only support a brand-name product.

Figure 11.1   Target Market Analysis

Market Potential

In this section, you should include sales potential for the next year, market potential of the targeted market, and market potential of the total market.

- *Next year's sales.* This number comes right from your market analysis chart. The market size for the hair crimping iron is 30,000 units in the Metro market. The locally based department store has 15 percent of the market, or 4,500 units. The sales potential of the product, based on input from the store's buyer, is 20 percent of what the store sells, or 900 units.

- *Potential of the targeted market.* You should be able to penetrate new retail outlets every year. Go back to your market analysis chart for an estimate of the sales potential of the targeted market. For the hair crimping product, the local market took 30,000 units per year. Based on the first sales period, and estimates from local buyers or insiders, an entrepreneur might estimate a 15 percent market share, or a sales potential of 4,500 units.

- *Potential of the entire market.* I personally hate making this estimate. The number is usually meaningless because nationwide sales can't be reliably projected based on a local market. However, everyone wants to know the product's "true" sales potential. Take the market number from the market analysis and multiply it by your projected market share. For example, the sales potential for the hair crimping iron would be 2 million times 15 percent, or 300,000 units. This is the number of units you may be able to sell after being in business five to ten years.

If you are not able to obtain a total market size number, try to find another product to use as a sales base. For example, Product Y might be the top-selling crimping iron, at 1.2 million units per year. Your estimates could then be based on selling 20 percent of Product Y's volume. Base your percentage of sales either on actual results from the first sales period or on insider or buyer estimates.

Competition

When introducing a product, entrepreneurs typically are offering a product that fills a void or need, is the next logical step in the evolution of a product line, or takes advantage of an opportunity. For example, a box for feminine hygiene supplies meets the need for an all-inclusive feminine box. An easier-to-use windsurfing board is a natural extension of a product line. T-shirts with Desert Shield and Desert Storm emblems took advantage of a marketing opportunity.

Base your section on competition on one of these three points so that people can understand the logic of a product's introduction. Explain the competition and tell why your product fills a void, is a logical extension, or capitalizes on an opportunity.

Product feature charts or function comparison charts are helpful in illustrating how a product is different. Figure 11.2 is a comparison chart for a new rake. *Consumer Reports* magazine is a good source for samples of product comparison charts.

Product category:	Rakes	
Production description:	A rake with two rows of tines; greatly decreases raking time. Every other tine on this rake is an inch shorter than the longer tines. The rake ends up with two rows of raking tines when the tines are bent at a 60-degree raking angle.	
Competition:	Traditional bamboo, metal, and plastic rakes.	

Product	Price	Speed	Dethatching Capabilities	Anticlogging	Ease of Use	Effectiveness
Bamboo rake	$ 4.95	Poor	Fair	Some	Good	Poor
Plastic rake	6.95	Fair	Poor	No	Fair	Fair
Metal rake	8.95	Good	Good	No	Fair	Good
New rake	12.95	Excellent	Excellent	Minimal	Good	Excellent

Figure 11.2   Competitive Product Chart

Distribution Plan

So far, your plan has explained who your targeted customers are, what type of outlets you'll cultivate, and what the distribution network is for those outlets. For example, suppose you're selling to walleye fishing enthusiasts in Minnesota, through bait and tackle shops as well as a small chain of three discount stores. Sales to bait and tackle shops are typically made through fishing distributors, and sales to the discount store chain are through a manufacturers' representative.

You've already presented the framework for the distribution plan. Now you need to add the necessary details: the actual distributors, manufacturers, representatives, or other sales network components involved in selling the product. If you have a key contact who will help, mention that person in your discussion. Figure 11.3 is an example of a distribution plan for the fishing product.

Distribution Network: Two distributors—Minnesota Fishing, and Lures and Jigs—will sell to bait and tackle shops, and Peterson's Manufacturers' Representatives will sell to Merlin's Discount Stores.

Minnesota Fishing has a line of 11 products that it sells through 41 bait and tackle shops in Minnesota. The company's sales manager has been a consultant on the project for six months, and he feels he will be able to place the product in half of those stores in 1992.

Lures and Jigs carries a line of 24 fishing products that it sells to 117 stores in central Minnesota. One of the company's salespeople has field-tested the product for over a year. He feels that he can place the product in 24 stores in 1992.

Peterson's Manufacturers' Representatives: The owner of this company has close ties with a small chain of discount stores. He currently sells 14 products to the chain. The owner has agreed to sell the fishing lure provided we offer him a 20 percent commission and offer the chain 60-day terms and guaranteed sales.

Figure 11.3   Sample Distribution Plan: Walleye Lures

Current Sales Status

Give a brief overview of where your product is selling. List each outlet and the approximate number of units that it sells per month. Detail how many units have been sold by manufacturers' representatives or distributors.

Your goal in this section is to show that your product has had some initial sales success. Mention any trade shows or fairs you have attended. State not only what your sales were, but also what the sales were at booths around yours. Include, as an attachment, your sales comparison chart (Chapter 10, page 187).

Detailed Sales Forecast

New entrepreneurs are absolutely horrible at sales forecasting. To them—in fact, to most people—a sales forecast might start with 100 units the first month, move to 120 units the second month, and then proceed nicely up to 220 to 250 units per month by year's end. I wish sales could build that smoothly, but they don't. If a fishing store buys a product in April, it might buy again in May, but, more probably, it won't order again until the next year. A fishing product might have 90 percent of its sales in a 2- to 3-month period. Entrepreneurs sometimes make another faulty assumption: if three stores order one month, then four stores will order the next month. New products often have a burst of sales in the beginning, when stores bring in their initial stocking orders. Those initial stores are usually "friendly"; the product creator has a friend or helpful contact there. After that initial burst, sales can be hard to come by. When you do your sales forecast, list each customer and when it is expected to buy.

Your sales forecast is the most important part of your budget. Not only does it drive your revenue, but it also provides the information you need to prepare manufacturing and promotional budgets. A combined sales/revenue forecast for the fishing product is shown in Figure 11.4. Sales occur when a unit is sold; revenue occurs when payment is received. You need to know when sales will occur so that

Fishing Widget
Sales and Revenues

	Jan.	Feb.	Mar.	Apr.	May	June
Sales units (returns)	0	300[1]	600	4,800	210	100
Revenues[2]	0	0	$600	$1,200	$600	$420

	July	Aug.	Sept.	Oct.	Nov.	Dec.
Sales units (returns)	100	0	0	(300)	(300)	(100)
Revenues[2]	$200	$200	$9,000	0	$(600)	$(600)

Sales Explanation:

February

Distributor X has 6 stores that will buy early.[3]

Distributor Y has 4 stores that will buy early.

March

Distributor X will have 10 stores buy.

Distributor Y will have 10 stores buy.

April

Distributor X will have 4 stores buy.

Distributor Y will have 6 stores buy.

Each large store[4] will purchase 1,500 units.

May

Distributor X will add 3 stores.

Distributor Y will add 4 stores.

June–August

Small number of reorders expected to restock shelves.

October

Product returns. Payment within 30 days of return.

November

Product returns.

December

Product returns.

Notes:

1. Small fishing stores are projected (based on the first sales period) at 30 units per store. Each large store is projected to buy 1,500 units based on the buyers' preliminary estimates of 1,500 to 2,000 units based on 90-day dating, guaranteed sales, and a television ad campaign.
2. Based on an average selling price of $2. Payment expected in 30 days from small stores.
3. Sales projections are based on half of Distributors X and Y's customers purchasing. This is consistent with the results of the first sales period and with the distributors' own sales projections.
4. Five large discount chains have indicated they would buy 1,500 to 2,000 units each. The plan calls for selling only 3 of the 5 stores. [List the names of the stores.]

Figure 11.4   Forecast of Sales and Revenues: 12-Month Projection

you can plan production. You need to know when you'll receive revenue so that you can determine cash flow requirements.

Notice several points about the forecast. There is a considerable difference between when you make the sale and when you collect the money; neither sales nor revenue shows a consistent pattern; and the sales in the transitional period's first year aren't very high.

Promotional Activities

List month-by-month every activity, from point-of-purchase displays to television advertising, that you plan for the next year. This list will tell you how much money is needed and will provide an action plan to follow.

Figure 11.5 shows what the fishing entrepreneur's promotional list might look like.

This schedule budgets $4,000 for promotion against a sales budget of $11,200—not bad, considering that the product is still becoming established. You have to promote your product if you expect to sell it.

Month	Activity	Cost
January	Print 250 11"-by-14" point-of-purchase displays emphasizing the product's benefits and the fact that the product is new.	$ 400
March	Produce a 15-second TV commercial for April and May TV spots.	400
April	Run 100 ads on cable-TV fishing shows carried by small cable systems in northern Minnesota.	1,500
May	Run 100 ads on cable-TV in northern Minnesota.	1,500
June	Prepare 100 point-of-purchase cards with a $1 instant-rebate coupon offer, to help clear out remaining store inventory.	200

Figure 11.5   Schedule of Promotional Activities: Fishing Widgets

The cost allowances are extremely low. You won't get these prices by walking into a TV station and saying you want to buy some ads. You'll have to call up every cable station in your sales area and ask for discounts. Tell each TV ad salesperson that you're an entrepreneur with a new product and that you're trying to save money. Promise to run more ads if the product is successful. Be willing to take unsold time at a discount, provided it will reach your target audience.

Concentrate on a market where you can afford to run your ad in at least 25 to 50 spots; you'll need the repetition to convey your message to consumers. No one will see all 25 runs, but if you advertise that much, some people might see the ad 5 times.

Be sure that the timing of the promotional programs ties in with your sales forecast. For example, the discount stores will want to have an ad campaign to promote the product when it first comes into the stores. Your promotion budget should show a campaign in the month when the discount stores buy. The fishing entrepreneur needs to have ads running in April and May to coincide with the discount stores' April purchase.

Manufacturing Overview

This section explains how you plan to have the product manufactured and contains a manufacturing budget.

Manufacturing plan. Figure 11.6 shows a month-by-month manufacturing plan. According to the sales forecast, the fishing entrepreneur needs to manufacture 6,110 units. The cost to produce the units in a garage is 73 cents. The costs from a contract manufacturer are: 95 cents for up to 5,000 units; 75 cents for up to 10,000 units; and 67 cents for over 20,000 units. Packaging adds 12 cents to each unit's cost, no matter how it's produced.

Both manufacturing options should be explained so that potential investors can see that the units produced in a garage will end up costing about the same as if they were made by the contract

August	Order packaging artwork.
	Order inventory to build 1,500 units. Note: Shipment lead time is 12 weeks.
September	Order inventory to produce 1,500 units.
October	Order inventory to produce 1,500 units.
	Order packaging supplies for 6,500 units.
November	Order inventory to produce 1,500 units.
December	Hire a part-time worker for the December–March period.
	Produce 1,500 units.
	Order supplies to produce 500 units.
January	Produce 1,500 units.
February	Produce 1,500 units.
March	Produce 1,500 units.
April	Produce 500 units.
May	Rework product returns.
June	Rework product returns.
July	Determine manufacturing plan for next season.

Figure 11.6   Manufacturing Plan: Fishing Widgets

manufacturer. The entrepreneur should make the product in a garage, rather than invest $3,000 to $4,000 in inventory.

Manufacturing budget.   The first step in preparing a budget is to list when you need to produce your product. Refer back to your sales forecast and your production capability. If you need 4,800 units to ship in April, and you can produce only 1,500 units per month, then you need to start producing four months before April, or in December.

Work backward from your production schedule to determine when you need to order supplies and when you'll have to pay for them. A supplier might have a 12-week lead time; if you need to start production in December, you'll need to order supplies in September. You may have to pay for supplies 30 to 60 days after shipment, or give cash on delivery, or make a 50 percent deposit before a supplier will accept your order. Include in your budget not only when you must place the order, but also when you'll have to pay for it.

Another expense to include is packaging. Again, what are your lead times and payment terms? Packaging costs almost always have dramatic price drops; for example, 1,000 units might cost 45 cents each, and 5,000 units might cost 22 cents each. New entrepreneurs tend to buy large quantities to "save" money. Don't do that. Your goal is to preserve working capital. Figure 11.7 shows the fishing entrepreneur's manufacturing budget. Study it along with the manufacturing plan (Figure 11.6). With a part-time helper, 1,500 units per month can be produced; without a helper, 500 units can be produced. As you can see from the plan, a product entrepreneur has to be planning 3 to 6 months ahead and has to faithfully execute every action item.

Start-Up Expenses

These expenses can be quite numerous. Beyond tooling costs, they include: product liability insurance; incorporation costs; manufacturing and office supplies; logo design; moving expenses; engineering documentation; legal fees for partnership or contract manufacturing agreements; telephone; rent deposits, and so on. You should have a fairly good estimate of your major costs, such as tooling. But you may overlook many of the small, miscellaneous expenses. If at all possible, ask another entrepreneur (suggested by your Chamber of Commerce or named in magazine and newspaper articles) what his or her unexpected start-up expenses were. The fishing product might have the start-up expenses shown in Figure 11.8.

$1,600! And the product is being produced in a basement! None of the purchases is a major item; that's the nature of start-up costs. They're small, but the dollar total sneaks up on entrepreneurs.

Month	Comments	Month	Comments
August		*January*	
$1,000	Artwork	$450	Pay 75% on shipment
150	25% prepayment for supplies	500	Labor
$1,150		$950	
September		*February*	
$ 150	Prepayment for supplies	$450	Pay 75% on shipment
$ 150		500	Labor
		$950	
October			
$ 150	Prepayment	*March*	
300	Half of charge for package	$450	Pay 75% on shipment
$ 450		500	Labor
		$950	
November			
$ 150	Prepayment	*April*	
450	Pay 75% on shipment	$150	Pay 75% on shipment
$ 600		$150	
December			
$ 50	Prepayment		
450	Pay 75% on shipment		
500	Labor		
300	Payment for last half of package		
$1,300			

Figure 11.7 Manufacturing Budget: Fishing Widgets

Action Plan

In this section, you combine all of the actions you plan to take through the transitional sales period—marketing, manufacturing, and any other activity. Figure 11.9 gives an example.

Investors love action plans because they like to know whether things are going as expected. In your first few months, it may appear that nothing is happening. Your investors may panic. They'll be reassured if you can show that you're right on the action plan's schedule.

1. Two additional manufacturing fixtures	$ 400
2. Incorporation costs	125
3. Company name registration	225
4. Business phone deposit	250
5. Stationery, invoices, statements, bills of lading forms, and business cards	275
6. Miscellaneous manufacturing and cleaning supplies	150
7. Shrink-wrap equipment	175
Total	$1,600

Figure 11.8   Start-Up Expenses: Fishing Widget

And if you're not on target? You can expect to have upset investors. The action plan gives you and your investors a guide for tracking your performance. It will help to keep you on schedule. Without a plan, dates can slip by without any action occurring.

The Budget

Refer to Figure 11.10 (page 226) as you read the next few paragraphs. There are four key points that I want you to note:

1. The highest cumulative profit/loss amount is in May, a loss of $10,650. To survive the first year, the company needs, either from the entrepreneur's resources or those of investors, an additional $10,650.

2. The year shows a loss of $2,630. Many entrepreneurs don't want to show a loss. What appears to be the only area that can be cut back? Promotion. Cutting promotion is exactly what most people do, and it's a mistake. Without promotion, stores won't carry your product. You need point-of-purchase displays, selling boards for distributors, or co-op advertising programs if you are to move out of the first sales period.

3. The monthly profit/loss figure acts like a scorecard; it tells how you're doing. In May, after nine months of operations, if you

August	Order packaging artwork. Order inventory to build 1,500 units. Confirm shipment lead time is 12 weeks.
September	Order inventory to product 1,500 units. Order manufacturing fixtures.
October	Order inventory to product 1,500 units. Order packaging supplies for 6,500 units. Order stationery, invoices, etc. Start procedures for incorporating and filing for company name registration. Obtain any necessary local licenses.
November	Order inventory for 1,500 units. Start development of a point-of-purchase display. Order miscellaneous office, manufacturing, and cleaning supplies. Order shrink-wrap machinery.
December	Put down deposit for business phone. Hire a part-time worker for the December–March period. Produce 1,500 units. Order inventory to produce 500 units.
January	Produce 1,500 units. Order 250 point-of-purchase displays. Note: Order extra point-of-purchase displays to replace those that will get damaged.
February	Produce 1,500 units. Develop the concept for the 15-second TV commercial. Find low-cost producer to put together TV ad.
March	Produce 1,500 units. Produce 15-second TV commercial.
April	Produce 500 units. Run 100 ads on cable-TV shows carried by small cable systems in northern Minnesota.
May	Rework product returns. Develop point-of-purchase display to help clear out inventory.
June	Rework product returns. Print point-of-purchase return coupons.
July	Determine manufacturing plan for the next year.

Figure 11.9   Action Plan: Fishing Widgets

	Aug.	Sept.	Oct.	Nov.	Dec.	Jan.	Feb.	Mar.	Apr.
Sales (units)	—	—	—	—	—	—	—	600	4,800
Production (units)	—	—	—	—	1,500	1,500	1,500	1,500	500
Revenue	—	—	—	—	—	—	—	$ 600	$ 1,200
Expenses									
Manufacturing									
Supplies	$ 1,150	$ 150	$ 450	$ 600	$ 800	$ 450	$ 450	$ 450	150
Labor	—	—	—	—	500	500	500	500	—
Overhead	—	—	—	—	—	—	—	—	—
Promotional	—	—	—	—	—	400	500	400	1,500
Start-up	—	400	625	325	250	—	—	—	—
Other	50	50	50	50	50	50	50	50	50
Total expenses	1,200	600	1,125	975	1,600	1,400	1,500	1,400	1,700
Profit/loss	(1,200)	(600)	(1,125)	(975)	(1,600)	(1,400)	(1,500)	(800)	(500)

	May	June	July	Aug.	Sept.	Oct.	Nov.	Dec.
Sales (units)	210	100	100	100	—	(300)	(300)	(100)
Production (units)	—	—	—	—	—	—	—	—
Revenue	$ 600	$ 420	$ 200	$ 200	$9,000	—	$ (600)	$ (600)
Expenses								
Manufacturing								
Supplies	—	—	—	—	—	—	—	—
Labor	—	—	—	—	50	—	—	—
Overhead	—	—	—	—	—	—	—	—
Promotional	1,500	200	—	—	—	—	—	—
Start-up	—	—	—	—	—	—	—	—
Other	50	50	50	50	50	50	50	50
Total expenses	1,550	250	50	50	100	50	50	50
Profit/Loss	(950)	170	150	150	8,900	(50)	(650)	(650)
Cumulative profit/Loss	(10,650)	(10,480)	(10,330)	(10,180)	(1,280)	(1,330)	(1,980)	(2,630)

Figure 11.10 Budget: Fishing Widgets

show a cumulative loss of $10,650, your investors won't say: "What's going on?" Instead they'll say: "Ah yes, you're right on budget."

4. The budget is strictly on a cash basis. Don't consider any other accounting method. Project when you'll receive the cash, and when you'll spend it.

Your budget gives you a basis for putting a value on your business. The budgeted sales revenue for the year is $11,000. A new, growing company is worth about two to three times its current sales volume. Fishing Widgets is worth about $25,000 to $30,000. A 20 percent share in the business should sell for about $5,000.

Your transitional plan and budget are very important documents in your entrepreneurial path to success. Every step I've introduced has been designed to help you create a workable transitional plan. For most new product entrepreneurs, however, things don't always go smoothly. Let's discuss some tactics you can use to overcome problems that might arise.

Problem-Solving Tactics

New product entrepreneurs typically face the serious problems of not enough money, not enough sales, and/or a manufacturing cost that's too high. Frequently, the first two problems are tied together: an entrepreneur doesn't have enough money to promote his or her product and consequently sales are too low. Fortunately, a wide variety of tactics can be used to overcome these problems.

Find a Smaller Market

The rallying call of every financially pinched inventor seems to be: "I need some investors." The true cry should be: "I need a smaller market." The goal of the transitional period is to become established in *a part of* the market. Being established means that consumers have heard of your product and that you have a fair number of sales outlets carrying it. Whether the market is a town with 75,000 people or a metro area with 2 million people, what matters is that you choose a market where you can afford the promotion costs.

You are much better off away from the standard consumer market. Turn your product into a specialty consumer or industrial item; these markets have much lower promotional costs. Jim McCoy created a great-tasting ice cream which he marketed under the name McConnell's. Can you imagine a worse product for a new entrepreneur? Think of the packaging, distribution, and advertising expenses involved in reaching consumers. Because the product was difficult to market, Jim repositioned it as a premium ice cream for restaurants. He made the sales calls himself and was able to persuade 60 restaurants to start buying his product.

Enlist More Insiders Who Will Help You

Insiders can take pressure off you in the transition period by placing a product in key stores, finding cooperative distributors, and generally endorsing the product. Their support can cut your promotional requirements because sales outlets may be willing to help you even if you don't have a promotional program.

If you're having trouble getting enough help from insiders, increase your attendance at trade shows, association meetings, and Chamber of Commerce gatherings. One or two contacts isn't enough. More inside contacts will give you more opportunities for lining up investors.

Arrange Exclusive Agreements

Earlier in the book, I mentioned the value of an "exclusive," a sales agreement in which you promise to sell a product through only one outlet. Most exclusive agreements are for one year, but they can be for periods of from six months to five years and may even be permanent. An exclusive is a powerful tool for both an entrepreneur and his or her customer. The entrepreneur receives the benefit of having a distributor or store that wants to promote a product. The benefit to a store or distributor is that it will be the only place where a product can be purchased. A chain of stores called the Museum Shops carries only museum replicas that no other stores stock. That strategy makes the Museum Shops special places to visit. People go out of their way to shop there. Think of the ads you've seen that end with "available at Macy's," or "available only at Macy's." Exclusivity is a strong sales tool if a product is unique and advertises well.

Most entrepreneurs hate exclusive agreements because they cut a product's sales potential. However, as you saw from the first budget of the fishing inventor, the main concern is to get a product established, and I know of no better way to do that than by signing an exclusive agreement with an important sales outlet.

The exclusive helps you in two ways:

1. You might be able to get by with a lower promotional budget because the sales outlet might promote the product;
2. When the outlet has an interest in promoting a product, your sales should rise because you'll receive better shelf space.

An exclusive is only worth something to an outlet if your product is recognized as being unique. Use all your market research findings when trying to sell an exclusive. A disadvantage of an exclusive is that the sales outlet will pressure you for a lower price. I recommend you grin and bear it. Next year, when the exclusive is over, you can say: "This product was carried, and heavily advertised, by Sales Outlet X last year."

You can take an exclusive one step further by offering a contest or other promotion. For example, you could have a drawing for a free weekend, or dinner for two, or a $250 savings bond, or some other prize, available at only one store. This is an especially strong tactic when you want to place a large point-of-purchase display in an outlet.

Sell Through Co-op Advertising Programs

When you see a full-page newspaper ad for Herman's Sporting Goods, promoting Head Skis, for example, you are probably looking at a co-op advertising campaign. Half the cost of the ad is paid by Herman's, which is promoting a sale at its stores. The other half is paid by Head Skis, which receives favorable exposure in the paper. Co-op ads are also run on radio and television.

Co-op advertising offers an entrepreneur a lot of advantages. If you give a sales outlet a discount in the form of a co-op advertising program, you get a promotional benefit from a price reduction. For example, rather than giving a 15 percent discount on a hardware item, you could offer to pay for half of a newspaper ad.

The name of your product becomes associated with a big store. As XYZ Product Entrepreneurs, no one knows who you are. If you're advertised by a large retailer, your product gains tremendous credibility, which will help all your other promotional efforts. Co-op ads also give you leverage when you sell a product to other customers. Businesspeople, as a rule, don't like to be trend setters; they like to jump on the bandwagon of a winning product. Once you have a few co-op ads to show, you'll find other outlets more receptive to a sales presentation.

The big disadvantage of co-op advertising is that ads are expensive, and you have to go along with the rates negotiated by the retailer. Always put a top-dollar limit on a co-op program. For example, you might agree to a 15 percent co-op advertising allowance, with the total not to exceed $500. Personally, I like co-op programs. I believe that they deliver a lot of exposure for their cost and offer entrepreneurs long-term sales benefits. Be sure to sign up for a co-op program if you get a chance to run one with a big sales outlet.

Offer Guaranteed Sales

Your offer will mean that you'll take back anything a store doesn't sell. This clause is very bad for entrepreneurs, but you will probably have a tough time getting around guaranteed sales. Most outlets receive those terms from even some large suppliers. This is one of the reasons for proving that a product can sell in the first sales period. You don't want to ship some large orders, only to end up taking the product back and issuing a refund.

Check with your insiders to see whether guaranteed sales are a requirement in a market. If they are, resign yourself to them, but always specify a date when you'll take unsold products back. For instance, you'll want your fishing product to be on the store shelves at least four months before taking it back. If you have to take guaranteed sales, ask for prepaid orders. Small convenience stores, drugstores, and variety stores are accustomed to having to pay for small orders up front.

Guaranteed sales hurt when products are returned and you can't afford refunds. Put aside at least 10 percent of your sales volume to handle returns.

Ask for Deposits

Entrepreneurs should ask for deposits, or even full payment, a lot more often than they do. You aren't going to check a distributor's or store's credit rating when you get a $250 order. Instead, ask for a 50 percent deposit with the order. In that way, you won't lose money if the account doesn't pay. You can get deposits from large companies if you offer a corresponding discount. For example, you can offer a 5 percent discount with a 25 percent deposit, and an 8 percent discount with a 50 percent deposit. Deposits can be an ideal negotiating tool if a large potential customer is pushing for a lower price. Offer a discount, but only if the company will give you at least a 25 percent deposit.

Deposits are common for nonconsumer products sold to companies. For example, Skyline Displays of Burnsville, Minnesota, sells a booth that companies can use at trade shows. The booth's benefit is that it can fold up into a little container and be carried to and from each show. Prices range from $1,500 to $3,000 depending on size. Skyline was started by a couple of partners in a garage. From the beginning, the company always insisted on a 50 percent deposit with every order. Today, after 10 years of operations, Skyline has $40 million in sales and still demands a deposit.

Collecting money is an enormous problem for product entrepreneurs. Most businesses in the United States are short of cash. Most eventually pay their bills, but slowly. When a business is strapped for money, it first pays suppliers whose products or services it needs to keep operating. A convenience store will pay its soft drink suppliers, to keep stock of a product that's important to its customers. Because new product entrepreneurs rarely have a key item that a business needs to keep ordering, their invoices fall to the bottom of the pile. For this reason, I always prefer to sell through distributors. I may have to give up a percentage of profit, but the distributor will be a better bill collector than I am.

Allow Cash Discounts

Your discount might be 10 percent off for payment on delivery, or 10 percent off for cash with an order, or 8 percent discount if an account is paid in 10 days. These are all forms of cash discounts. They will greatly speed up payment and remove some of the financial pressure on an entrepreneur.

Another way of collecting money right away is to factor your receivables. Commercial finance companies and some banks will buy a receivable (an invoice that shows how much a customer owes) for a discount ranging from 5 to 10 percent of the receivable's value. For example, if a large retailer owes you $10,000, the factoring organization might give you $9,200 for the receivable. It then becomes their job to collect the $10,000.

Negotiate with Contract Manufacturers

Earlier in the book, I said that contract manufacturers have a lot to gain by working with a product creator. They get increased production and profits and they have little risk. As the product's creator, you are in a favorable position to try and push more costs back on the contract manufacturer. Absorption of product liability costs, six-month payment terms, collection help, and outright loans are all possible if you can make a strong enough case that your product will succeed. You should have ample evidence of your product's potential from the first period sales evaluation and the transitional plan. If your current contract manufacturer won't help you, look for another one that will.

At times, your manufacturing cost will end up being too high. For example, your costs might total $1.25 for a product that has a perceived value of only $2. Address this problem immediately, and don't proceed until your costs are back to an acceptable level. In my experience, manufacturing problems never go away; they only get worse.

Join Other Product Creators, or Sell Through Another Manufacturer

I've mentioned both of these tactics before, but they're worth repeating because they illustrate the value of a broader product line. When you run a co-op ad with a retailer, the retailer wants its name spotlighted. It doesn't care whether you list one, two, or three products. By joining products into a line, you can cut your promotional costs in half. The same principle applies to the costs of sales calls, trade shows, and virtually any other promotional expense.

Joining forces with another entrepreneur or company makes it easier to have *workable* promotional programs. Most promotional programs are based on a percentage discount, such as a 10 percent discount on sales given as a straight discount or as a co-op advertising discount. A 10 percent discount on a $400 order is only $40—not a very exciting amount.

For the program to be effective, your 10 percent credit has to amount to something. If two or three entrepreneurs joined as a unit can raise the sales level to $2,000 to $3,000, the promotional money will look more attractive. Substantially more benefit can come from placing a product with a company that sells 10 to 15 other products. (See Chapter 6.)

This tactic can be used backward: you can become a distributor for other products. In that way, you can offer a broader product line, one product of which happens to be yours. Brian H. once talked to me about marketing a fishing product that was primarily geared toward deep-sea fishing charter boats. The product didn't generate enough volume by itself to justify the promotional cost. I found another entrepreneur who had a product geared to the same market, and I might have been able to market the two products together if I could have worked out a favorable deal.

Dreaming Possible Dreams

The first sales period proves that a product can sell. In the transitional period, you show that a product can become established in a small market. You are now ready to enter the next phase of a business: selling the product through a much larger part of the market.

Some entrepreneurs' ideas are one- or two-year phenomena. The slap bracelets that sold millions of units in the fall of 1990 probably won't be on the market in 1992. Entrepreneurs like to go for broke (one of the most appropriate phrases in the language) and plunge into national exposure in one short swoop. I don't agree with that philosophy, though it works for some people. I like to think that I'm selling a series of new products, not widget X. I'm not concerned if I can take the first product only so far in the market. I've built up contacts and I'm going to do a lot better with my next product.

At the beginning of the chapter, I mentioned Pepin Heights Sparkling Cider. Their first-year transitional plan was short and simple. They ran a joint promotion program with a radio station; had a booth at some fairs attended by upper-income people; placed their product in about a dozen restaurants, and sold the product off the shelves of several delicatessens. Theirs was not the most exciting plan, but it worked because it had limited, achievable goals. The plan began to establish name recognition in a small, targeted market, and it set up a distribution network that placed orders each and every month. By setting up the same type of simple, achievable goals, you can keep your sales volume growing.

12

The Business Plan: Turning into an Operating Company

Some readers may be surprised that discussion of the business plan doesn't appear until Chapter 12. I know that many other books emphasize that a business plan is the *first* thing to do when starting a business. I don't think a new product entrepreneur can say that he or she is ready to start a business until after the transitional period.

Business plans have two purposes: to raise money and to prepare an operating plan. These are the objectives of the transitional plan. The difference is that a transitional plan is for a small market, and it is geared only to raise enough money to show that a product can penetrate a small market. A typical transitional plan won't show much, if any, profit. A business plan is designed to expand sales to a larger market where a product's sales will increase to a level where they generate profits.

A business plan is usually not a one-time event. You'll normally do one right after the transitional period, when you're ready to expand to a larger market. But you might need to expand in three or four stages before your company is penetrating the entire market. As you approach each expansion, do a revised business plan.

A business plan is a well-known action item. A transitional plan is a new concept that I firmly believe in. Most product entrepreneurs face a tremendous leap from the development stage (making a prototype and conducting some research) to the business plan stage (setting up a full-fledged operating company). Only businesspeople with a proven record of success can risk that leap. Most new product entrepreneurs come toward the end of the development stage and then watch their efforts die because they don't have the momentum needed to carry them across to the business plan stage.

The small entrepreneurs that I've seen succeed have invariably found a middle ground, a stage between development and the business plan, where they have proven that their product can support a profitable company. Most of these people didn't necessarily plan a transition period; they fell into it because they were short on money, or because of the nature of the product, or because it was a toehold when they were scrambling for a place to sell their product.

There are more similarities than differences between a transitional plan and a business plan. I prefer to separate them because of their different goals and the different amounts of money entrepreneurs are trying to raise in each stage.

Let me mention again that the purpose of this book is to help you establish a product in a market. Many other books offer specific information about business plans and raising money. This chapter's overview of the business plan will help you to understand its importance and its place in a product's introduction cycle. When you're ready to write your own business plan, you may want to look for a book that's entirely devoted to the subject.

Business Plan Myths

Recently, more than ten university classes on the subject of business plans were offered during one term in the Twin Cities area.

Bookstores routinely carry three or four (and sometimes many more) books on how to write an effective business plan. Business magazines run an article on business plans at least every few issues. As a result, most entrepreneurs have begun to regard the business plan as *THE Document* that determines whether a business will succeed or fail.

Business plans are now elevated to a status that they definitely don't deserve. They're important, but they have become overrated. The key to attracting investors is not how good the plan is, but rather how good the company behind the plan is.

Myth 1. Business Plans Are All-Important

A business plan is a reflection of how the plan's author feels a company is now operating and will grow in the future. That's all the plan is and says. Most investors, if they like what a plan has to say about a product, will still want a thorough evaluation of the product.

For investors, an evaluation is essential. A business plan provides some operating details, but it doesn't show any underlying weaknesses that a business might have. For example, a business plan might list product costs that are correctly broken out as raw material costs, production costs, packaging costs, and so on. On the surface, the company may seem to have costs under control. But the product costs may not be reliable at all. An important supplier may not be able to meet a surge in demand without raising prices. A contract manufacturer might have quoted a low price to receive initial orders; after one year, its own plan may call for raising prices 15 to 25 percent. The product cost might include a 5 percent scrap rate for both product returns and manufacturing defects; the actual scrap rate may be 15 percent.

Investors are always worried about unseen problems. Until a company is actually running, an investor can't be sure of how many unexpected problems the company will encounter. I feel it's imperative to establish a business's basic functions before doing a business plan. It's not time yet to hire people for each projected position. You may still be doing most of the work yourself, but you should be producing and selling products.

Most advice regarding business plans does not recommend that you have ongoing operations before writing a plan. My advice is different because product creators have a much more difficult time raising money than do other entrepreneurs. There are three reasons for the resistance they encounter:

1. Product creators do not have a successful company to use as a comparison. If I'm going to open up a new restaurant in Omaha, and there is a successful one just like it in St. Louis, I should have a good chance of finding financing. Investors would have confidence in my venture because someone else has already proven that such a business can work. Product entrepreneurs are introducing a product that has never been on the market before.

2. Product creators tend to be short on management experience; they are usually people who think about new ideas and take time to tinker around with them. This type of person is rarely found among business managers. In contrast, most other entrepreneurs have a track record of management success.

3. Product entrepreneurs have a high failure rate. Investors and bankers, who know that, are leery of any investment in a new manufacturing venture.

The all-important element is to have the basic operations of a company thought out, documented, and proven.

Myth 2. *Every Business Always Needs a Business Plan*

Some product entrepreneurs establish a product in a small niche market during the transitional sales period. Then, either because they can't find financing or because they're happy with their small sales volume, they increase their sales slowly every year. Earlier, I mentioned Scott Turner, the inventor of specialized semiconductor inspection equipment. Over seven years, Scott built his business up to annual sales of $1 million. He was in a small niche market, but he could have expanded and gone after other markets. He decided that his small business, with only 12 employees, was just right for him. He never borrowed any money, and he never had a business plan until he decided, after 14 years, to buy his own building.

What would have happened to Scott if he had decided to expand into a broader market? Immediately, he would have faced increasing competition. He wouldn't have been able to adapt his product readily to the specific needs of his niche market. He would have had to cope with intricate financial problems, an increasing number of employees, and a loss of control of his business. To Scott, it wasn't a pretty picture. On the downside, Scott's earning power was limited in the smaller market.

Some experts recommend writing a business plan because it offers an operating budget. I certainly agree that you need a budget. But, as I showed in the discussion of the transitional plan (Chapter 11, pages 227-234), a budget can be generated from sales, marketing, and production plans, and these documents are much easier to prepare than a business plan.

Myth 3. A Business Plan Guarantees That You'll Find Financing

I don't want to belabor this point; I've covered it earlier. Instead, let me update you on Jamie Leach and her husband, a couple that seemingly did everything right, but still couldn't get financing. Their product, the Wiggle Wrap, was a cloth and Velcro™ restraint that keeps babies in high chairs. Jamie and her husband sold 8 percent of their company to private investors to raise money during their initial and transitional sales periods. They had some start-up sales success and eventually increased sales to $1,000 a month, at which point they needed more financing. Unable to obtain any money from conventional sources, they had to factor their receivables. The Leaches kept increasing sales, using factoring as their financing tool, until sales hit $20,000 to $25,000 per month. At this

point, they were rejected again for conventional financing because they didn't have any equipment or real estate to pledge as
collateral.

Important Points

Business plans are typically 10 to 30 pages long; some are even
longer. You can increase your chances of receiving a favorable response to a plan if you can (truthfully) stress these facts:

- All your sales efforts to date have been for market research;
- Your current equity position is favorable;
- Your product has already had some limited market penetration;
- You need a particular amount of money.

Market Research

"Last year, Product X was successfully introduced with sales in
excess of $45,000. This year, if this plan is implemented, sales
should exceed $2 million." How does that sound to you? $45,000 to
$2 million in one year! That's almost impossible.

"Last year, I completed the final phase of market research on
Product X, successfully selling $45,000 of the product in a limited
area. Based on those market research sales, Product X should sell $2
million with a full-scale marketing effort in Illinois, Wisconsin, and
Iowa." That projection sounds a lot more believable; the product creator was careful to perform extensive market research. Still, he or
she must be an entrepreneurial genius to be able to sell $45,000 dur-
ing a market test.

Be careful when you're calculating your sales projection. If you
sold $45,000 with earlier sales efforts, what makes you think you can
increase sales to $2 million? No matter how much explanation you
give, that growth seems out-of-line. When you say you've done market research, people will assume that you had a limited advertising

and promotion budget. They'll be more receptive to your notion that a "real" marketing program will increase sales tremendously.

I don't feel that you're misrepresenting your business by calling the transitional period a market research phase. You are establishing, in a test market, that a product will sell through a distribution network. That qualifies as market research by almost anyone's definition.

Equity: How Much Money Do You Have Now?

The Leaches had trouble raising money because they didn't have any collateral, another term for money. The Leaches were out of cash. As I discussed in Chapter 2, almost no one will loan money to someone who is broke.

At least 80 percent of all product entrepreneurs don't try to raise money until they've spent all of their own. How much money an entrepreneur is investing is one of the first queries an investor will have. If you have reserved cash, be sure to point that out. Include a funding history in your business plan. Show how you've spent your money to date and how much money you have available for future expansion.

Figure 12.1 shows the funding history for a hardware product. Note that the entrepreneur lists funds available from personal assets ("from inventor"). These funds could include cash from a home equity line of credit, credit cards, and personal savings. (You don't have to indicate that your available funds are primarily from credit sources. All that is important is the amount that you're personally responsible for repaying.)

Compare that funding history with a report in which an entrepreneur tells how he and two investors have spent $100,000 on their product and are now looking for additional capital to market the product. To investors, the first entrepreneur has been prudent, has managed his or her product well, has controlled expenditures, and, most importantly, still has money to invest in the product. Those same investors will sense that the second entrepreneur has simply run out of money and is now looking for someone who can bail the project out.

Original funds invested by inventor: $5,000

	Budget	Actual Costs	Revenue	Net Cost	Funds Left
Product's preliminary stages: prototypes, market research, initial sales period, etc.	$4,500	$ 3,800	$ 600	$3,200	$1,800
Funding prior to transitional sales period:					
From inventor $10,000					
From inside investor 5,000					
Total $15,000					
Transitional period: initial penetration of Rochester, MN market (or market test in Rochester, MN)	$6,000	$19,200	$10,000	$9,200	$7,600*
Funding for market expansion throughout Minnesota and Wisconsin:					
From inventor $10,000					
From original investor 5,000					
From new investor 15,000					
Total $27,500					
Total funding required to expand throughout Minnesota and Wisconsin, including manufacturing, marketing, and cash flow requirements		$60,000			
Funding to be provided by inventor and investors		$27,500			
Additional financing required		32,500			
Total		$60,000			

*$7,600 cash reserve to continue to be used for operating cash.

Figure 12.1   Funding History: Hardware Widgets

Strong Operating Position

Three points are crucial in this area: management, cost control, and sales reliability.

1. **Management.** To an investor, you're not a strong manager until you've taken a product successfully onto the market. Because most new entrepreneurs haven't done that, they have to lean for support on their insiders. Your management team will look strongest if some insiders are investors, members of the board of directors, or members of an advisory council. An advisory council might meet once every three months to offer input regarding the activities of the business.

2. **Cost control.** This element is crucial to any company's success. All types of hidden expenses seem to rise up and swallow profits. Installation of phone lines, sales training expenses, unemployment insurance, property and equipment maintenance, incoming freight charges, and office supplies are all potential sources of totally unexpected charges. The best way to show that you have a good handle on costs is to be in operation for a year or so, even if you've spent the time on market testing. By actually operating, you'll know what the miscellaneous charges are because you'll be paying them.

3. **Sales reliability.** Will you really sell the units listed in a plan? I've prepared dozens of sales forecasts for new products, and I can tell you from hard experience that sales are never easy, no matter how wonderful the product is. Potential entrepreneurs are taking wild guesses when they estimate sales for a product that's never been sold. After completing your transitional sales period, you will have *actual sales* to base your forecast on. Your investors can have a certain degree of confidence that you'll reach your budgeted sales levels.

How Much Money Is Needed

You must state why you need the money and how much the investor is going to obtain for his or her contribution. For their Wiggle Wrap product, the Leaches might need $50,000 for operating cash so that they can stop selling their receivables. Investors might receive 10 percent ownership of a company in exchange for financing the additional growth that will improve operating margins.

Telling people how much money you need and why you need it may seem like a simple task, but you'll find it's surprisingly easy to write a 30-page document that never states plainly what you're looking for.

The Business Plan Format

Business plans can vary in format, to represent a particular product or situation. Make any changes that are needed to stress the points listed in the previous section. At a minimum, your business plan should have the following sections:

1. Executive summary
2. Product information
3. Activities to date
4. Strengths and weaknesses
5. Company operations
6. Management team
7. Funding requirements
8. Business pro forma
9. Action time line
10. Formal offer

Executive Summary

Keep this section to no more than 10 to 12 sentences that tell:

- What you're doing—you're introducing product X;
- What your sales proposition is—why people will buy your product;
- Why you feel your product will be successful—you sold $X,000 of product during your initial market test;
- How much money you need—you need $25,000;
- Why you need the money—to expand into a larger market;

- What your expected sales are for both the first and second expansions—you expect initial sales of $1 million to grow to $10 million in the second expansion period.

An executive summary for my tire cutter venture might have read as follows:

> ETC Corporation has introduced a tire cutting device that separates a tire's treads and sidewalls. The result is that old tires are easier to store and ship, and that a tire's high-quality tread can be recycled. Twenty-five units were sold at $99 each through a tire equipment distributor, during an initial market test. ETC Corporation currently needs an additional $30,000 to support sales in eight midwestern states. Based on initial market tests, sales in the eight-state area should be $85,000 per year. Once the product is sold nationally, sales are expected to reach $400,000 per year.

Product Information

You can use the same information and format that you used for the first six points in your transitional plan (see Chapter 11, pages 208-215). As a quick review, those six points are product description, targeted customers, targeted geographic area, where targeted customers buy, market potential, and competition.

Activities to Date

Include in this section a brief review of your accomplishments, a sales and profit summary, an explanation of your distribution strategy, and a summary of how you're currently manufacturing the product.

Entrepreneurs sometimes have long delays in their product introduction efforts. These delays are frowned on by investors and bankers, who prefer to see continuous progress. If you've kept up your momentum, include a timetable that shows how your product is building on its past success. If you have had long delays, either don't mention them or, if they eventually had a positive effect, explain why they occurred.

Strengths and Weaknesses

You'll be covering the product's strong and weak points in the product information section. In this section, describe strengths such as a favorable attitude across the distribution network, or an advantageous manufacturing arrangement; weaknesses may include difficulty in locating good salespeople, or the business's requirement for strong seasonal promotions.

Every business has obstacles to overcome, many of which have nothing to do with whether a product has merit. The lottery pen I discussed earlier had several problems. It had to be sold at lottery sale locations (bars, convenience stores, hotels, legion halls, and a variety of other installations). The market was scattered and I couldn't find any distributors or rack jobbers that sold to the entire market. Another problem was that retailers needed to see the point-of-purchase display before they bought a box of pens. There was no easy way to set up a sales force for a short, one-time promotion. My solution was to concentrate on convenience stores, where I reached about 20 percent of the market.

Don't feel bad if you have problems; everybody has them. What's important is to show that you've figured out how to solve them. Your company's operations should be at least partially designed around your product's strengths and weaknesses.

Company Operations

Don't make this section longer than one or two paragraphs. Review the following areas: sales strategy, distribution network, promotional plans, manufacturing plans, and administration plans. I've given a considerable amount of space to the first four points throughout the book. Like most entrepreneurs, I tend to overlook administration plans. Billing, collecting, taking orders, paying bills, handling legal affairs, and keeping the books are tasks that take a tremendous amount of time and effort and are a big part of a company's success. They may require one or two clerical people as well as professional legal and accounting consultation.

Management Team

Management is a part of a company's operations, but potential investors consider it important enough to deserve a separate section. Earlier (pages 20, 243), I talked about how to make a favorable impression with a management team. Management and money are probably the only true go/no-go decisions that an investor or lender makes. If the management isn't sound, no one will invest. Sound management will overcome a host of problems.

Funding Requirements

Why do you need money, how much do you need, and where will it come from? Give details; don't announce that it's needed to "penetrate a target market." Instead, develop a list of major expenses such as:

1. Promotional programs $15,000
   - 300 TV ads
   - Point-of-purchase displays
   - Attendance at three major trade shows
2. Manufacturing expenses   35,000
   - Inventory to support sales
   - Packaging equipment
   - Two pieces of machining equipment
3. General and administrative   20,000
   - Office supplies
   - Rent deposit
   - Computer and other office equipment
   - Professional services (lawyer and accountant fees)
4. Operating cash   <u>20,000</u>
       Total   <u>$90,000</u>

To explain where the necessary money will come from, the funding history (page 242) is an excellent tool that can be adapted to show how much money you plan on investing, and how much money you need from outside sources.

Business Pro Forma

This section is really your budget for the next 12 to 18 months. The pro forma should contain, at a minimum, the entries shown in Figure 12.2.

To demonstrate the reliability of your sales forecast, include a sales chart similar to the one in the transitional plan (Chapter 11, page 218). You should also include a cash flow chart. I've created a model in Figure 12.3.

Action Time Line

Investors look for two time lines, a tight one for the action steps in your initial market and a very loose one for expanding into the entire market. The time lines for initial operations don't have to be

	Jan.	Feb.	Mar.	Apr.	May
Sales					
Cost of goods sold					
Gross profit					
Marketing expenses					
Administrative expenses					
Other expenses					
Total expenses					
Operating profit					

Figure 12.2   Business Pro Forma

	Jan.	Feb.	Mar.	Apr.	May
Starting cash					
Revenue					
Materials and labor					
Marketing expenses					
Major purchases					
Other expenses					
Total spending					
Cash flow					
Ending cash					

Figure 12.3   Cash Flow Chart

as specific as the transitional period's time lines, but they should list major advertising, sales, and manufacturing efforts. Your time line for further expansion can be stated as a number of years or a specific future date, such as 1995. You don't have to be precise, because you can't know how market conditions might change.

Besides your targeted time for your next expansion, investors will also want to know how much additional investment will be needed. You won't be able to give a precise estimate, but you should provide a ballpark figure. For example, you might state that your current expansion, which will raise annual sales to $1 million in the Upper Midwest, will require an investment of $200,000. In three years, when you will expand again to sell throughout the entire United States, you will require an additional $1 million investment. Provide a back-up chart that itemizes what the additional money will be used for. For instance, to sell to the entire market, you might need to hire a sales manager and four new salespeople, run a national ad campaign, and increase operating cash by $250,000.

Formal Offer

What are you offering potential investors? This is a very difficult area for most entrepreneurs. They believe their product is worth millions because of its sales potential; however, they might *have* ongoing sales of less than $50,000 per year and fixed assets of less than $5,000. That's why I favor starting off with the formula given in Chapter 8: a new, growing business is worth about twice its projected sales volume for the next year.

The funding chart (page 247) details how much money you need, and how much money you need from investors. The next step is to briefly state your offer. If your company expects to have $50,000 in sales next year, then you might offer an investor a 10 percent share of the company in return for a $10,000 investment. If you want to borrow money from a bank, ask for a loan for a specific period of time, for example, a $10,000 loan for three years.

Financing

A comprehensive review of potential financing sources is beyond the scope of this book. Chapter 2 briefly reviewed several financing sources open to entrepreneurs. Offered here is a quick review of the three-step approach most product creators take to obtain funds for their sales expansions.

First, they contribute, from their own resources, about 10 to 25 percent of the money they need to expand. In Chapter 2, I warned that you need money to raise money. Perhaps money projects an image of success, or shows people that an entrepreneur is a prudent money manager, or assures investors and lenders that if they lose money, then the entrepreneur will lose money too. The fact is, you need to put up some of your own cash. Plan on having money available from personal assets or from credit cards or other loans.

The second financing step is to raise from investors another 15 to 35 percent of the money needed for expansion. Potential investors include family members, friends, insiders or salespeople in your chosen market, community leaders anxious to help a new business, suppliers, and your contract manufacturer.

Another way to find an investor is to take on a working partner. Many product creators ask where they'll ever find a working partner. Retired or laid-off managers can be ideal working partners. Not only can they provide money, but they also may have a great deal of experience in running a company. Many of these managers who are having a hard time finding a job are searching for an opportunity to join an up-and-coming company. Advertise for potential working partners in the Sunday paper under Business Opportunities. State that a new manufacturing company, with a successful product (mention its sales potential), is looking for a working partner. Add that you prefer a partner with experience in, for example, marketing hardware products. I've received five to ten qualified responses per ad when I've run ads similar to this one:

> New manufacturing company looking for working partner. Dental product has completed successful market test and is ready for sales expansion. Need individual with sales/marketing experience to help product reach its $1 million potential.

After you've lined up funding for 25 to 50 percent of your financial requirements, the last step is to apply to a bank, commercial finance company, or government agency for a loan. You should be able to borrow the money if you have a strong business plan and if investors have purchased a share of your company.

Before you even start your business plan, get copies of loan applications used by banks, commercial finance companies, and government agencies. You'll be able to tell how much financial information needs to be included in your business plan. Banks and government agencies almost always have an information package for business loans.

You can learn what banks are making small business loans by calling the Chamber of Commerce or individual banks. Commercial finance companies are in the Yellow Pages under either their own heading or the heading for factoring companies. Trade shows for small businesses and ads in local business papers are other information sources. For information on government loans, contact the nearest Small Business Administration office or your state's small business assistance agency.

Part III Summary:
Entrepreneurs Need Mental Toughness

Part III has covered all the steps you need to take to put a product on the market. Entrepreneurs fail to sell their product 70 to 80 percent of the time. That doesn't mean that their products fail; even the most successful salespeople typically sell a product only 20 to 30 percent of the time. But entrepreneurs spend most of their time facing rejection. Many people are surprised to learn that product creators who spend $20,000 or more on a product may drop it after a minimal sales effort. That doesn't surprise me at all. A person has to have a tremendous amount of mental toughness to avoid being discouraged by repeated rejection.

When people create a product, it becomes their "baby." Someone who doesn't buy an entrepreneur's product isn't necessarily saying that the product is a bad idea. The person might not have the money, might not need the product, might need another product instead, or might be saving for another purchase. Some entrepreneurs have a hard time accepting those possibilities. Instead, they look at turn-downs as personal defeats.

I place successful product entrepreneurs into two categories. At the top of my list are people with a strong belief that their product has potential, who keep pursuing their idea against all odds. I once worked for an inventor who quit his job and worked on a product 70 to 100 hours a week, for four years, before he produced any revenue. Besides incredible commitment, he had a tremendous amount of mental toughness. Next are people who are lucky enough to get immediate positive reinforcement for their ideas. Dr. Robert Cade, a faculty member of the University of Florida, developed Gatorade for the football team. Other schools wanted to know what the drink was, and the product started selling. You can't count on being lucky, so you should try to join those who believe in their ideas and keep pursuing them against all odds.

People who want to introduce a product know that they must make a commitment of time, money, and energy. They may not know that they must be mentally prepared to face rejection of their idea. To succeed, entrepreneurs have to realize that there are few products that *most* of the market will buy. To succeed, they have to avoid becoming discouraged and keep plugging away to capture their part of the market.

Part **IV**

Now You're Ready

By now, you should have a pretty good grasp of all the details involved in introducing a product. You know the struggles you'll face, and you know how to overcome the problems that might arise. The last two chapters are intended to help motivate you to believe in your product and see whether it has a million-dollar potential.

13

New Product Failures: Nine Reasons Why Entrepreneurs Don't Succeed

According to *Statistical Abstracts of the United States*, 110,000 people reported a loss from manufacturing operations on their income tax return in 1987. Virtually all of those people were product entrepreneurs who failed to successfully market their product. Why did they fail? There are numerous reasons, but I believe the nine reasons explained in this chapter cause most of the problems.

An Inadequate or Nonexistent Distribution Plan

Products go from manufacturers to final consumers through a distribution network that might consist of distributors, wholesalers, manufacturers' representatives, and retail stores. A distribution plan shows how, and through whom, an entrepreneur plans on moving a product to the final customer.

Product distribution can be brutally tough. Leo is an entrepreneur who developed a new line of nifty sunglasses. The glasses didn't have conventional bows (the pieces that rest on the ears).

Instead, the glasses wrapped around the eyes and hugged the wearer's temples. When the glasses weren't being worn, they could be rolled up into a canister that was about the size of a roll of film. The totally unique product had a tremendous amount of appeal, but it was very difficult to place on store shelves.

Leo didn't consider the distribution system when he was designing the product. Sunglasses salespeople take back all unsold sunglasses for full credit when they sell a rack of new ones. The system works fine, as long as the salesperson is selling comparably priced glasses. For Leo's sunglasses, the suggested retail price was $2.99, versus the traditional sunglasses' price of $8 to $14. Leo couldn't afford to take back any unsold sunglasses.

A second distribution problem was that sunglasses salespeople typically set up a rack in each store. No one in the distribution network wanted to handle the new glasses because their price was too low. There wasn't enough profit in the product to justify anyone's time.

A third problem was that sunglasses are sold off a rack. The new sunglasses didn't fit on a traditional rack, so people couldn't try them on. The glasses didn't cost enough for Leo to furnish his own rack. The sunglasses were new, unique, and relatively inexpensive—an ideal impulse purchase at a store checkout counter. Leo's point-of-purchase display box was 10 inches square, too big for most counters. The product had to be relegated to a shelf that lacked the visibility needed for sales. Leo ended up selling the glasses, but most of his sales were to companies that purchased glasses, put their name on them, and gave them away as a promotional item. The glasses never did well in stores, the market Leo had hoped to enter.

What should Leo have done? His first move, after developing the product concept, should have been to figure out how he would sell the product. He should have followed this procedure:

1. Determine where the product could be sold. Leo's product might have succeeded at discount stores such as K mart and Target, drugstores, and convenience stores.

2. Find out how those sales outlets buy their products. Each target market will probably have a different type of supplier. Leo could have found this out by calling on the companies, talking to people in the industry, or reading industry trade magazines.

3. Find out what the distributional network requires. What size racks are needed? What type and size of point-of-purchase display should be prepared? What pricing discounts are necessary? What types of promotional programs should be run? What is the ideal order size?

4. Find out whether the distribution network will carry a product. Will distributors buy from a small, one-line manufacturer? Will they carry a product for $2.99 when traditional glasses cost $8 to $14? Does the network have any long-term contracts with other manufacturers that would prevent them from carrying a product?

If Leo had researched this basic information, he would have been able to adapt his product and its package so that they were suited to at least one or two of his targeted markets. Research would have given him a much better chance to succeed.

Inadequate Help from Industry Insiders

A manufacturer's marketing person, a general manager at a key distributor, or a manager of a large retail outlet are all industry insiders who know a market and the steps necessary to introduce a product. Without help from insiders, most new entrepreneurs end up making critical mistakes.

Ken F. developed a line of exercise equipment that could be used for schools and sports clubs. Ken didn't know anyone in the exercise market, and he wasn't sure how to market his product. Not knowing what else to do, Ken decided to donate equipment to two local high schools; he hoped that potential customers would somehow learn about his equipment gift. The equipment didn't get publicized, and Ken lost his investment.

What should Ken have done? He should have found one or two sales representatives who call on schools and sports clubs and asked them to explain the market's distribution network. In back issues of fitness trade magazines, Ken should have looked for companies or distributors in his area. Ken could then have contacted some companies with noncompeting equipment, in an effort to locate an insider-advisor. Ken could have found the best magazines by asking gym teachers what fitness equipment magazines they read, or by looking up fitness magazines in *Gale's Source of Publications* at his local library.

Finally, to meet helpful insiders, Ken should have attended some of the fitness equipment trade shows listed in the industry's trade magazines.

Contrast Ken's situation to that of Steve Hed, creator of the Hed Disk bicycle racing wheel. Steve's wife competes in triathlon events, and Steve had ready access to many people in the market's distribution network. Steve knew what types of products the market wanted, how products were distributed, and who the market's key contacts were. Steve was able to utilize this knowledge to start his own company, HED Designs.

Imprudent Spending Habits

Entrepreneurs need enough financial resources to create, develop, test, and start to sell their products. For most products, entrepreneurs should be able to handle these steps for $5,000 to $10,000. Entrepreneurs usually have enough money or can borrow enough from credit cards or personal sources to cover this expense. Unfortunately, most entrepreneurs spend their money so fast that all they end up with is a garage full of inventory or a pile of unpaid bills.

Jerry L. was marketing a religious medallion at a retail price of $24.95. Jerry paid $8,000 for an inventory of 1,500 units, produced a TV commercial for $2,500, and then spent $6,500 for eight commercials on a national cable-TV network. Jerry sold 31 units from the commercials. Jerry had hoped that the initial sales from the TV spots would fund additional TV exposure. Instead, Jerry was out of money. Jerry didn't have a bad product; he just couldn't afford to run ads with the frequency he needed to produce results.

Wayne D. created a new key chain that was lighter and easier to use than a conventional chain. Wayne invested $78,000 in patents, tooling, and a small initial production run, but he didn't save any money for operating cash. Wayne couldn't afford to take an order with 30-day terms; he had to receive cash. Needless to say, Wayne's product never got off the ground.

Both Jerry and Wayne assumed that they would be able to find investors, once they had their product ready for the market. They found out that investors are only willing to support a product that has had sales success. Jerry and Wayne should have started out small and worked at selling 100, instead of 10,000, units. They probably wouldn't have made money on so few sales, but they could have conserved their cash, while they developed a small sales base that would prove whether their product could make money. With that history, the entrepreneurs would have been in a much stronger position to obtain loans or attract investors.

Another reason to start small and proceed slowly is that a product might need to be changed. Kurt L. introduced an ice-fishing product for clearing ice off a fishing hole. Kurt tied up all his money in producing 3,000 units, and then found out that he needed a change in his product's package. Unfortunately, Kurt couldn't afford a package change, and his product died.

Other problems besides packaging can waylay a product creator. I did some testing for Jerry, the creator of the religious medallion, to see why his product didn't sell. The medallion was priced too low. Because Jerry wanted as many people as possible to be able to afford his product, he priced it at $24.95. I found that people expected a high-quality medallion to cost $39.95 to $49.95. They considered Jerry's product "cheap." Unfortunately, that information didn't help Jerry. He had no money left for promotion of the product at the new price.

Entrepreneurs need to limit their spending to no more than 30 to 40 percent of their resources for initial product development, which includes any necessary models, prototypes, and product testing. Another 30 to 40 percent should be used for a small initial production run that serves as a market test to prove that a product can be sold. If the product sells in its market test, the entrepreneurs should use the remaining 20 to 40 percent of their resources to establish sales to a small target market. After those three steps are successfully completed, the entrepreneur should be able to raise some additional capital.

Large-Market Targeting

I talked recently to an optometrist who had a vision-correcting product that could be sold to optometrists and to the general public. The optometrist had enough research to sell the product in his field, but he needed another 12 to 18 months of research before he would be ready to sell to the public. The optometrist was disappointed that he wasn't ready to go after the general-public market. Actually, he was lucky. The optometrist market has a few major distributors and 20,000 potential customers—a market that is easy and inexpensive to reach.

The consumer market is a different story. Potential customers are widely scattered, and the distribution system has hundreds of potential outlets. Those facts would have made the product hard and expensive to market.

Entrepreneurs who want to sell a product to the greatest number of customers add a great deal of complexity to their product's introduction. In a large market, the entrepreneur might compete with 20, 30, or more new products. In a small market, the entrepreneur might compete with only two or three other new products. A large market might require a six-figure advertising budget. An entrepreneur might be able to sneak by with a budget of under $10,000 in a small market.

Susan and Charlie Schwartz are selling their Dakota Seasoning products in over 250 stores. Their product line consists of spices, seasonings, and scone and dried soup mixes. Susan and Charlie's product could potentially be sold in every supermarket in the country. But that fiercely competitive market would have been difficult, if not impossible, for Charlie and Susan to penetrate.

Charlie and Susan decided, instead, to target North Dakota gift stores. The stores were anxious to sell quality products from North Dakota entrepreneurs. Charlie and Susan's marketing expenses were limited to a mailing campaign that included free samples. The Schwartzes expanded to other markets only after they had a secure sales base in North Dakota.

Entrepreneurs need to follow the Schwartzes' example and target first a small, easy-to-penetrate market. Then they can expand when their product has a proven sales base.

Vague Product Benefits

Consumers may look at a product in a store or a mail-order catalog for, at most, two or three seconds. A product's benefit must be immediately understood. Cardboard windshield shades offer an easy-to-understand benefit: the shades keep cars from becoming too hot. Consumers also understand quickly why the product will work: shading the windows keeps the cars cooler.

Lyle H. developed a product that had a hard-to-understand benefit. The small, 4"-by-8" product, which made it easy for salespeople to do their sales follow-up work, looked like a plastic phone directory. The top popped open to reveal a series of tabs, one for each of the phone tasks a salesperson needed to perform each day. Lyle's product forced salespeople to have daily goals and helped them track their effectiveness.

Salespeople could understand the product's benefit (improved sales performance) but they couldn't understand why Lyle's product would work. Wasn't the product just another plastic phone number directory? The product didn't sell. Salespeople weren't willing to spend two or three minutes to understand why the product worked.

There are only two ways to sell a product that has a hard-to-understand benefit: advertise the product (an expense most new product entrepreneurs can't afford) and demonstrate the product, usually with a sales force (hiring salespeople is an impossible expense for most new entrepreneurs).

The Halloween Leaf Bag has an easy-to-understand benefit. When filled with leaves, the big orange bag with a jack-o'-lantern's face looks like a huge pumpkin. The product was a big seller in the fall of 1990.

Shortchanged Sales Effort

Each year, 10,000 new consumer products, from major corporations and new entrepreneurs, have a noticeable introduction. Ninety percent of those products are off the market within three years. Products do not sell themselves, and they rarely benefit from word-of-mouth advertising. Products sell because of an intensive sales effort.

I stopped by a booth at a state fair to talk to Charlie R., the creator of a convertible topper (a product that covers a pick-up truck bed). When I asked Charlie how his sales were going, he told me they were slow. Charlie was hoping to find some dealers at the state fair, and to receive orders from a few pick-up owners. He did receive a few orders, but none from dealers. I asked Charlie what he was going to do next. He thought he might come to the fair the following year.

Charlie had spent over $30,000 on his idea, yet that was all the sales effort he was willing to devote to his product! He didn't have a chance of succeeding. Charlie should have had a sales action plan that included: identifying key retailers in his local market; approaching each retailer to introduce his topper in person; and offering retailers a demonstration model, sales brochures, and favorable pricing and terms. Charlie should also have planned on contacting each retailer three to five times to get orders. I would have recommended that Charlie agree (1) to pay for half of any store ads that would prominently mention his topper, and (2) to work in the stores every Saturday in an effort to generate sales.

At a sales seminar that I attended, the trainer asked us to estimate the average number of calls a salesperson makes on an industrial buyer before getting a sale. Most of the people at the seminar estimated three or four calls. The correct answer was seven sales calls in order to make a sale.

When I try to set up initial appointments with distributors, retailers, or manufacturers, I'd estimate that it takes me an average of at least three calls to set up a meeting, and an average of four to five follow-up calls before I make a sale. Sales requires plenty of persistence and hard work. Buyers have countless products to choose from. An entrepreneur's success will depend heavily on his or her effectiveness at selling. Greg Balzic is the U.S. distributor for Fisherman's Friend cough lozenges, which is now the third top-selling product in the market. Greg says his start was rocky: "I was thrown out of so many places in the early years, it was incredible." But Greg persevered with good salesmanship. Every product entrepreneur has to be prepared to do the same.

Failure to Plan for the Transitional Period

The transitional period, when an entrepreneur penetrates a small target market, comes after an entrepreneur has had some initial success at a few sales outlets.

Roy L. created one of my favorite dice games, Spell It. The game has three 18-sided dice, and each side has a different letter on it. The game is very simple: a player rolls the dice and then spells out as many words as possible that include the three letters. The words can have additional letters, but they must include the three letters on the dice.

Roy had successfully called on many schools, which purchased the game to help improve children's vocabulary. Roy was also able to sell quite a few units at a large discount store. Much of Roy's success at the store was credited to his game demonstrations on Saturdays. Roy sold the game for $3.98.

Roy's introduction status was that he had created a game, tested it, and proven it could be sold at various sales outlets. Roy thought the next step was to jump out and start selling his product nationally. Unfortunately, games are hard to sell unless an entrepreneur commits several million dollars to an advertising campaign. Roy couldn't afford that, and his sales success was too limited to generate any outside financing.

Roy needed to develop a transition plan, to establish a steady sales base in a small market. Roy had several options for his transitional period. He could have concentrated on selling the product to PTAs as a fund-raising item. He could have placed the game in children's bookstores, selling it as a learning aid. In a small market, he could have cosponsored, with either a bookstore or a toy store, a citywide Spell It contest. Roy might also have negotiated an exclusive one-year sales agreement with a catalog supplier selling to educational toy stores. Any of these markets would have been much easier to target and penetrate than the general toy market.

Poor Product Packaging

Entrepreneurs run into two problems with packaging: the package looks cheap, and the package doesn't convey the product's benefits.

James S. created several travel toys for children. My two boys liked the collection. But the package was plain, with no pizzazz. The product always sold well with a demonstration, but never sold well in a store. Why? People thought the toys were out-of-date because of the package.

I picked up Joy L.'s product, "liquid magnet." I loved the name; it sounded as though the product would have a great benefit. I looked at the package for five minutes and finally realized the product was a glue stick. The name of the product was misleading and the package didn't convey the product's benefit. The product didn't sell.

Another common entrepreneurial mistake is to make the package too complex. Buyers typically want only two pieces of information: what the product is, and why they should buy it. The package for liquid magnet was 4" by 7$\frac{1}{2}$". On it were 240 words! Entrepreneurs should say just enough for customers to understand the product.

High Manufacturing Cost

Entrepreneurs should follow two simple rules regarding manufacturing cost. First, their cost must be less than 25 percent of their product's suggested retail price. If the cost is higher than 25 percent, the product won't produce any profits. Contrary to popular opinion, manufacturers don't make a high percentage of profit. Most companies are content with a 10 percent profit on their sales volume, or $10,000 in profit for every $100,000 in sales. Manufacturers usually have a cost that's lower than 25 percent of the suggested retail price. What happens to the rest of the money? It goes to distributors, retailers, the sales force, marketing expenses, engineering expenses, and administrative expenses.

The second rule on manufacturing costs is that a product can't sell for more than its perceived value. If it's priced too high, the product won't sell.

The rules seem simple, but they have one complication: almost every entrepreneur has very high costs on an initial production run. How entrepreneurs negotiate the pitfalls in initial pricing and manufacturing often determines whether they make money on their product.

Earlier, I mentioned George T., who developed a gardening product that would route a garden hose around a flower bed. George knew from his market testing that a set of four hose rollers had a perceived value of about $10. George's manufacturing options were to produce 300 units for $375 ($1.25 per unit, and $5 for a set of 4 units), or to produce 2,800 units for $2,520 ($0.90 per unit, and $3.60 for a set of 4 units).

To maintain a manufacturing cost less than 25 percent of the suggested retail price, George would need to sell a set of 4 units for $20 to cover his $5 cost, or sell the set for $14.40, to cover his $3.60 cost. Both of those prices were over the product's perceived value. George must sell for $10 or people won't buy the product.

George's high cost was to be expected on small production runs. Should George move ahead and produce some units to test his product? I don't think so. George should first make sure that, at some reasonable volume level, he can get his product produced for $2.50. George might go back to a contract manufacturer and determine a price for 50,000 units. If that unit cost is $2.50 or less, then George could go ahead with 300 units and a small market test. If the cost doesn't come down to $2.50, George shouldn't do the market test. There's no point in testing a product that won't make money.

Doug S. developed a fishing product that helped keep leaders and other fishing gear from becoming tangled in a tackle box. When the product sold well in some small test runs, Doug proceeded to produce and sell another 3,000 units. However, after those sales, Doug had less money than he started with. What happened? Doug was producing the product for 35 percent of its eventual retail cost. By the time Doug paid marketing and administrative expenses, he had lost money. Doug had to eliminate some product features, use lower-cost materials, or find a cheaper manufacturing method, or he would shortly be forced out of business.

14

Exhilarating Times:
You Too Can Be Successful

John Naughton was selling lounge chairs at the Iowa State Fair when a dentist came up and asked him whether he could make one of those chairs work in a dental office. John and his brother went to work modifying the lounge chair and eventually introduced the first reclining dental chair. John's company, Dental-Ez, sold as many as 7,000 dental chairs per year.

John's path to success wasn't easy. He took a year to develop the product, and he sold only 10 chairs the following year. But John did succeed: he had a product that was unique; he had the help of dentists who really wanted the product; he entered a market that had only three large distributors; and he was able to cut his development costs by modifying an existing product.

Susan Anderson has created a line of kits for cleaning dust and lint out of computers. She started her line with $20,000 of borrowed money, and now sells $250,000 a year. The secrets to her success were: a small, niche market; an easy-to-make product; and experience in the computer field.

I believe that almost everyone, with the proper desire, can be a new product entrepreneur. The secret to success is to control the introduction process. To do that, follow the guidelines in this book. Not every product can be a winner, but you can find the winners if you learn to evaluate ideas without spending too much time or money.

Ken Hakuta made $10 million from his Wacky Wall Walkers, little plastic spiders that crawl down a wall. Bob Ayers found an investor to help him introduce a line of rocking wheelchairs. Eldon Jones built a $3.1 million company based on his design for a dump truck hoist. With less than $1,000, Keith Kendall started a line of fashion clothing, now selling $400,000 annually. Domingo Tan invested 10 years of his time before receiving an order for 25,000 of his Instant Car Koolers. King Gillette was a salesman who had a fling of inspiration while shaving on a train. Estée Lauder started out toting jars of home-brewed "magic potion" to local beauty shops. William Hewlett and David Packard started out in a garage with only $538.

Most entrepreneurs I talk to are either sky-high with optimism after a few successes, or down-low with depression from a series of rejections. I don't want you to be at either extreme. Know exactly where you stand during the entire introduction process, how to capitalize on your product's positive points, and how to work around its negative points.

Few experiences are as exhilarating as working on an idea, molding it based on market input, and then selling it as a final product to a customer. I know several entrepreneurs who couldn't sleep past 4:00 A.M. because they were too excited about their idea. Product creators will also start to be enveloped in the mystique of power that successful businesspeople have. Graham Lovelady was a dental dealer servicer, a pretty low notch on the totem pole. He never forgot the first time he walked in to meet with the dealer hierarchy, some of whom hardly knew his name, and then walked out with his first large order. His self-confidence from that encounter helped push him to build a $5 million business.

How are you going to be successful? Your number-one action has to be to find the right idea. Keep referring to the five key criteria that determine whether a product can be introduced by an under-financed entrepreneur. These criteria will help you to quickly scan ideas when you are searching for one that might succeed:

1. Will the product be easy to distribute?
2. Is the product's technology simple? Can the entrepreneur build the necessary models and prototypes?
3. Do potential customers perceive the product to be unique?
4. Is the product's benefit obvious?
5. Can the product be sold at four to five times its manufacturing cost?

When you find a product that looks like it has a chance, learn everything you can about the product's market. You can't succeed without knowing the process by which products are bought and sold, the distributors that control the market, and the typical dis-counts and promotions that manufacturers offer. With this knowl-edge, you will make a professional presentation to your key contacts, and you will avoid making costly mistakes.

After you have a product, and the necessary knowledge, the next action step is to proceed cautiously, following the step-by-step intro-duction process outlined in this book. No entrepreneur can know whether a product will succeed until it is on the market and selling. An entrepreneur's primary goal in an introduction cycle is to preserve cash—a goal that can be attained only by moving cautiously.

The last action step is to work hard. Introducing a new product is not an easy path to instant riches. It calls for an expenditure of plenty of time and effort.

Every month, people walk into my office with an idea and an attitude of "Here I am; make me rich." Success doesn't happen that way. No one will help someone who is not willing to invest any personal time or money.

There are no magic formulas or secret techniques that will turn your product into a success. But if you get the right idea, and learn how to introduce it, you can get your "million-dollar idea" onto the market.

John Naughton was once selling contour lounge chairs at the Iowa State Fair. Today, he lives in a large home, retired after a very successful business career. You can join John as a success story. Work smart, and work hard.

Appendix

Sample Patent Documents

Sample Patent Disclosure (Partial)

The United States of America

The Commissioner of Patents and Trademarks

Has received an application for a patent for a new and useful invention. The title and description of the invention are enclosed. The requirements of law have been complied with, and it has been determined that a patent on the invention shall be granted under the law.

Therefore, this

United States Patent

Grants to the person or persons having title to this patent the right to exclude others from making, using or selling the invention throughout the United States of America for the term of seventeen years from the date of this patent, subject to the payment of maintenance fees as provided by law.

Acting Commissioner of Patents and Trademarks

Attest

United States Patent [19]

Klawitter

[11] Patent Number: **4,896,879**

[45] Date of Patent: **Jan. 30, 1990**

[54] **ADJUSTABLE WEIGHT DEVICE FOR HUMAN JOINT OR MUSCLE EXERCISE**

[76] Inventor: Ronald J. Klawitter, 321 Fifth St., West, Hector, Minn. 55342

[21] Appl. No.: 212,564

[22] Filed: **Jun. 28, 1988**

[51] Int. Cl.⁴ A63B 21/12
[52] U.S. Cl. 272/119; 272/DIG. 4; 272/96
[58] Field of Search 272/96, 130, 119, 143, 272/145, 122; 128/25.3

[56]   **References Cited**

U.S. PATENT DOCUMENTS

D. 271,408	11/1983	Bauer	D21/197
2,114,790	4/1938	Venables	272/57
2,214,052	9/1940	Good	272/57
2,689,127	9/1954	Silverton et al.	272/145 X
2,849,237	8/1958	Simithis	272/119
3,231,270	1/1966	Winer	272/84
3,380,447	4/1968	Martin	272/145 X
3,406,968	10/1968	Mason	272/119
4,079,932	3/1978	Schuetz	272/122 X
4,357,009	11/1982	Baker	272/96
4,575,074	3/1986	Damratoski	272/119
4,602,784	7/1986	Budden et al.	272/119
4,621,808	11/1986	Orchard et al.	272/119
4,650,183	3/1987	McIntyre	128/25 B X

Primary Examiner—Richard J. Apley
Assistant Examiner—H. Flaxman
Attorney, Agent, or Firm—Kinney & Lange

[57]   **ABSTRACT**

An adjustable boot-shaped weight for exercising a human joint or muscle group, such as a knee, by strapping onto the foot and filling the container with liquid or other flowable material in the hollow body of the device. The ball of the foot extends beyond the base of the container, and the concave leg support partially surrounds the back portion of the leg while extending above the ankle to prevent slipping. The retainers over the instep and the lower leg keep the leg in place while the lining provides comfort for the user.

5 Claims, 2 Drawing Sheets

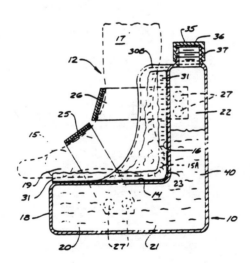

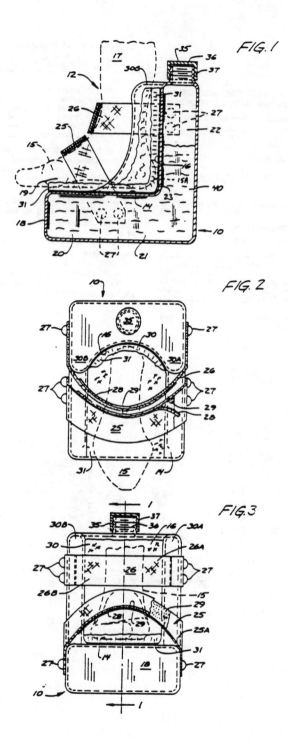

FIG. 1

FIG. 2

FIG. 3

SUMMARY OF THE INVENTION

10   An adjustable weight device for exercising a human leg joint or muscle group, such as a knee, comprises a container having at least one material holding compartment in the hollow body of the device. A first surface of the container is adapted to engage the bottom of the

15   foot of a user, and a second surface extends upwardly at substantially right angles to the first surface. The surfaces support the leg and foot and hold them while exercising. The ball of the foot extends beyond the base of the container and the first surface so the toes are not

20   constrained. The leg support is concave and partially surrounds the back portion of the leg. Preferably, the container is a hollow, molded hard plastic body which, as shown, has a single top opening with a threaded neck that could be closed by a screw-on cap, or a friction-cap

25   type closing.
    The foot is positioned on the device and retainers are provided for strapping the foot firmly onto the user to prevent slipping. The retainers placed over the instep and the lower leg keep the weight in place. A lining is

30   provided for comfort of the user, if desired. The use of retainers in two places prevents the apparatus from slipping around and being uncomfortable. The retainers can be straps employing Velcro hook and loop fasteners or with plastic snap-type buckles on a adjustable length

35   band, attached by cap screws to the device. Plastic gripping straps could be molded as part of the container.
    The container can be filled with water, for example, or with dry particulate material such as sand, salt or

40   gravel, or other liquids, to increase the weight. A typical size would weigh up to in the range of 19 pounds when filled. Varying the amount of liquid would provide a range of loads to be carried by the user capable of

45   being changed to reflect the wearer's needs. The preferred amount of weight will vary with the physical condition of the individual and with the particular exercise being performed.
    An exercise for strengthening muscle groups in the

50   leg could be lifting the foot with the device outwardly and upwardly while sitting with the leg swinging freely from the knee. Another exercise could be done while sitting with the lower leg swinging freely and lifting from the thigh muscle, keeping the lower leg substan-

55   tially at right angles to the floor plane to exercise the muscle groups in the upper leg and hip joint.

BRIEF DESCRIPTION OF THE DRAWINGS

60   FIG. 1 is a vertical sectional view of an adjustable weight device for human joint or muscle group exercise shown engaged on the foot of a user;
    FIG. 2 is a top plan view of the device of FIG. 1; and
    FIG. 3 is a front elevational view of FIG. 1.

DETAILED DESCRIPTION OF THE PREFERRED EMBODIMENTS

65
    Referring to the drawings, in FIG. 1, an adjustable weight device for exercising human joints or muscle groups is indicated generally at 10, and is supported on a foot and lower leg region shown generally at 12. The weight device comprises a first surface 14 substantially perpendicular to a second surface 16 which extends upwardly from the first surface 14. Surface 14 supports the foot 15 and is designed to engage the foot no farther then the ball 19 of the foot 15. The surface area 16 which extends upwardly from the surface 14 supports the lower leg 17. The device 10 comprises a hollow, molded plastic container 18 which has at least one compartment 20 defined therein. The container is preferably constructed from a rigid or semirigid, molded plastic. The compartment 20 has a first section 21 and a second section 22 defined on the interior of the device 10.

As shown in FIG. 2, a concave shape 30 of upward surface 16 is formed to provide wall portions 30A and 30B which partially surround the back portion of the leg of the user. A heel 15A of the user seats back at junction region 23 of first and second surfaces 14 and 16, shown best in FIG. 1.
    First fastening means 25, comprising strap sections 25A and 25B, fits over the instep of the foot 15. Second fastening means 26 comprises strap sections 26A and 26B that fit around the forward portion of the lower leg 17. The fasteners secure the general leg region 12 and foot 15 against the surfaces 14 and 16 and prevent slippage.
    The fastening means 25 and 26 comprise adjustable straps having ends of the respective strap sections fixed on the container side walls with cap screws 27 or other suitable fasteners. The ends of fastener sections 25A, 25B and 26A, 26B are held together by means such as hook and loop fastener (VELCRO) straps 28, 29 or snap type buckles so that the straps can be fitted as desired or required, as shown in FIG. 3. The fixed ends of the strap sections 25A, 25B, and 26A, 26B can be attached to the container 18 with adhesives or other fasteners.
    A cushioning liner 31 is supported on the first and second surfaces 14, 16 between the foot area 15 and the lower leg 17 of the user and the container 10. This liner is preferably an absorbent pad that provides comfort or reduces slippage of the foot, for example, sheepskin or other absorbent and soft materials. Foam of various types could be used, and no pad has to be used. The foot can rest on the plastic surface 14.
    A single access opening 35 with a threaded neck 36 is closed by a cap 37 as best shown in FIG. 3. The cap could also be a type of friction cap that would allow easy access, and would be attached to the device by a loop to prevent losing the cap while adjusting the weight by pouring liquid in or out.
    The walls of the container preferably are not flexible, but retain a distinct shape so the container keeps the weight from shifting excessively. While some liquid flow back and forth will occur in the container, the secure support from the fastening means and the use of the liner 31 will prevent slipping between the foot and the container.
    The shortened length of surface 14 permits toe movement and also fits a wide foot size range. The outer shape can be varied as desired, of course, but the support of the foot and leg is important.
    The device is easily portable, easily made, and easily used, as well as being reliable because of its simple construction and readily available weight adjustment. Water can be filled in from a tap to add weight and the compartment 20 can be filled with granular solid materials, if desired. Sand, salt, gravel, lead or steel shot can be used, if desired. The filling is shown at 40. This adjustable weight device for human joint or muscle group exercise is designed for convenient installation and removal from the body.

5   Although the present invention has been described with reference to the preferred embodiments, workers skilled in the art will recognize that changes may be made in form and detail without departing from the spirit and scope of the invention. Normal knee therapy

10   wuld be to lift wieghts, beginning at approximately 3 lbs., and continuing gradually upwards to 20 lbs.
    What is claimed is:
    1. A foot and lower leg mounted exercise device for exercising a human knee under external weight com-

15   prising:
        a substantially rigid L-shaped container having a base section and an upright section joined together and at least one compartment defined on the interior thereof, and an access opening to the compartment

20   at an upper portion of the upright section;

foot and lower leg support surface means formed on such container defining a first surface on an upper side of the base section and adapted to engage the bottom of the foot of a user and support such foot along the instep region, and a second surface joining the first surface and formed on the upright section extending upwardly and substantially at right angles to the first surface to be adjacent and in contact with the calf of the leg of a user when a foot of a user is supported on the first surface, the compartment including a first compartment portion below the first surface and a second compartment portion to the rear of the second surface, the second compartment portion extending upwardly along substantially the entire upright section;

a first adjustable strap fastener mounted on the first section and adapted to be positioned over an instep of a user above the first surface; and

a second adjustable strap fastener mounted on the upright section and positioned for engaging and encircling a lower leg of a user and extending outwardly from the second surface, whereby the container can be filled with a variable amount of liquid including the compartment portion extending up-

wardly along the upright section of the container for adjusting the total weight carried for exercise, and wherein the ankle of a user is retained in substantially one position for such exercise when the container is in place on a user with the fastener means fastened to support such foot and lower leg.

2. A foot mounted variable weight exerciser comprising a substantially rigid L-shaped container having a base section and an upright section rigidly molded together and defining a liquid tight compartment on the interior thereof, the compartment including compartment portions substantially coextensive with both the base and upright sections, and an opening to the compartment for filling liquid into the compartment and removing liquid from the compartment;

foot and lower leg support surfaces formed on the respective base and upright sections of such container, including a first surface on an upper side of the base section and adapted to be engaged by the bottom of a foot of a user and support such foot, the container having sufficient rigidity to support the weight of a user, and an upright surface joining the first surface and formed on the upright section and extending upwardly and substantially at right an-

Sample Issued Patent

United States Patent [19]

Chisholm

[11] **Patent Number:** **Des. 290,787**

[45] **Date of Patent:** ⁂ **Jul. 14, 1987**

[54] **COMBINATION PHOTOGRAPHIC FRAME AND CLOCK**

[76] Inventor: Dell T. Chisholm, 1010 Fairmount Ave., St. Paul, Minn. 55105

[**] Term: 14 Years

[21] Appl. No.: 483,213

[22] Filed: **Apr. 8, 1983**

[52] U.S. Cl. D6/301; D10/2

[58] Field of Search .... D6/300-303, D6/309-312, 314; D10/2; 40/152, 152.1, 158 R, 154; D10/122-126, 127

[56] **References Cited**

U.S. PATENT DOCUMENTS

D. 3,396	3/1869	Sadler	D6/302
D. 31,165	7/1899	Stiles	D6/300
D. 118,026	12/1939	Scott	D10/127 X
D. 129,998	10/1941	Lamothe	D10/2
D. 213,843	4/1969	Summers	D10/123
D. 245,833	9/1977	Dystant	D10/125
D. 247,612	3/1978	Lucich	D10/2

Primary Examiner—Bernard Ansher
Assistant Examiner—Terry Pfeffer
Attorney, Agent, or Firm—Thomas B. Tate

[57] **CLAIM**

The ornamental design for a combination photographic frame and clock, as shown.

DESCRIPTION

FIG. 1 is a top, front left side perspective view of a combination photographic frame and clock showing my new design.

FIG. 2 is a left side elevational view thereof.

FIG. 3 is a right rear perspective view thereof.

FIG. 4 is a top plan view thereof.

FIG. 5 is a bottom plan view thereof.

U.S. Patent   Jul. 14, 1987   Sheet 1 of 2   Des. 290,787

FIG. 1.

Glossary

amortize: Turning a large payment into a series of smaller payments. For example, if a $10,000 tooling charge is amortized into the cost of a product, an inventor pays off part of the $10,000 cost on every production run.

backorders: Orders that are not shipped on time. For example, if normal delivery is 2 weeks and an order can't be shipped for 8 weeks, the order would be identified as a backorder.

blister pack: A piece of clear, hard, molded plastic that is glued to a paperboard backing. A popular package, especially for small toys.

brand name: Any well-known product or company name. Examples are Pillsbury, Betty Crocker, Mr. Coffee, Toro, Sony, and a host of others.

cannibalizing: The practice of taking one product apart so that its parts can be used to make another product.

card pack: A package containing, usually, 15 to 120 postcards advertising products or services, that is mailed to a target market.

cavity: A part of a mold that can produce one unit. Injection-molded parts are usually produced from 2-, 4-, or 6-cavity molds, which means that 2, 4, or 6 products are manufactured at once.

clip art: Black-and-white drawings of people, places, or events that can be cut out and used for ads, sales fliers, or promotional materials. Books of clip art are available at art and office supply stores as well as larger libraries.

co-op advertising: A promotional program in which manufacturers and retailers split the cost of ads promoting the manufacturer's products. A co-op advertising allowance is the percentage of a customer's purchases that a manufacturer will pay for ads. For instance, when a manufacturer offers a 10 percent co-op advertising allowance, it will pay for ads a dollar amount equal to 10 percent of a retailer's purchases.

consignment: Giving a product, at no charge, to a store, sales representative, or dealer, with the understanding that the product will either be returned at a later date or paid for when it is sold.

contract manufacturer: A manufacturer that agrees to make another manufacturer's, or an inventor's, product for a fee.

copy: All the words used on an ad, package, or promotional display.

direct mail: Any type of promotion in which materials are mailed or delivered to homes, apartments, or businesses.

distributor: A company that buys products from a supplier and later resells them to retailers, other companies, or consumers. A distributor owns the products it sells, in contrast to a manufacturers' representative, who never buys the product.

due diligence: A thorough company evaluation completed by an investor or venture capitalist prior to deciding whether to invest in a company.

factoring: The practice of selling receivables for immediate cash. For example, if a manufacturer ships a $20,000 order to a customer, the invoice or statement is a receivable. If the manufacturer needs immediate cash, it will sell the receivable, or factor it, to a commercial finance company. The charge for factoring ranges from 4 to 10 percent of the receivable's value.

focus group: A market research term for a group of 5 to 15 people brought together for the sole purpose of evaluating a product.

four-color artwork: Another term for full color. Printing is done with only black, yellow, red, and blue ink. All colors are produced by mixing these four. One-color artwork means only one color of ink is used. Two-color artwork uses two colors. Four-color artwork is expensive because it requires (1) a color separation (the process that turns a photograph into four printing plates, one for each color ink) and (2) a larger printing press.

guaranteed sales: A manufacturer's or distributor's promise to issue a refund for any unsold merchandise.

injection molding: A common way of making small plastic parts. An injection mold shoots plastic into a mold, cures it (heats and then cools the plastic so that it becomes a solid), and then pops the part out of the mold. Ideal for high-volume, automated production. The process has high start-up costs because of expensive tooling charges.

letter of credit: A statement from a bank that it will transfer money to a supplier's bank once a shipment has been received. Sometimes required by suppliers before they will ship products. Before a letter of credit will be issued, a manufacturer needs either a line of credit or an escrow account equal to the amount of the letter of credit.

license: A contractual arrangement in which an inventor agrees to allow a manufacturer to produce his or her idea in return for a royalty (a predetermined share of either the manufacturer's sales dollars or its profits). A 5 percent royalty based on sales will give an inventor an amount equal to 5 percent of a company's net sales of the inventor's product.

manufacturers' representative: A person who acts as a sales representative for several manufacturers, never taking possession of a product, but funneling orders to the manufacturers in return for a commission (usually 10 to 15 percent). Manufacturers' representatives are used by companies whose sales are too low to justify having their own sales force.

margins: The percentage of profit that a company makes. Gross profit margin is equal to the selling price minus the manufacturing cost, divided by the selling price. Net margin is the selling price minus all costs—manufacturing, marketing, administration, and so on—divided by the selling price.

markup: The percentage a retailer or distributor increases the price of a product. If a retailer buys a product for $1 and sells the product for $2, the retailer has a 100 percent markup. The formula for determining markup is:

$$\frac{\text{Dollar amount increase in the product's price} \times 100\%}{\text{Purchase price of the product}}$$

mockup: A crude model of a product that helps an inventor to visualize what the final product will look like. Often made out of cardboard, papier mâché, or other easily shaped materials.

model: A representation of what the product will be like; usually structurally sound and functionally similar to a production unit. A model is different from a prototype in that a model will not be quite like the final product; it may have different materials, a different size, or some other different feature. A prototype is very close to, if not exactly like, the final product.

niche market: A small segment of a large market. For example, Mercedes-Benz targets people with incomes of over $100,000, a market that is a small segment, or niche, of the total car market. Chevrolet appeals to buyers looking for a $7,000 to $25,000 car, a very big part of the market.

overhead: Any expense that occurs regularly—rent, salaries, utilities, telephone, and so on. Sometimes referred to as fixed expenses.

per-unit surcharge: A charge by which a contract manufacturer recovers tooling or other costs. If a manufacturer has absorbed $10,000 in up-front set-up costs, those costs might be recovered by charging 25 cents per unit over and above a product's manufacturing cost.

placement: Refers to the process by which a manufacturer or inventors puts their products in locations where customers can see and buy them.

point-of-purchase display: A display located near where a product is placed for sale in a store. Liquor-store displays promoting certain brands of liquor are point-of-purchase displays.

private label manufacturing: A manufacturer's production of an item that is then sold under another company's name. Manufacturers that make the products sold under the Sears brand name are producing private label products.

pro forma: A projected income and cash flow statement. Most loan documents require an income and cash flow statement for at least 12 months in the future.

promotional allowance: A type of price discount that pays for a customer's promotional programs. A 10 percent promotional allowance, for instance, gives a retailer reimbursement for its promotional costs in an amount equal to 10 percent of its purchases.

promotional mix: How a company spends promotional money. Sales brochures, trade shows, advertising, promotional allowances, and coupons are only a few of the promotional tactics a company might use. The promotional mix refers to how much a company uses each tactic.

prototypes: A sample of what a product will look like once it's produced. Prototypes are usually manufactured with a different technique than will be used for the final production unit.

rack jobber: A distributor who contracts with stores to furnish all of a certain type of product, such as hair care products, stationery products, or toys. Rack jobbers can typically put whatever they want on the rack, but they agree to charge the store only for what is sold. Because of their contracts, rack jobbers often control certain markets.

receivables: The money that is owed by customers to a manufacturer or distributor.

rotational molding: A manufacturing process in which plastic is charged into a mold, and the mold is then rotated so that centrifugal force will push the plastic into the proper configuration. Typically used for large parts, such as plastic drums.

shrink-wrap: A common packaging technique in which a sheet of thin, usually transparent plastic is placed around a product, and then pulled tightly over it and held with a heat-seal. The wrapping looks like thick cellophane.

slotting allowance: A payment to a store that is required before a manufacturer can obtain shelf space. Grocery stores are among the stores that require this payment.

targeting: A process in which a manufacturer or inventor identifies a small segment of the market as having potential customers, and then directs all of its promotion at that segment. Targeting and niche marketing are often used interchangeably.

temporary tooling: Tooling that is expected to last for only a short production run.

terms: A period of days after which payment is due. For example, 30-day terms means payment is due for a product or service 30 days after the product is shipped or the service performed.

trade shows: Conventions that are geared toward one market, such as tire wholesalers, gift galleries, novelty distributors, or semiconductor manufacturers.

turnover: How long it takes for a store to sell its inventory. If a store sells out a product in two months, then the product has a two-month turnover.

vacuum forming: A manufacturing process in which a sheet of plastic is placed over a mold. Then the plastic is heated and vacuum is applied to draw the plastic tight over the mold. Used for fairly large products where high strength is not required.

vendor: Another term for supplier.

wholesale price: The price at which a product is sold to distributors.

References

Beauty Products Magazine, September 1988.

Changing Times Magazine: August 1989, May 1990.

Direct Marketing Magazine, April 1990.

Fortune Magazine, March 14, 1988.

Freeway News, November 29, 1989.

Gardener's Supply Catalog, Summer 1990.

Guide to Intellectual Property Protection. Merchant, Gould, Smith, Edell, Welter and Schmidt P.A. in collaboration with Minnesota Small Business Administration. Minneapolis: Minnesota Department of Trade and Economics, 1989.

Home Office Computing Magazine, July 1990.

Inc. Magazine: October 1988, December 1988, October 1989, May 1990.

Keane, J. Timothy. *Coping with Invention Development Firms.* Rolla: University of Missouri Press, 1986.

Knapp, Phillip B., PhD. *Inventing.* Blue Ridge Summit, PA: Tab Books, 1989.

MacCracken, Calvin. *Handbook for Inventors.* New York: Charles Scribner's Sons, 1983.

Merrill, Ronald E., and Henry D. Sedgewick. *The New Venture Handbook.* New York: AMACON, 1987.

Minneapolis Star and Tribune:
    1989—September 10, September 17, November 11, November 19.
    1990—February 25, March 1, July 15, October 28, November 16.
    1991—January 10, December 24.

Minnesota Ventures, November/December 1990.

New Brighton Bulletin, December 13, 1989.

New Business Opportunities Magazine: January 1991, February 1991.

Park, Robert. *The Inventor's Handbook.* Whitehall, VA: Betterway Publications, 1986.

Patents (kitty litter boxes): 4,807,563; 4,807,564; 4,819,580; 4,846,103; 4,846,104; 4,846,105; 4,858,559; 4,870,924; 4,872,420

Pressman, David. *Patent It Yourself.* Berkeley, CA: Nolo Press, 1988.

Sales and Marketing Management Magazine, July 1989.

Statistical Abstracts of the United States. Washington, DC: Government Printing Office, 1990.

Success Magazine, May 1990.

TIME Magazine, April 2, 1990.

Washington Monthly Magazine, January 1989.

Helpful Sources

Artmaster, 500 N. Claremont Blvd., Claremont, CA 91711. Supplier of a wide range of clip art.

Castolite Inc., P. O. Box 391, Woodstock, IL 60098. A great source of liquid plastics, fiberglass, and mold-making compounds. Its catalog is informative, and I recommend it for anyone interested in making models or prototypes.

Color Graphics Press, 11-20 46th Road, Long Island City, NY 11010. Printing source for low-cost catalog sheets.

Creations Unlimited, 2939 Montreal Drive, N.E., Grand Rapids, MI 49505. Source of small tools and files for producing prototypes.

Direct Marketing Magazine, 224 Seventh St., Garden City, NY 11530-5771. Contains numerous sources for mailing lists, catalog houses, and card packs.

Dremel, Division of Emerson Electric, 4915 21st St., Racine, WI 53406. Source of miniature power tools.

Edmund Scientific Co., 101 E. Gloucester Pike, Barrington, NJ 08007. One of my favorite catalogs. The first place I look for small motors, optical parts, and miscellaneous parts.

Fair Times Magazine, P. O. Box 455, Arnold, MO 63010. Targeted at people who sell products at fairs and flea markets. Has a fairly complete list of upcoming shows. Also has ads for flea market-type products.

Fine Scale Modeler Magazine, Kalmbach Publishing Co., 21027 Crossroads Circle, P. O. Box 1612, Waukesha, WI 53187. Contains numerous ads for small parts and small-scale modeling equipment.

Graphic Products Corp., 1480 South Wolf Road, Wheeling, IL 60090. Source of clip art books.

Great Catalog Guide, Consumer Affairs Dept., Direct Marketing Association, 11 W. 42nd St., P. O. Box 3861, New York, NY 10163. The *Great Catalog Guide*, available for $3, lists virtually every catalog sold in the country.

Hobby Stuff, Inc., 11239 9 Mile Road, Warren, MI 48089. Manufacturer of a small vacuum forming machine. Also has a line of small hardware parts.

Hysol Electronic Chemicals, 15051 East Don Julian Road, Industry, CA 91746. Supplier of casting and laminating compounds that are ideal for an inventor. Catalog #T 6-15, 5/88 is especially helpful.

Light Machine Corp., 669 East Industrial Drive, Manchester, NH 03103. Manufacturer of small lathes, machining centers, and milling systems.

Micromark, 340-835 Snyder Ave., Berkley Heights, NJ 07922. Source of modeling tools.

Model Maker's Handbook, by Albert Jackson and David Day (New York: Alfred A. Knopf, 1981). Excellent book for anyone interested in making models or prototypes.

Morgan Industries, 3311 East 59th St., Long Beach, CA 90805. Manufacturer of a small prototype and short-run injection-molding machine.

Patents, General Information Concerning, U.S. Department of Commerce, Patent and Trademark Office, Washington, DC 20231. This helpful pamphlet is available for only $2.

PDI, P. O. Box 130, Circle Pines, MN 55014. Produces Plasti Dip, a product that will coat metal or other materials with a protective plastic layer.

Pyramid Products, 3756 South 7th Ave., Phoenix, AZ 85041. Makes small foundry furnaces and supplies.   •

Rapid Color Corp., 101 Brandywine Parkway, West Chester, PA 19380. Will print as few as 100 color catalog sheets.

Start-Up Money: Raise What You Need for Your Small Business, by Jennifer Lindsey (New York: John Wiley & Sons, 1989). Sources of financing for sales expansions.

Stock Model Parts, Division of Designatronics, Inc., 2101 Jericho Turnpike, New Hyde Park, NY 11040. Great assortment of small parts such as gears and drives, and of prototype kits. Excellent source for small, hard-to-find parts.

Total Marketing: Capturing Customers with Marketing Plans that Work, by Don Debelak (Homewood, IL: Dow Jones-Irwin, 1989). This has been called an excellent book to help you map out a marketing strategy.

Uniform Code Council, 8163 Old Yankee Road, Suite J, Dayton, OH 45458. Organization that assigns bar code numbers. Send for their free information pamphlet.

U. S. Press, P. O. Box 640, Valdosta, GA 31603. Source of inexpensive color printing.

Index

Action plans, in transitional
    period, 223–224
Action time line, 248
Adjustments:
    during first sales period,
        183–184
    in distribution network,
        183
    in packaging, 184
    in price, 182
    in product features, 182
Administrative plans,
    246–243
Advertising:
    co-op, 212, 224, 230, 233
    effectiveness of, 82
    first sales period, in the,
        166
    magazine,
        choosing the best
            magazine, 179
        distribution network,
            as a, 70, 183
        profit potential,
            checking, 178
    market research tool, as a,
        103–104

newspaper ads, 104
pitfalls of, 82, 190
support, as product, 99
sales comparisons,
    importance in, 190
targeting an audience,
    104, 199
TV, 220
Advertising specialty
    companies, 83
Advisory Council, 243
*Almanac of Business and
    Financial Ratios*, 51
Amortizing expenses,
    130–131
Anderson, Susan, 89, 269
Artwork, 118, 129, 140,
    167
Atomizer, the, 71
Attitude, important
    characteristics, 47–49

Balloon Wrap, the, 97
Balsa wood, 122
Balzic, Greg, 265
Bank loans, 19–20, 29,
    250–251

Bankruptcy:
    avoiding, 22
    finding companies in, 21
Benefits, product:
    communicating properly,
        201
    definition, 200
    evaluating in a sales
        comparison, 188–189
    evaluating low sales, 200
    problems when not
        obvious, 263–264
    testing, 168
Big, the movie, 94
Billing, 60-day terms, 174
Blister pack packaging, 117
    artwork, 118
    mold charges, 118, 167
Bonnette, Andy, 205
Boo-Boo Tubes, 109
Book of Associations, the, 73
Brand names, 85, 100, 190
Brown, Len and Lisa, 211
Budget:
    financial, 226
    manufacturing, 223
    sales, 218

Business experience,
    importance of, 20
Butts, Dave, 148
Business plans:
    executive summary, 244
    financing, as it relates to,
        239–240, 247
    format, 244
    formal offer, the, 224
    funding required, stating,
        243, 247
    importance, 237, 238
    need for, 236
    points, important to make,
        240–244
    unimportant, when,
        238–239

Cade, Robert, 253
Cannibalizing products, 128
Card packs, sales, to
    generate, 178
Cash:
    Cash-on-delivery
        (C.O.D.), 27, 222
    conserving during
        introduction cycle,
        222, 260
    discounts, 232
    flow-through charts, 52
    needing your own, 19
    operating, 75–78, 226
    selling for, 25
Castings:
    permanent, 53
    sand, 53, 136
Castolite, 124, 128
Categories, established
    product, 110-111
Cavity, as a property of
    plastic molds, 53
Chambers of Commerce:
    insiders, for meeting,
        149–150
    research help, for, 60
Chip Clips, 97
Christianson, Jerry, 16
Clarifying questions, 49
Collateral, loans, for
    obtaining 335

Commercial finance
    companies, 26–27,
    9, 232
Communications:
    benefits, explaining, 96
    clear, ensuring they're
        short and, 201
    problems, overcoming,
        201–202
    target market, to, 201
Community groups, 171
Comparative products:
    costs, tool for estimating
        manufacturing,
        55–56, 115
    market research, for,
        97, 99, 101, 107,
        109–110
Competition:
    feature comparison
        charts, 215
    small markets, in, 80
    stealing ideas legally, 32
    transitional period, 215
Confidential statements, 41
Consignment units, 141,
    165, 175
Consultants, hiring insiders
    as, 103, 142, 143, 148
Consumers, targeting,
    81–82, 211
Consumer Reports, the
    magazine, 215
Contact file, 50, 147–148,
    171
Contract manufacturers:
    aid from, 197
    amortizing expenses, 130
    choosing, 14, 113
    conflicts with, 132
    definition, 130
    design help from, 42
    finding, 21, 131–133, 145
    negotiating with, 232–233
    prototypes shops, 130
    surcharges, 130
Co-op advertising:
    advantages of, 230
    budget item, as a, 224
    definition of, 230

effectiveness, 233
exclusive agreements,
    reasons for, 212
Coping, demonstrating the
    trait, 129
Copy, 129
Copyrights, 42
Costs:
    control, 243
    corrective measures when
        high, 202
    manufacturing, 119
    product liability
        insurance, 170
    quotes, manufacturing,
        118, 133
    start-up, 137–141
    tooling, 133, 134, 137
Courtier, Dennis, 144
Credit cards:
    as a source of financing, 22
    as a source of payment,
        174
Criteria, to successfully
    market a product, 1,
    158, 271
Customers:
    evaluations, after first
        sales period, 193–195
    surveys, 194
    targeted, 211
    where they buy, 212

Dakota Seasonings, 85, 262
DeCube Health Care
    Mattresses, 67
Demonstrations, product,
    192
Dental chair, 115
Dental-Ez, 269
Deposits:
    negotiating tool, as a, 231
    suppliers, to, 137, 222
Development financing,
    22–23
Discounts:
    distributor, 78
    rack jobbers, 76, 79
    retailer, 78
    starting sales, when, 175

Displays:
  floor, 188
  point-of-purchase, 225,
    229, 246
Distribution:
  correcting problems,
    203–204
  definition, 68
  Real estate lock boxes,
    for, 2
Distribution mechanics,
    204–205
Distribution network:
  changing, 183
  concentration of, 82–84
  definition, 68
  dental, 90
  driving business through,
    90
  evaluating, after first
    sales period, 191–193
  finding one, 141
  food, 84
  initiating a new one,
    92–93
  openness, 84–85
  overlooked, why it's, 68
  problems, resolving,
    87–92
  resistance from, 98
  support, product required,
    69–70
Distribution outlets:
  analysis, 213
  simulating selling
    situation, 168
  testing, 168
Distribution plan:
  problems when
    nonexistent, 258
  sample plan, 216
  sunglasses, for, 257–258
  transitional plan, in, 217
Distributors:
  approaching, how to,
    180
  discontinue products,
    why they do, 193
  first sales period, use
    during, 199

medical equipment,
    67, 70
  points, sales to make, 180
  sales, expected, 251
Document Disclosure
    Program of U.S. Patent
    Office, 41–42
Down payments, overseas
    manufacturers, with,
    203
Draftsman, engineering, 139
Dutton, Jan, 22, 67

Emotional appeal, 108-109
Endorsements, 9, 70, 175
Engineering documentation,
    138–139
Engstrom, Arthur, 200
Equipment leasing, 29
Equity:
  business plan, as reported
    in, 241
  ratios, 19–20
Exclusive agreements:
  benefits of, 228–229
  with distributors, 83, 180,
    229
  with mail order catalogs,
    46
  with manufacturers, 46
  with retailers, 83, 192,
    212, 229
*Great American Catalog
    Guide*, the, 74

Factoring, 232, 239
Fairs, 173
Fiberglass models, 125–126
Fiber optic handpieces, 36
Flea markets:
  market research tool, 105
  sales outlet, 173
Features, product:
  adding to increase value,
    203
  charts, product feature,
    215
  testing, 168
Finance companies,
    commercial, 26–27, 29

Financial:
  goals of first sales period,
    165
  plan, 226, 247, 248
Financing:
  borrowing against orders,
    24
  business plan, from, 238,
    244
  cash sales to consumers, 26
  credit from suppliers, 27
  development stage, the,
    22–23
  finding investors, 250
  growth stage, 28–30,
    250–252
  receivable sales, 26–28,
    232, 239
  transitional period, 23–28
First sales period:
  funding, 22
  goals, 164
  problems during,
    181–183
  production runs, 134
Fisherman Friend's Cough
    Drops, 265
Fixed expenses, *see*
    Overhead costs
Follow-up system for sales
    calls, 204
Food distributors, 84
Formula, to determine
    product's worth,
    154–155
French Meadow Bakery, 10,
    152
Frookies, R. W., 24, 90
Funding:
  history, 241–242
  requirements, 247

Gale's Source of Publications,
    57, 122, 178, 260
Gatorade, 253
Geographic markets, target,
    212
Goals, of first sales period,
    164
Gordon, Lynn, 10, 153

Guaranteed sales, 175, 182, 216, 230

Hakuta, Ken, 36
Halloween pumpkin leaf bags, 5, 97
Hawkins, Howard, 200
Hed Designs, 260
Hed, Steven, 260
Hockey mouthguard, 7
Hysol Electronics, 123

Income tax losses, from manufacturing operations, 257
Incorporation, 170
Indexes:
  newspaper, 58
  New York Times, 58
Insiders:
  definition, 146, 259
  essential, why, 259–260
  examples of, 146–147
  finding, 181–183, 146–150
  initial meeting, 209
  investors, as, 202
  market research, source of, 144–146
  utilize, when to, 150–152
Instruction:
  manuals, 140–141, 202
  product packages, on, 201
Insurance, product liability, 57, 170
Interplak, 91
Inventory:
  costs, 137, 139
  loans, 29
  turnover, 192
Investments:
  from insiders, presentation package, the, 156
  request, how to, 155
  size, appropriate, 157
Investors
  approach, how to, 155
  insiders, 17, 152–154

sales success, need to show, 261
venture capitalists, 16
working partners, 251
worth, of a product, 154–155

Kitty litter, disposable, patents, 35
Knowledge:
  need for, 51

Labor costs, 139–140
Leacho, C.J., surviving the transition period, 27
Lemelson, Jerome, 37
Liability insurance, 57, 170
Library, the, market research tool, as a, 57–58
Licensing, 3
Line card, of manufacturers' representatives, 181
Loan programs:
  government, 29
  specialized, 29–30
Lock boxes, real estate, 213
Lottery pen, 167
Lovelady, Graham, 147

Machining parts, 127
Magazine ads:
  choosing the best magazine, 179
  distribution network, as a, 70, 183
  profit potential, checking, 178
Magazine articles, method of finding investors, 149–150
Mail order:
  catalogs, 70
  disadvantages of, 82
  discounts required, 178–179
  selling through in first sales period, 177
  selling through other manufacturers with, 178

Management, need for in business plan, 243
Manufacturers, see also Contract manufacturers
  selling with other, 126–127
Manufacturing costs:
  comparative products, using to estimate, 55–56
  corrective steps when high, 202–203, 267–268
  estimates, preliminary, 114–117
  quotes, 113–114
Manufacturing:
  budget, in transitional period, 221, 223
  plan in transitional period, 221
Manufacturers' representatives:
  agents to discount stores, 71
  dropping, why they do, 192
  finding them, 59
  line cards, 181
  sporting goods, 71
Manufacturing start-ups, number, iii
  success rate, iv, 9, 10, 32
Manufacturing techniques, knowledge needed, 53–55
Margins, industry, 51
Market history, insiders, learned from, 144
Market leaders:
  definition, 73
  resistance to new competitors, 86, 98
Market potential, 214
Market research:
  business plans, in, 240
  comparison with other products, 133
  distribution network, determining sales potential, 258–259

experts or insiders,
utilizing, 34, 103,
142–144
fairs and flea markets, at,
173–174
first sales period, in,
166–167
friends, utilizing, 102
initial, 95, 100–101
low cost methods, 144
need to show an idea, 33,
34
packaging, 167–168
panels, 102–103
preliminary, 141–143
simulating the selling
situation, 94,
107–108
small markets, in, 80
store owners, utilizing,
31, 59, 104–105
warranty cards, using,
193
why people don't buy,
171–172
Market size, estimating,
73–74
Markets:
openness, 84–87
regional, 288
small, benefits of, 80–81
targets, 199, 201
Marketing:
background, 56
costs, 44–45, 72
joint ventures, 233
lingo, 56
small market, to a, 80–81
Mark-ups (also see
discounts), 45
McConnell's Ice Cream,
228
McCoy, Jim, 228
McGuiness, Dale, 109
Million Dollar Directory, 58
Mock-up, 115, 150
Models:
building, 120–130
cannibalizing products,
128

clay, 122–123
cost quotes, for, 116
definition, 120
fabric, 127
insiders, showing to, 151
machined models, 126
metal models, 127–128
modifying existing parts,
126, 135
one part, 123
packaging, 128–129
plastic, 123–126
reference sources, 120
sheet metal, 127
temporary tooling, 124
two-part molds, 124
wood, 122
Momentum:
business plan, as reported
in, 245
first sales period, during,
15
introduction process,
during, 180, 183
Money:
accumulating, 21, 22
business plans, raising
with, 239–240
personal assets, 19, 20
private versus public
sources, 16
problems raising, 238–240
raising during,
development period,
22–23
growth stage, 23–30
transitional period,
23–28
Mr. Coffee, 32
Murphy, Mike, 67
Murtha, Greg, 38
Museum Shops, a retail
store, 229

Names, product, as a
promotional tool, 111
Nada chairs, 26
Nakamatsu, Noshiru, 5
National Association of
Female Executives, 29

Naughton, John, 90, 147, 269
New York Times Index, 58
Niche markets:
benefits of, 68
Dakota Seasoning, story
of, 263
lace products, 68
targeting to in transitional
period, 23
why target, 199–200
NordicTrack, 70, 190
Notebook:
engineering, 40
inventor's, 40

Operating cash, 75–78, 226
Ortho-flex saddles, 211
Overhead:
as affecting borrowing
capabilities, 21

Packaging:
adjustments, 182
blister packs, 117, 167
budget item, as, 222–223
costs, 117–118, 139
in transitional period,
222
effectiveness, 109
evaluating in a sales
comparison, 187
idea, an, 61, 132
back-up materials, 62
initial materials, 61
models, 127–128, 165
molds, 140
products, 109
results when poor, 266
shrinkwrapping, 129, 167
upfront costs, 117
Packaging suppliers, as a
source of market
research, 60
Paper White, 22
Park Tool Company, 200
Pasta Mama's, 19
Patents:
applying for your own,
42–43
benefits, 35–37

companies, why they
    obtain, 37–38
design, 42, 43
disposable kitty litter, 35
fees, 42, 43
grace period, one year, 33
lawsuit costs, 36
novelty, 35
original purpose, 35
pending status, 37–38
percentage overturned, 36
products introduced
    without, 40
utility, 42
Patent Gazette, 91
Pepin Heights Sparkling
    Cider, 207, 212, 234
Perserverance,
    demonstrating it, 47–48
PGL syndrome, iii
Phone directories:
    business-to-business, 60,
        116
    Yellow Pages, 60, 116, 137,
        203
Photography, 141
Plastics:
    bending into new shapes,
        125
    fiberglass lay-ups, 53, 125
    molds: 53
        for models 123
    vacuum forming, 53
        for models 125
Premises, as market
    research tool, 100–102
Premium items, 88
Prepaid orders, 231
Presentation package for
    investors, 156–157
Price:
    adjustments, 182
    analyzing in a sales
        comparison, 189–190
    low vs. high, 167
    testing, 167
    value chart, 110
    value relationship, 109,
        198
Pride, James, 34

Private labeling, 72, 89
Product:
    adjustments, 182
    benefits, 96–97, 99
    categories, 111
    changes, 182
    costs,
        firm quotes, 133
        preliminary estimates,
            114–117
    deficiencies, 211
    demonstrations, 99–100
    description, 210
    design, as it relates to a
        distribution network,
        79
    flyers,
        preparation, 14
        use with tire cutter, 4
    information, 245
    introduction criteria, 1,
        158, 271
    introductions,
        number, 9
        success rate, 32, 257
    liability insurance, 32, 257
    life cycle, 81
    nuances, 81
    review, 144
    support, amount needed,
        97–102
    types entrepreneurs
        introduce, 215
    uniqueness, 97–98
    worth, 153–155, 250
Production runs, initial,
    134–137
    modifying existing parts,
        135–136
    temporary tooling,
        136–137
    using other materials,
        136
Production schedule, 221
Professional behavior,
    45–46
Profit margins:
    definition, 80
    presentation package,
        156

small markets, of, 80
    typical, 267
Profit potential, 159
Proforma statements, 156,
    248–249
Promotions:
    co-op advertising
        programs, 230
    correcting problems, 205
    name, potential of, 111
    pitfalls in reducing, 224
    plans, in transitional
        period, 219
    possibilities, 111
    programs, with radio
        stations, 144
    purchases, 49
Promotional:
    discounts (also called
        allowances), 98
    input from insiders, 146
    items, 88, 258
    programs that keep a
        market closed,
        86, 98
    sales, to generate, 183
Protecting an idea, 40–43
    copyrights, 42
    Document Disclosure
        Program of U.S.
        Patent Office, 41–42
    inventor's notebook, 40
    patents, applying for your
        own, 42–43
Prototypes, *see also* models:
    bypassing, danger in,
        121
    building, 120–130
    definition, 120
    price quotes, for
        generating, 116
    shops, at manufacturers,
        130
    tire cutter's, 142

Questions, clarifying, 49

Rack jobbers, 76, 148
*Reader's Guide to Periodic
    Literature*, 58

Receivables:
  collecting, 75
  selling, 26–27
Regulatory approvals, 57
Retail Stores:
  discounts to, 175
  disadvantages of, 82
  friendly, 217
  initial sales outlets, as,
    174–175
  market research at, 59–60,
    168–169
Risk/reward ratios, 64–65
Ronchak, Andy, 12
Root canal cleaner, 163–164
Rotational molding for
    plastic parts, 54
Royalties, arrangements, 33,
    153

Sachetti, Terry, 92
Sales:
  analyziing the results, 187
  budget, 187
  call frequency, 86
  combining with other
    inventors, 91
  comparison chart, 184
  comparing sales made to
    different outlets, 197
  effort,
    entrepreneurs, by, 177
    first sales period, in, 169
    shortchanging, 204,
      264–265
  finding the right outlets,
    145
  forecasts,
    sample, 218
    transitional period, in,
      210
    transitional plan, in,
      217–218
  incentives, 183
  market research tool, as a,
    240–241
  momentum, 13, 183–184
    first sales period, in, 182
    mail order catalogs,
      from, 178

worth, as it relates to a
    product's, 153
people, retired, as
    employees, 152
premiums, 87
proposition, 210, 244
reliability, 243
strategy, 204
support, as a selling tool,
    181
threshold, 191
through other
    manufacturers, 72,
    89, 184, 233
Scheduling, during first
    sales period, 169
Santille, Paul, 19
Second tier companies, 73
Self-employed people as
    credit risks, 21
Self-service marketing
    environment, 95
Selling;
  cards, 181
  cash, for, 25
  manufacturers, with
    other, 91
  receivables, 26–27
  sheets, 175
Set-up charges, 114, 165
Schwartz, Charlie and
    Susan, 262
Sheet metal models, 127
Shelf space, premium, 155
Skyline Displays, 231
Slap bracelets, 38
Small markets:
  benefits of, 80–81
  examples of, 81
Solar Stat, 179
Spector, Stuart, 26
Sperling, Dennis, 199
Sporting goods stores as a
    sales outlet, 71
Start-up:
  documentation, 138,
    222
  expenses, 222
  instruction manuals, 140
  inventory, 132

labor, 139–140
manufacturing, 138
operating cash, 32
packaging, 140
tooling, 138
Stealing a product legally, 32
Suggestions, welcoming,
    48–49
Suji, knowledge, 5
Suppliers, receiving credit
    from, 27
Surcharges, 130

Target markets:
  analysis chart, 213
  communicating to,
    201–202
  definition, 200
Targeting:
  customers, 81–82, 211
  definition, 199
  finding smaller markets,
    227
  markets, 199–200,
    205–206
  sample, 211
  need for, 262
Terms:
  cash, a way of raising, 26
  receivables, time to
    collect, 75
  retailers, to, 174
  suppliers, from, 139
Testimonial letters, 208
Theft, why an idea probably
    won't be stolen, 33
*Thomas Registry of American
    Manufacturers*, 33, 58,
    116
Time management for new
    entrepreneurs, 13–15
Timetable:
  first sales period, for, 169
  patents, for obtaining, 33
  tire cutter, for, 169
Timing, importance of,
    92–93
Tooling:
  costs, 137–138
  temporary, 124, 136–137

Toso, Victor, 26
Trade associations, place to
        find insiders, 148–149
Trade magazines, 57, 122,
        131
Trade shows:
    cash, method of raising, 26
    discounted booths,
            obtaining one, 174
    finding ones to attend, 106
    manufacturers, contract,
            place to meet, 132
    research tool, as a,
            105–106
    sales outlet, as a, 173
Transitional period:
    definition, 23, 207
    funding, 23–28
Transitional plan: 207–224
    competition, 218
    distribution, 216

manufacturing,
    budget, 221
    plan, 220–221
    market potential, 214
    need for, 209, 265–266
    product benefits, 210–211
    promotion activities, 218
    sales forecast, 217–218
    targeted customers,
            211–213
Turner, Scott, 147, 177, 238
TV advertising, on a
        commission basis, 183

Underwriter's Laboratory
    (U.L.), 57

Vacuum-formed parts, 125
Value:
    determining company's,
            153–155

perceived versus
        manufacturing cost,
        109, 198
Venture capitalists, 16, 30
Venture economics, 16

Wacky Wall Walkers, 36–37
Want ads, as a research
        resource, 116
Warranty cards, as a market
        research tool, 193
Waste tires:
    disposal system, 11
    recycling possibilities, 12
Wiggle Wrap, 27, 239
Wind surfboard patents, 36
Working partners, 251
Worth, Richard, 24, 90

X-ray screening device, 186